cx2 c7

GRIFFITH COLLEGE CORK
WELLINGTON HOUSE
9/11 PATRICK'S HILL
CORK   IRELAND
TEL: 021 4507027 FAX: 021 4507659

D1357677

303.4'09415
McC

MODERNISATION, CRISIS AND CULTURE IN IRELAND, 1969–1992

Modernisation, Crisis and Culture in Ireland, 1969–1992

CONOR McCARTHY

FOUR COURTS PRESS

Set in 10 on 13 Janson for
FOUR COURTS PRESS LTD
Fumbally Lane, Dublin 8, Ireland
e-mail: info@four-courts-press.ie
and in North America by
FOUR COURTS PRESS
c/o ISBS, 5804 N.E. Hassalo Street, Portland, OR 97213.

A catalogue record for this title
is available from the British Library.

ISBN   1–85182–475–8 hbk
1–85182–479–0 pbk

Printed in England
by MPG Books, Bodmin, Cornwall

For my mother

Contents

Preface

This book could not have been written without the help of a number of people: family, friends and colleagues. My debt to my mother is inexpressible: to her the book is dedicated with love and admiration. To my regret, my father did not live to see this project, which he supported generously, come to fruition.

The doctoral study upon which this work is based would never have been completed without the support, encouragement, advice and example of Norman Vance. His warmth and intellectual liberality led me over many hurdles. I have had the privilege of the intelligence and assistance of brilliant teachers: Seamus Deane, Thomas Docherty, Ellen Goodell, Declan Kiberd. I have learnt enormously from the sustained conversation and comradeship of Joe Cleary, Dara Fox, David Johnson, Andrew Kincaid, Chris Lee, Peter McAuley and Prem Poddar. The solidarity, talk and kindness of many friends have made intellectual work a pleasure to me: Lucy Collins, Richard Curran, Sally Eberhardt, Patricia Garvey, Glenn Hooper, Tiernan Ivory, Sean Kennedy, Richard Kötter, Mark McGovern, Laurence Marley, John Monaghan, Caoilfhionn Ní Bheacháin, John J. O'Dowd, Lionel Pilkington, Olwen Rowe, Michael Trainor, Derval Tubridy and David Wheatley. Jonathan Bate, Terence Brown, Marianne Elliot, Tadhg Foley, Luke Gibbons, Nicholas Grene, John Hobbs, Siobhán Kilfeather, Geraldine Mangan, Christopher Morash, Christopher Murray, Riana O'Dwyer, Antoinette Quinn, Shaun Richards and Kevin Rockett have all given me generous support over the years. More recently, conversations at the Red Stripe Seminar in Maynooth and Dublin have been a continuing source of ideas and illumination for me. For their kindness and patience in difficult circumstances, I am indebted to Sunniva O'Flynn and Liam Wylie at the Irish Film Archive. Michael Adams, Ronan Gallagher and Martin Fanning at Four Courts Press could not have been more helpful or tolerant in guiding a neophyte through the publishing process.

A version of part of Chapter 3 was published in the *Irish University Review*, vol. 27, no. 1 (spring/summer 1997), under the title 'Ideology and Geography in Dermot Bolger's *The Journey Home*'. I am grateful to the editors for permission to reproduce that material

Introduction

This book provides a series of readings of the work of contemporary Irish activists in the field of culture – writers, critics and film-makers in this case – with a view to drawing out the ideological implications of their work in the context of the rapidly evolving social, political and economic conditions of Ireland in the 1970s and 1980s. The book is intended, therefore, as a kind of hybrid that lies between the sort of cultural history that has been pioneered in Irish studies by scholars like F.S.L. Lyons (1979), Terence Brown (1985), and David Cairns and Shaun Richards (1988);[1] and the volumes of more discrete essays, or monographic studies, that literary critics tend to favour. In practical terms, what emerges from this format is a collection of essays that, while treating of separate figures or movements, will be found to return repeatedly to a particular ideological or conceptual contradiction. Another way of putting this would be to say that I am trying to write a thematic, as against a narrative, cultural history in that I have found in my somewhat diffuse range of activists a common ideological conflict. This conflict has been visible in the patterns of recent Irish history, both political and cultural, since the early 1970s, so it is with a brief account of that history that I will begin.

In 1979, Charles Haughey, Taoiseach of the Republic for much of the 1980s, described Northern Ireland as a 'failed political entity', in his first speech as Fianna Fáil leader (Haughey, 1986, pp. 327, 335). By this, Haughey meant that the Northern political unit had not succeeded in gaining the consent and loyalty of the overwhelming majority of the population residing within it. It was not, therefore, fully legitimate, and this explained its ongoing crisis. In a pamphlet published in 1990, *From Cathleen to Anorexia: The Breakdown of Irelands* (Longley, 1990), the critic Edna Longley picked up Haughey's phrase, arguing that both the Northern and Southern Irish states had 'failed', as *cultural* units. I will be pursuing a similar argument, but in a different direction from that pursued by Longley. In her essay, she goes on to suggest that the principal failure has been that of nationalism, which has been an oppressive state ideology in the Republic and has fostered irredentism in the Northern minority. I will be arguing here for a more nuanced critique of

---

1 It will rapidly become obvious to the reader the degree to which I am indebted to the work of Brown and Cairns and Richards. Without that work, a book like this would simply not have been possible.

nationalism, and that the failures of the Northern and Southern polities have been related, in the absence of a Left-modernist critique. My founding premise has been that the period from, roughly, 1968 to 1973, witnessed a profound alteration in Irish society, North and South. This could be described, in the terms of Antonio Gramsci, as a 'crisis of authority' (Gramsci, 1971, pp. 275–6). By this I mean that the political and cultural dispensation that had obtained on both parts of the island began in this time to show signs of breaking down. Clearly, this breakdown was more dramatic and violent in Northern Ireland, but the impact in the Republic of the return of violence in the North, combined with economic slowdown and the shift in cultural, social, economic and political horizons implied by membership, finally achieved in 1973, of the European Economic Community (as it then was known), is not to be underestimated.

Both Northern Ireland and the Republic had been undergoing a process of modernisation for some time. The process in the North can be understood in terms of the broader development of social democracy in the post-1945 United Kingdom. There (most famously in the shipbuilding and linen industries) economic modernisation and industrialisation had been in train since the nineteenth century. After 1945, infrastructural development in the North was financed from Westminster, but even this economic progress eventually produced its own variation of the sectarian violence that had long lurked in the background of Northern political and social life. Post-war economic development required educational expansion, which came in the form of the 1947 extension to Ulster of the 1944 Butler Act. This enabled the education of a generation of often radical young intellectuals, from both main confessional groupings, who came to prominence in the 1960s. David Cairns and Shaun Richards point out that the equalising, transcommunal impulse of modernisation and education undermined the ruling ideology of Ulster Unionism. This was predicated on the maintenance of certain visible differentials in living standards and education between Protestants and Catholics/Nationalists (Cairns and Richards, 1988, pp. 141–2). The Prime Minister of Northern Ireland, Terence O'Neill, was the local vehicle and focus for this modernisation, as Lemass was in the Republic, and his meetings with the latter, starting in 1965, and with Cardinal Conway, Roman Catholic Primate of All Ireland, convinced extreme Protestants that he was not to be trusted. The emergence of the Civil Rights movement only seemed to confirm them in this belief.

In the Republic, the process can be dated a little later, to the late 1950s. Up to this time, a chauvinistic economic nationalism had been pursued, that found its ideological basis in post-Independence isolationism, wartime neutrality and the ambivalences of the political and economic relationship with Britain. This issued in policies based on the development of the agricultural sector, import substitution and protectionism that had been pursued since the Second World War. These policies had now been revealed to be wholly inadequate to the country's needs. Unemployment was running very high; over 400,000 people emigrated between 1951 and 1961 (Foster, 1988, p. 578). John Kelleher described the Republic in 1957 as a society suffering an 'implosion upon a central vacuity' (Brown, 1985a, p. 241). In 1958, the then Secretary of the Department of Finance in Dublin, T.K. Whitaker, published a White Paper, *Economic Development*, which proposed a radical re-think of economic policy. Whitaker proposed an approach based on a series of five-year plans, the relaxation of protectionism, the provision of incentives to foreign corporations interested in setting up industries in the Republic and a newly rigorous approach to economic planning. When Fianna Fáil won the 1959 general election, with Sean Lemass as Taoiseach, the new policy was adopted wholeheartedly in the form of the First Programme for Economic Expansion. The results were dramatic: the 1960s witnessed the arrival of over 350 foreign corporations in the Republic, and the establishment of export-led growth rates of Gross National Product of 4 per cent in the period 1959–63 (Brown, 1985, p. 242). Alongside the new economic policies, the Lemass government and its successors began a wider process of cultural and political relaxation, opening the state television station, Radio Telefís Éireann, in 1962 and applying for membership of the EEC (which was initially blocked by de Gaulle) in 1961. In 1964, the Minister for Justice, Brian Lenihan, liberalised the law in relation to film censorship, and in 1967 he introduced a bill into the Dáil relaxing the censorship of literature. The same period witnessed the warming of relations with the Northern statelet, with the meetings between Lemass and O'Neill.

The apparently encouraging progress implied by Southern modernisation and O'Neillist reformism started to unravel with the arrival on the Northern scene of more radical reformist movements in the form of the Civil Rights movement, and the nationalist Trotskyism of People's Democracy, which demanded more rapid progress. These were answered by forces of reaction most obviously represented by the virulent Protestant Loyalism of the Reverend Ian Paisley. Between these two irreconcilables, the moderation proposed by O'Neill was caught and crushed.

The Northern crisis eventually bled into the Southern political arrangement, in the explicit form of the Arms Trials, where Taoiseach Jack Lynch of Fianna Fáil found himself facing a situation in 1970 where two members of his cabinet were rumoured to be involved in the smuggling of weapons to the Irish Republican Army in the North. The ministers concerned, Charles Haughey and Neil Blaney, were tried and acquitted, but not before the impression had been created of a government-within-a-government, acting without either a democratic mandate, or the authority or knowledge of the Taoiseach.

In the meantime, the long post-war boom in the Western capitalist economies, on which the Republic's putative modernisation can be viewed as having ridden, ground to a halt in the 1970s, marked by the oil crises of 1973 and 1979. In Britain, this apparent discrediting of social democracy brought forth the new conservatism of 1980s Thatcherism, with its ferocious attacks on the welfare state, and its ideology of the free market, but also its new nationalism and stress on defence policy. In Ireland, these developments were felt most obviously in Northern Ireland, where the Thatcher government's approach of regarding the 'Troubles' as a law-and-order problem contributed to the H-blocks hunger-strikes of 1980 and 1981. This in turn produced a considerable upswing in support for Provisional Sinn Féin in Northern Ireland in the early 1980s, and led to the negotiation of the Anglo-Irish Agreement in 1985, in an effort by the FitzGerald government to impress upon the Thatcherites the potential for all-Ireland destabilisation if the rise of Sinn Féin was allowed to continue unchecked. In the meantime, the approach of the Fianna Fáil government of 1977–81 to the gathering economic crisis had been one of running up a considerable deficit in public spending. It was a policy predicated on the continuance of economic growth, and this was not to be. The result was a massive, spiralling national debt in the South, creating the need for tough controls and restrictions in public spending in the late 1980s. This took place against a background of continuing economic crisis, with mushrooming unemployment, the return of high levels of emigration, and political instability caused by the inability of any one party to obtain an overall majority in Dáil Éireann.

This overall transformation and historical pattern has been predominantly understood in Ireland in terms of *modernisation* and *nationalism*, terms which at this point I think it is necessary to reflect on in a critical manner. I will first discuss modernisation, and then nationalism. I will use the term 'revisionism', a term that has a number of valencies in Irish debates, to articulate the two. Frequently, it seems to me, these terms have been understood in rather attenuated and limited ways in Irish academic discussions. This has been the case for several reasons. Firstly, because of the influence in the academic humanities in Ireland since the 1950s of 'modernisation theory'. This is a theory of development that was promulgated in the academic social sciences in the United States after the Second World War by Clark Kerr and others, and was the intellectual analogue in the Republic of Ireland of the opening-up of the economy in the wake of the Lemass/Whitaker liberalisation begun in 1959. Modernisation theory suggests that the chief forces for change and development in society are industrial technology, entrepreneurial skills and capital investment. Under the influence of these forces, societies change in their structures and their divisions of labour, tending to 'converge'. From being *traditional* – characterised by face-to-face social relationships, identities defined in local terms, the extended family, clientelist relations with political authority – societies change to being *modern* – meritocratic, centered around the nuclear family, having a much more diffuse set of social relationships and a principally bureaucratic relationship with political authority. Ideological struggle is replaced by bureaucratic bargaining, as social conflict is reduced from being about the basic nature of society to being concerned with internal checks and balances. This theory assumes that technology alone is the engine of development, that it leads to industrialisation, and that that leads to the convergence and increasing similarity of societies (and, not coincidently, their increasing similarity to the United States). Modernisation theory envisages this process as taking place largely smoothly, without great social or political trauma or rupture, in a consensual manner (see O'Dowd, 1986, p. 200; Wickham, 1986, p. 72). It assumes that this move from tradition to modernity is socially, economically and politically positive and progressive.

The weaknesses of this theory are not far to seek. In its faith in the beneficial effects of technology, it is crudely materialistic, in a manner that would gratify the most vulgar Marxist. It presupposes that the simple diffusion of technology will alter an entire social formation. It is unable to foresee that such diffusion may have unlooked-for or contradictory effects, especially in the cultural or intellectual realms. It assumes its applicability in widely divergent geographical regions of the globe. In its relationship to the work of American social and political scientists who in the late 1950s believed that ideology was no longer a useful category of analysis (see Bell, 1960), it reveals its inability to recognise its own ideological status. Indeed, as O'Dowd points out, 'the strength of modernisation theory may be gauged from the extent to whcich its assumptions are taken for granted as common sense by its adherents who frequently fail to realise or acknowledge that they subscribing to a particular theory of social change' (O'Dowd, 1995, p. 168). Thus, as I have suggested, the blockage to critical views of Irish modernisation has worked on the level of ideology, where a particular set of ideas has been accepted as 'common sense', and very little space is available in which to assess the adequacy of this theory to the Irish case, or to suggest alternatives.

Modernisation, in the terms of modernisation theory, has been understood as standing in opposition to tradition, or effecting a radical break with it. In Ireland, the chief repository of tradition has come to be seen as the discourse of the *nation*, and the political movement known as *nationalism*. To the degree that modernisation theory takes it as given that the shift from tradition to modernity is progressive and desirable, tradition is, in this formulation, seen as regressive, something to be left behind or discarded. Hence, nationalism comes to be seen as atavistic, authoritarian, provincial, chauvinist.

However, I will argue that it is more accurate and more helpful to look at modernisation and nationalism as related, intertwined but contradictory phenomena. Nationalism, as I will demonstrate below and as has been argued by Ernest Gellner and Benedict Anderson (Gellner, 1983; Anderson, 1991) is itself an element of modernity. To dismiss it or to launch negative critiques of it, as has been the ideological trend of much of recent Irish critical, historiographic, political, social scientific and cultural work, is simply to misread it or to fail to attempt to recover any of the liberatory or progressive impulses that may be found embedded in the discourse of nationalism.

Benedict Anderson points out the close relationship to be found between the rise of nationalism in the eighteenth century in the Americas and Europe, and the existence of mass literacy and what he calls 'print-capitalism' (Anderson, 1991). The existence of cheap means of mass communication, of a mass audience or constituency able to consume such material, as well as such earlier developments as the decline of the great sacral languages (most obviously Latin) all combined to produce a situation where the geographical reach of a community's capacity to imagine itself expanded dramatically. This imagining took place in the context of the rise of national languages, the development of powerful state apparatuses, and the unleashing of secular ideologies of emancipation and enlightenment. These conditions of possibility permitted the self-narration of a new kind of community, the 'imagined community' we now call the nation.

Anderson famously demonstrates the importance of the cultural institutions of the novel and the newspaper – the products of 'print-capitalism' – to the 'imagining' of the nation. He distinguishes between the conception of simultaneity characteristic of the mediaeval period, and that of the modern period. The former is marked by a sense of what he calls, after Walter Benjamin, 'Messianic time', where past and future merge in a continuous present. Modernity, on the contrary, is marked by a sense of 'homogeneous, empty time', where simultaneity is conceived as 'transverse, cross-time, marked not by prefiguring and fulfilment, but by temporal coincidence, and measured by clock and calendar' (Anderson, 1991, p. 24). Anderson suggests that this modern sense of simultaneity can be summed up in the term 'meanwhile', and that it was technically made representable by the forms of the novel and the newspaper, two new and important cultural forms that emerged in Europe in the eighteenth century. Both of these forms enable the representation of a 'sociological organism moving calendrically through homogeneous, empty time', the latter being exactly analogous to the idea of the nation, a solid community moving steadily through time (Anderson, 1991, p. 26).

Thus, Anderson links modernity and nationalism, the material conditions of the one being conducive to the emergence of the other. Thus, it seems crucial to me to understand that nationalism and modernity are not necessarily mutually exclusive discourses; on the contrary, in Europe and the American colonies, and in more recently colonised regions, modernity has been driven by nationalisms. Nationalism is not simply a Romantic discourse, but one that draws on Enlightenment ideas of Progress, liberation, co-operation and equality. To see nationalism as exclusively atavistic, racialist, nostalgic and militant is fatally to misunderstand the situation of countries like Ireland that still sit on the boundaries of tradition and modernity. I would argue, in fact, that such a narrow view of nationalism is the product of a shallow cosmopolitanism, a limited modernity. In seeking to examine the political limits of cultural forms here, my desire is to suggest the benefits of a more sophisticated view of culture, critical of tradition and of the legacy of cultural nationalism, but also aware of the liberatory moments contained in these discourses, and finally capable of a kind of reflexiveness and self-criticism. For the point must be that not only does nationalism look to the past, but also to the future. Not only is it a Romantic reaction to the pains and confusions of modernity, but it is a strategy, in both culture and politics, of giving back to the individual subject or to a community, a sense of hope and coherence, in the face of the shattering, fragmenting experience of modernity. Nationalism is a movement that seeks to restore to a subject or a community its own potentiality. Nationalism seeks to make history heroic or adventurous.

The dismissively negative view of nationalism has advanced itself in the Republic under the title of 'revisionism', and it is my argument here that much of what is termed 'revisionism' in the Irish academic humanities is in fact traceable to the influence of modernisation theory. It is under the rubric of this term that most of the purely negative critique of nationalism that I referred to above has taken place. This term has a specific set of meanings in international and Irish debates. Originally 'revisionism' was a term of abuse deployed by Marxist thinkers against colleagues who began, in the early part of this century, to call into question the value of certain categories of Marx's thought, especially his ideas of the inevitability of socialist revolution and the evolution of capitalism. Later, especially in the post-1945, so-called Communist states of Eastern Europe, the Soviet Union, China and various countries in the developing world, 'revisionism' became a term by which Communist parties in power denigrated the ideas and policies put forward by rival indigenous socialist parties or by rival Communist governments. The term was introduced into Irish debate by the writer Desmond Fennell, who, in a series of books published since the 1960s, has questioned the modernisation process initiated by Whitaker and Lemass, suggesting that this process has led to the abandonment of most of the goals that the young Free State (subsequently the Republic) set itself in the immediate post-Independence period. The most important of such goals were the project of political unification with Northern Ireland and the revival of the Irish language. More specifically, and most heatedly, the term has come to refer to an alleged tendency in a substantial number of influential Irish historians to belittle the nationalist tradition, arguing its conservatism, its sectarian Roman Catholicism, its myth-making impulses, or its non-existence before the nineteenth century. In Chapter 2, I will discuss this historians' quarrel in some detail, but I wish to make clear here that my interest in the term 'revisionism' is as much in trying to blow it open and place it in the wider intellectual context of Irish modernity, as it is in its specifically historiographic sense. So, in other chapters, I will try to point out the pervasiveness of this approach in much of Irish intellectual life. My argument is that 'revisionism' is not only a historians' argument but is the historiographic outrider of the discourse of modernity as it has come to be understood in Ireland. That understanding, as I suggested above, has come to be dominated by the rather attenuated discourse of modernisation theory, and consequently the more contradictory but also more exciting and radical Marxist vision of modernisation and modernity has never been able to gain much purchase in Irish intellectual debates or political or social movements. Fennell uses the term to refer to the critique that has been mounted, initially in intellectual and cultural arenas, but increasingly in the popular culture of the Republic, of state-nationalism as it appeared before the Lemass/Whitaker liberalisation. Much of this book will consist of examinations of the clashes and contradictions in radical or avant-garde cultural and intellectual practice between nationalism and what might be called Left-culturalism, or Brechtianism. By the latter I mean a self-consciously materialist approach to cultural and intellectual activity, which I would like to advance as a more genuinely radical approach to Ireland's ersatz modernity, than the putative radicalism of modernisation theory. So I will be using the term 'revisionism' to discuss not only historiography, but also the work of novelists, playwrights, film-makers and critics. If the historians' debate can be crudely characterised as one over nationalist interpretations of the past, it is possible to suggest that the 'national question' has impinged on other areas of study and discussion that frequently seem quite unrelated to history or politics. Hence my interest in retaining the term 'revisionism' (though I hope it will emerge from this book severely battered) as a way of articulating apparently unrelated areas of debate and practice with each other. In these areas, the nation, nationalism, nationality can appear as a kind of significant absence. This has serious implications for debates in various fields. It is not that the critical re-examination of the categories of the 'nation' or the 'national' is not devoutly to be wished, but that in the Republic the intellectual and aesthetic forms of this revision have often been compromised and narrow, radical only in comparison to nationalism. In relation to an attenuated and restricted tradition, it is easy to appear 'modern'.

As a way of getting beyond the weaknesses and influence of modernisation theory, and the separation of cultural and economic practices it causes, I would suggest that a more radical and more useful view of modernisation is to see it as a *contradictory* or dialectical process, leading to a condition of modernity that produces various economic, political, social and cultural effects. In this, I am adhering to accounts of modernisation produced by Marxist writers such as Marshall Berman (1983) and David Harvey (1990). Berman and Harvey stress the degree to which capitalist modernisation leads to the positive developments pointed to by modernisation theory, but also to negative concomitant features such as the destruction of older forms of social arrangement, the uprooting of whole rural communites because of the mechanisation of agriculture, the resultant creation of an army of workers with nothing to sell but their labour-power, the powerful surge of migration from rural to urban areas, overcrowding in cities, the process of reification (where relationships between human beings are reduced to the logic of cash exchange). Berman and Harvey make clear, then, the fact that modernisation alters the material environment in which people live, profoundly, but also that it changes the climate of ideas, or ideological climate, in a society in just as profound a way. Not only is this cultural change profound, but it is unsettling. It is characterised by a sense of both cultural possibility, and cultural apocalypse; by a sense that everything is open to renewal, and at the same time, that all that is of value in a society – in the realms of culture, politics, ideas, social arrangements – may be destroyed arbitrarily overnight. Harvey uses the concepts of 'creative destruction' and 'destructive creation' to illustrate this situation. By these terms, he means that the rapid and seemingly perpetual transformation of society put in train by capitalism helpfully clears away stifling belief-systems (such as superstitions), authoritarian institutions (such as feudalism, or despotic government), unproductive systems of land-use or manufacture, very quickly and greatly to the benefit of people at all levels of society. But these transformations also and at the same time create great new poverty in their wake, new distortions of social life (urban slums, for example), new forms of power that working people must struggle with (large industrial corporations, or sprawling government bureaucracies), new forms of political violence (imperialism, for instance). So for Harvey and Berman, modernity is not simply the positive endpoint of a cheerful uplifting narrative of progress (as modernisation theory would have it), but an overwhelming, complex, confusing, liberating, disturbing condition of life under capitalism from the middle of the nineteenth century onwards. Berman sums this condition of modernity up well:

There is a mode of vital experience – experience of space and time, of the self and others, of life's possibilities and perils – that is shared by men and women all over the world today. I will call this mode of experience 'modernity'. To be modern is to find ourselves in an environment that promises adventure, power, joy, growth, transformation of ourselves and of the world – and, at the same time, that threatens to destroy everything we have, everything we know, everything we are. Modern environments and experiences cut across all boundaries of geography and ethnicity, of class and nationality, of religion and ideology; in this sense, modernity can be said to unite all mankind. But it is a paradoxical unity, a unity of disunity; it pours us all into a maelstrom of perpetual disintegration and renewal, of struggle and contradiction, of ambiguity and anguish. To be modern is to be part of a universe in which as Marx said, 'all that is solid melts into air'.

(Berman, 1983, p. 15)

So, a first advantage of Berman's thinking is that he, in his effort to recapture what he calls 'the experience of modernity' for Marxism, takes a holistic view of the process of modernisation, a view that encompasses culture as much as politics or economics. For Berman, Marx's originality lay in his insights on 'modern *spiritual* life' (Berman, 1983, p. 88; my italics). Berman's Marx believed that modern life assumed a 'unity of life and experience that embraces modern politics and psychology, modern industry and spirituality, the modern ruling classes and the modern working classes' (Berman, 1983, p. 88). Berman notes, in a manner similar to that of Jurgen Habermas (Habermas, 1987, pp. 1–5), that contemporary thinking has separated thinking about modernity into two areas, which rarely are permitted to intersect: 'modernisation' in politics and economics, 'modernism' in culture and ideas.

Further, modernisation theory, as an academic discourse, lacks the exuberance of Berman's writing. But it also lacks the senses of both possibility and menace that Berman seeks to invest modernisation and modernity with. To that extent, modernisation theory stresses the *rationality* of modernisation and modernity, of the process and of the experience. It presupposes that the modern world is one where all human action, and social interaction, is based on rational decision-making. To the extent that such rationality is held to be objective and non-ideological, modernity is thus envisaged to be progressive, fair, egalitarian. But there is another view of this rationality: Max Weber's alarming vision of the 'iron cage' of rationality as the negative legacy of the Enlightenment. While the original intention of Enlightenment thinkers was to end man's subjection to ignorance, superstition and the dominance of nature, in Weber's pessimistic vision, via the prevalence of the money economy and bureaucratic modes of government, the entire field of human activity – cultural, social, economic, political – is dominated by a coldly rational logic of balancing costs against benefits.

Now I have no wish to be misunderstood as suggesting that the ubiquity of modernisation theory in Irish social science and humanities study is equivalent to the dystopian vision of Max Weber. I *do* wish to suggest, though, that modernisation theory has succeeded in monopolising the field of the modern imagination in Ireland, and the various chapters of this book will attempt to examine some of the cultural and intellectual consequences of this somewhat attenuated vision.

This situation is perhaps best illustrated by some examples. John Waters noted recently the prevalence of 'technocratic and economistic prescriptions to solve the widespread and manifest failures of Southern society' (Waters, 1994, p. 12). Noting that such thinking has little to offer the Republic's socially and economically stagnant midlands regions, Waters attributed this to the discrediting of nationalist discourse caused by the Northern crisis and the violent campaign of the Provisional IRA. This leads to a difficulty in the articulation of almost any radical economic position, which is thus seen as either subversive or backward-looking.

One such position is that of 'dependency theory', as it is explained by the sociologist James Wickham, in the course of a discussion of the Irish industrial workforce (Wickham, 1986, p. 72). Dependency theory has been associated with Latin-American Marxist or neo-Marxist economists and development theorists such as F.H. Cardoso and André Gunder Frank. Its approach locates an economy in the context of a geopolitical division of labour, where 'core' regions draw profits and resources away from 'peripheral' regions. This leads, at worst, to economic stagnation, or, at best, to the 'development of underdevelopment'. This latter is the result of the penetration of peripheral economies by multinational corporations, which tend to locate the least technologically sophisticated, least skilled and least profitable (in terms of value added) stages of the production process in the peripheral economy. Executive control of production, and research and development projects, tend to be kept in the parent country of the multinational. Cardoso termed this 'dependent industrialisation', and rather than resulting in 'convergence' as predicted by modernisation theory, it results in an *increase* in structural economic differences between core and periphery. This unequally structured relationship can obtain between nation-states, or within economies (between the south-east of England and the 'Celtic Fringe', for example; or between the European core of south England, the Benelux countries, the Netherlands, the Paris basin, Germany and Northern Italy, and the European periphery of the Italian Mezzogiorno, Spain, Portugal, Greece, Ireland and Scotland). The important point is that dependency theory seeks to analyse economies in relational terms – hence its ability to place economic issues in a context of unequal power relations – whereas modernisation theory sees modernisation as a dynamic that emerges from within an autonomous economic system. This capacity of dependency theory to examine an economy as a totality, from without, is a major asset, as it is a weakness of modernisation theory that it sees social conflict as being reduced by the modernisation process from being about the fundamental nature of society to being concerned with internal checks and balances. That is, modernisation theory assumes the fundamental stability of the social, economic and political system in which it is deployed. It cannot deal with a situation in which that dispensation is open to question, hence its tendency to shut out alternative thinking.

To Wickham we can perhaps add the recent work of the political geographer, Jim MacLaughlin. MacLaughlin utilises 'world-systems theory', which is related to but complicates dependency theory. Seeking to explain Irish emigration, he posits the idea of the island's peripheral *status* within the world capitalist economy, as against its peripheral *location*. This status is that of what MacLaughlin calls an 'emigrant nursery', and that, in fact, has been Ireland's status since the eighteenth century (MacLaughlin, 1994, p. 3). He suggests that, since the 1960s, a 'blame Britain' traditional nationalist approach to the woes of emigration has been replaced by geographical and behaviourist explanations, that tend to sanitise and voluntarise the issue, viewing emigration as a matter of rational choice and cultural tradition. This, MacLaughlin argues, is related to historical revisionism (see Chapter 2), which has stressed the inevitability of emigration and de-politicised its causes. So Irish historians have been poor defenders of the 'moral economy' of the rural poor and the urban working class, the communities struck hardest by emigration. This, of course, was John Waters' point.

When MacLaughlin suggests that historians have overplayed the inevitability of emigration, seeing it as a matter of rationally-exercised choice and cultural tradition, he is in fact alluding to the influence of modernisation theory, now in the field of historiography (see Chapter 2 for more on this). Modernisation theory tends to de-politicise social and economic issues, insofar as it does not see ideology as a useful analytical category. Therefore it cannot admit the possibility that social and economic choices are made by human beings in ways that are crucially influenced by ideology. Moreover, in its assumption of the stability of the political and socio-economic formation it is trying to analyse, it cannot adequately deal with a problem like that of emigration (MacLaughlin's topic here) as it involves incentives from outside the system that operate to influence the putatively rational choices made by people within that system. Overall, modernisation theory, lacking a geopolitical vision that enables it to see the political and socio-economic system as a totality (because to do so would call into question the viability of that system), cannot cope with conflictual issues like emigration in ways other than the sanitising and rationalising ones MacLaughlin describes here.

The result of this has been what MacLaughlin calls the 'deterritorialisation' of the political units in terms of which social and historical events are explained; other peripheral European nations, such as Scotland, Wales, Greece and Portugal have experienced the same phenomenon as a concomitant of integration into the European Union and the global economy. But in the Republic the process has been exacerbated by the intellectual and discursive effects of the Northern crisis. MacLaughlin quotes journalists Mary Holland and Nell McCafferty as suggesting that nationalism has become, in the Republic, 'an embarrassment' and the 'love that dare not speak its name' (MacLaughlin, 1994, p. 33). MacLaughlin's point is that the loss or 'revision' of the concept of the 'national', and its replacement with nothing else, has contributed in large measure to our inability to tackle our economic problems. 'Modernity', equated frequently and superficially with 'Europeanisation', has meant the discarding of the one synthetic or totalising intellectual concept available to us. MacLaughlin goes on to suggest that revisionism has been an essential ingredient in shifts in thought and policy-making in the Republic in various fields, and he explicitly links revisionist historiography and political economy. In public discourse, 'modernisation theory' has become 'politically correct' as the dominant paradigm of explanation of economic, social and political issues. This leads MacLaughlin to conclude that

> In Ireland, revisionism and modernisation theory literally marked the coming-of-age of a new institutionalised and state-centred Irish intelligentsia who have sought to break from what they perceive as the 'narrow nationalism' of the nineteenth century by embracing the narrow logic of cost-benefit analysis. This intellectual project has 'sanitised' Irish social problems and the Irish historical record to such an extent that problems like emigration, poverty and unemployment hardly appear as social problems any more, let alone as national social problems.
>
> (MacLaughlin, 1994, p. 44)

According to MacLaughlin, this has produced a 'blame the victims' approach to these problems. This approach originated in the United States, and was adapted to the Republic in the late 1960s. It attributes Irish social problems to the social-psychological attitudes and characteristics of individuals, and also to the various 'cultures' of poverty, emigration and unemployment in which those individuals are embedded.

This trend was highly ideological, in spite its claim to 'objectivity', based on scientific terminology and detailed and rigorous empirical investigation. This has resulted in a resistance to theoretical approaches. MacLaughlin concludes that revisionism created for itself a position of such centrality in Irish intellectual life that to oppose it 'has variously been considered unwise, unfashionable, radical, irresponsible and even unenlightened' (MacLaughlin, 1994, p. 45).

The historian J.J. Lee has noted that 'the growth in the number, status and influence of economists has been a striking feature of the intellectual market since the 1960s' (Lee, 1989, p. 582). But he also notes that the dominance of the 'policy studies market' by economists is not necessarily a good thing. For Lee, at least three problems arise out of this dominance. Firstly, there has been a considerable gap between the knowledge of academic economists and the realities of Irish business and industrial decision-making. Secondly, the dominant paradigms of economics are not necessarily suitable to the Irish situation. Lee tells us that

> Most Irish economists have clung to neo-classical models with a diligence which largely precludes conceptual originality even while fostering technical virtuosity.
>
> (Lee, 1989, p. 583)

Yet the economists 'have devoted little time to pondering their own assumptions'. Thirdly, the 'economic perspective' and the figure of the economist have come to dominate discussion of the condition of Irish society. Alan Matthews noted that 'economists can get away with playing the philosopher king because there is so little challenge to the dominant orthodoxy' (Matthews, 1985, p. 59). Yet Ireland tends to evade easy classification in terms of international economic orthodoxy. Lee suggests that the relations that have developed between the institutions of economic study and the State have led to a systemic tendency to 'short-termism'. An overly empirical approach has led to 'tunnel thinking, blind to either long-term perpective or lateral linkage' (Lee, 1989, p. 583). This, of course, is related to Jim MacLaughlin's critique of revisionism, modernisation theory and political economy in the Republic. But Lee's position is somewhat different from that of MacLaughlin, who provides an ideological critique of economic policy-formulation in Ireland as it affects emigration. Lee is much more cautious, telling us that

> The kernel of the problem is the desire to exclude 'non-economic' factors from 'economic' analysis. It is striking that a country with so distinctive a pattern of under-development has made so little contribution to development economics.
>
> (Lee, 1989, p. 583)

But Lee, in his commentary on Irish economists, makes scarcely any reference to, for example, Raymond Crotty, perhaps the best-known advocate of development economics in the Republic until his death in 1994. Crotty's major work, *Ireland in Crisis: A Study in Capitalist Colonial Undevelopment* (Crotty, 1986), is a sustained application of dependency theory to the economy of the Republic. But Crotty's interventions in public life, informed by this analysis, were deeply critical of the Republic's moves deeper and deeper into the European Union, and caused him to be dismissed as a crank, or an anachronistic reactionary, seeking to return to a de Valeraite idyll of isolationist economic nationalism. This fate is in accord with MacLaughlin's analysis cited earlier. The chief contradiction and weakness of Lee's assessment of what he calls 'Intelligence', coming at the end of a magisterial study of twentieth-century Ireland, is that he betrays his roots as an economic historian and assesses ideas overwhelmingly in the context of their production by what Noam Chomsky, discussing the Trilateral Commission, calls 'policy-oriented intellectuals' (Chomsky, 1982, p. 69). Lee is chiefly interested in what he calls 'performance', being mainly the economic performance of the independent Free State and then Republic. Ideas are significant, or achieve prominence in what he calls the 'market of ideas', to the extent that they are taken up by government for the purpose of policy-formulation. Yet when he comments on the stagnancy of economic theorisation in the Republic, he misses the irony that in using the 'market of ideas' as his dominant metaphor for intellectual activity, he is reproducing the performance-oriented cost-benefit model he is criticising for its tendency to filter out 'non-economic' ideas. Usefully, Lee compares the 'performance' of Ireland to that of other small European nation-states in this century such as Finland and Denmark, but at no point does he widen his comparatist parameters to include countries of the so-called 'Third World' or of Latin America. This is not to claim an exact identity of experience between Ireland, and, for example, Uganda, in the processes of the winning of independence and the struggle to establish a viable economy and democracy. Liam Kennedy has, in fact, disputed the relevance of the whole 'post-colonial' thesis to Ireland on precisely economic grounds (Kennedy, 1992). But what Kennedy ignores is the fact that social, political and even economic thinking takes place in the realm of ideology and culture, and it is here, as Colin Graham recently demonstrated, that the kind of 'post-colonial' analysis sponsored by groups such as Field Day might function to open up new areas of understanding (Graham, 1994, pp. 38–9). This is because, unlike positivist economic thought, 'post-colonial' cultural studies do not dismiss ideology out of hand as an intellectual space of unscientific error, or seek to set up another, properly rational, objective and non-ideological explanatory apparatus. However, Kennedy and Graham both reckon that the vocabulary of imperialism, colonialism and neocolonialism have been discedited by their use in the context of the Northern crisis by Provisional Sinn Féin. Further, Lee is unwilling to use the concept of 'ideology' except to refer to consciously-held belief-systems or political dogmas, perhaps because to do so would be to destabilise the entire field of intellectual disciplines and institutions, including the putative objectivity and authority of the historian.

Along with the limited sense of ideology in Lee goes an attenuated sense of the social construction of the public sphere. Lee blandly takes for granted the interpenetration of civil and political society in his market model of intellectual production. His focus on post-Independence 'performance' is predicated on an unjustified unitary image of the State and society. It leads him to concentrate on academic and intellectual services to power, without qualms or criticism. As a corollary of this, where such an instrumental relationship is not immediately obvious, as in the case with historical scholarship, he sees no relationship at all (see Chapter 2 for arguments against this view). For Lee, the intellectual works in a comfortable serviceable relationship with the state, but is in no way compromised by the fact that much of the meaning of her or his 'performance', being attuned to the 'performance' of the state and oriented to passing into common sense in the form of policy-formulation, is inevitably located within terrain mapped out by the state. Consequently, such criticism as can be practised is directed at the improvement of the functioning of the state, but rarely at that totality constituted by the state itself. Lee suggests that the orthodoxy in Irish academic economic study has tended towards the positive, empirical minutiae of economic management, not the formulation of broader economic, social or political goals. This is at once true and inadequate, the latter in the sense that it presupposes the non-ideological nature of empiricism. The problem is that, as the critic Seamus Deane puts it, 'Empiricists make good liberals; that is to say, all good liberals are empiricists, but not all empiricists are good liberals' (Deane, 1994, p. 238). Empiricism can call itself non-ideological, since it does not project an overt programme or a totalising explanatory system of nature or history. Rather, it portrays itself as pragmatic, realistic, attuned to realisable goals as against projecting a Utopian vision of the future, or retrojecting a traditionalist return to origins. To this extent, it buttresses the existing status quo rather than contesting it. Deane reckons that the goal of liberalism in the Republic is to improve the existing economic-political system to the point that individuals would no longer feel the need for recourse to such troubling or supposedly atavistic 'ideologies' as nationalism or Roman Catholicism. When Deane tells us that the 'buzz-word' of Irish liberalism is 'pluralism', and that its ideal is to organise the society of the Republic to the point that ideologies are replaced by individualistic 'lifestyles', chosen out of a 'free market' characterised by the tolerance of indifference, he is not simply enunciating a reactionary or traditional view. Rather, he is expressing irritation at the poverty of modernity as it has been conceived in mainstream bourgeois intellectual discourse in the Republic. If it seems that Deane is conflating economic with cultural modernity, then it must be admitted that such may be the case but only because that is the character of the intellectual terrain as he comes to it, where an economic modernisation driven by transnational capital finds its intellectual analogue in modernisation theory. This is the meaning of MacLaughlin's linkage of historical revisionism with modernisation theory. This also may be the reason why, as Terence Brown noted, Sean Lemass was able to nationalise the project of modernisation without causing ideological turmoil. Economic thought was understood in terms divorced from social, historical or political ideas. Modernisation was understood in a manner, as Desmond Bell writes, separated from the discourses of critical modernism, in the social, cultural or political sense (Bell, 1988, pp. 219–30).

The congruence between this style of economic thinking and the empiricism of 'revisionist' historical discourse will become very clear in Chapter 2, but what can be suggested here is that that historiography manifests a resistance to the idea of totality (which it vilifies in its manifestation in the form of the nation), a resistance to the influence of theory, ideas or ideology, a resistance to Utopian thought, resistance to a grand narrative of progress (as against the pragmatism of modernisation theory and the 'short-termism' Lee describes), a relative lack of methodological reflexivity and a desire to maintain a rigorous separation of academic fields. The literary historian W.J. McCormack notes the absence in Ireland (only matching that in Britain up to the 1960s) of a sociology of culture, whether classical or Marxist (McCormack, 1986, p. 46; also Bell, 1985. p. 95; Brown, 1985a, p. 105). It is entirely appropriate then, that the dominant conception of modernity in intellectual circles in the Republic should have been one of reform, adjustment and pragmatism, that advertised itself as non-ideological, technology-led, leading to economic take-off. The main discourse of critical or dialectical modernity – Marxism – is largely absent.

The case is illustrated further if one looks at a well-known earlier book of J.J. Lee's, *The Modernisation of Irish Society, 1848–1918*. In his Preface, Lee writes of the presiding concept of his study:

> ... a term widely, if ambiguously, used in international scholarship, modernisation may prove immune to the parochial preoccupations implicit in equally elusive and more emotive concepts like gaelicisation and anglicisation. Modernisation is defined as the growth of equality of opportunity. This requires that merit supersede birth as the main criterion for

the distribution of income, status and power, and this, in turn, involves the creation of political consciousness among the masses, the decline of deference based on inherited status and the growth of functional specialisation, without which merit can hardly begin to be measured.

(Lee, 1973)

In the anxiety to avoid 'parochial preoccupations' and 'emotive concepts', this passage betrays the lineaments of historical revisionism, which I will discuss in greater detail in Chapter 2. In the concentration on 'equality of opportunity', merit and functional specialisation, the traces of liberal individualism are visible. It is clear that Lee's concept of modernisation corresponds to the technocratic idea of development promulgated by modernisation theory. The concept of functional specialisation suggests a debt to structural functionalism, the dominant school of American sociology betwee the end of the Second World War and the late 1960s, when Lee was writing. As we will find in Chapter 2, Irish social and economic history owes much of its vocabulary to American social science of that period.

The critic Edward Said helps us to explain this. Writing on the political and ideological background of modernisation theory, he reminds us that it was formulated, and exported, in the context of the Cold War, when an extraordinary 'political correctness' pervaded American scholarship, even in the humanities:

A truly amazing conceptual arsenal – theories of economic phases, social types, traditional societies, systems transfers, pacification, social mobilization, and so on – was deployed throughout the world; universities and think tanks received huge government subsidies to pursue these ideas, many of which commanded the attention of strategic planners or policy experts in (or close to) the United States government. Not until the great popular disquiet at the Vietnamese war did critical scholars pay attention to this … the unexamined drive to global reach had the effect of depoliticizing, reducing and sometimes even eliminating the integrity of overseas societies that seemed in need of modernizing and of what Walt Whitman Rostow called 'economic takeoff'.

(Said, 1993, p. 351)

This is not to suggest that the United States saw in Ireland a refractory nationalism or communism of the kind it saw in Vietnam – such a claim would be plainly absurd – but that the concept of modernisation that came with American multinational penetration in the 1960s was far from the non-ideological purity in which it seemed to wish to cloak itself.

My purpose in this discursus on economics has been to demonstrate the degree of intersection and mutual reinforcement that has obtained between such disparate intellectual discourses as history and economics, and the degree also that both have been inflected and impoverished by the Northern crisis. However, it is important to note that while there has been intersection in ideological terms, there has been separation in discursive terms. Liam O'Dowd points out how Irish intellectuals have been preoccupied with the issue of identity and the ways that it is formulated in the realm of ideas and culture, but have neglected the 'material dimension', leaving it solely to the economists and the state bureaucracy. He traces this to the central importance of issues of identity to the cultural nationalism that drove the national revolution between 1912 and 1921 (though it found its own roots further back in the nineteenth century). This resulted in an intellectual stratum formed by the social changes effected via Westminster before Independence: the break-up of the estates of the Anglo-Irish landlord class and their consequent decline; the concomitant production of a class of peasant proprietors; and the rise of the commercial and professional middle classes. Such intellectuals took the new socio-economic order for granted, and thus were not disposed to think or seek its transformation (O'Dowd, 1988, pp. 11–12). Thus the generation of famous post-Independence intellectuals, exemplified by Sean O'Faolain, Peadar O'Donnell and their journal *The Bell*, produced critiques of the social order in which primacy was given to the realm of discourse, not to the material base. The stress was on 'critical exposure rather than systematic radical analysis' (O'Dowd, 1988, p. 12). Such thinkers did not affiliate their work to mass movements for change, but rather produced a somewhat self-validating discourse of greater cultural 'civility' than the prevailing norms. The Lemass/Whitaker modernisation changed this situation profoundly, with its new emphasis on the role of the state in economic planning, industrial development, policy research and the promotion of multinational investment. Later, a whole new level of the state bureaucracy was introduced with the accession to membership of the European Economic Community in 1973. All of this was accompanied by a substantial growth in education at all levels, but especially at second and third level. The result has been a marked shift from the intellectual scene being dominated by what Chomsky has called 'value-oriented' intellectuals, to a new technocracy (Chomsky, 1982, pp. 68–9). This appears to be common to all industrialised countries. Such figures offered an instrumental rationality adapted to specific tasks rather than the formulation of grand overarching or totalising projects of understanding the society in holistic terms. O'Dowd points out that this new intelligentsia were themselves immediate beneficiaries of economic modernisation, with economists themselves enjoying a massive boom in their job market. But he also notes that the 'increasingly technical and quantitative form [of economics] ... disguised an ideological stance which left little room for socialist or other non-conventional economists' (O'Dowd, 1988, p. 15). Involvement in various international bodies, chiefly the EEC, produced a wide range of new opportunities for work, training and research, and travel abroad by the new intellectuals. So now economic development seemed to be the engine of political and cultural development, not *vice versa*. But this relationship and process was itself untheorised and taken as self-evident: 'Social change was understood in typically élitist and idealist fashion as the spread of a virus of modern *ideas* through all sectors of Irish life' (O'Dowd, 1988, p. 15). Again, it is clear that what O'Dowd is describing is the effect on the Irish intellectual scene of modernisation theory: simultaneously an impoverishment of ideas and the creation of a particular intelligentsia which has been able to monopolise the field with its technocratic optimism. This cheerful scenario was seriously disrupted by the Northern crisis. That irruption, from the late 1960s onwards, has seemed to capture any space for radical intellectual projects that might exist in the public sphere. It has served, through its revelation of the persistence of militant nationalism and loyalism, combined with the economic crisis of the 1970s and 1980s and the apparent return of conservative Roman Catholicism in the Republic in the 1980s, to show that the modernisation project was inadequately understood in Ireland. This understanding took place at the level of both economics and culture, notably because of the separation of these discourses in critical terms. This separation has been one of the most powerful and pernicious ways that the Northern crisis has bled into the life of the Republic.

My point, then, is that the dominant conception of modernity in Ireland is intellectually impoverished. Terence Brown suggests that Lemass' chief success was his capacity to detach the notions of modernisation and Anglicisation, or, to nationalise modernisation (Brown, 1985a, pp. 246–7). I think that it might be more accurate to say that Lemass succeeded in making the opening-up of the society and economy that took place from the early 1960s onwards a viable project *for the society of the Republic*. Another way of putting this would be to say that modernisation became a narrative in terms of which the 'imagined community' of the Republic understood itself, and envisioned its future. The references to the Republic here are crucial, since Lemass was in effect abandoning, in terms of a communal project or narrative, the economic premises of state nationalism that had dominated the South since Independence. Ellen Hazelkorn and Henry Patterson recently suggested that the post-1959 modernisation amounted to a deepening rather than a widening of the nationalist project:

> The very process by which the southern state was extended domestically as it entered more spheres of production and reproduction grad-

ually reconstituted the basic structures of national sentiment. The dynamics of national aspiration became increasingly complex and cross-cutting as the 'external' horizon shifted increasingly to a European instead of a simple Anglo-Irish axis.

(Hazelkorn and Patterson, 1994, p. 57)

But the term 'national' here is operative only in the context of the Republic, and is therefore, in traditionalist terms, an oxymoron. What Hazelkorn and Patterson, in spite of their Marxist theoretical background, also seem not to notice is that the Lemass/Whitaker modernisation effected a separation between the 'national' community and the engine of its putative modernisation. The Lemass/Whitaker process effectively passed control of the modernisation of the economy and society of the Republic over to multinational capital. The future role for the business and bureaucratic élite of the Republic would be negotiating markets and financial assistance with the European Economic Community, and facilitating, by means of financial and other incentives, the penetration of the economy by multinationals. This brings us back to MacLaughlin's point about the 'de-territorialisation' of the terms in which social and historical events are explained. Thus Lemass' 'turn' can be understood as marking the definitive separation of state nationalism from its traditional ideological underpinnings. This is the moment when the partitionism of Southern policy became most obvious. But, I would argue, precisely *because* the process of modernisation was imagined in the impoverished manner described above, it was not recognised that a critique was also needed of the dominant state ideology: nationalism. It required the massive crises of the late 1960s and early 1970s to reveal this gap. From the moment of the Lemass/Whitaker initiative on, the relationship between economic base and ideological superstructure was contradictory, the first operating to delegitimate the second. This tendency was given considerable added impetus by the Northern crisis from the late 1960s onwards. As will be evident in much of the remainder of this book, the Northern conflict lent an edge of political immediacy and emergency to work undertaken in the fields of political and social science, history-writing and cultural criticism at this time. As activity by the Provisional IRA increased in the North, Southern intellectuals increasingly felt the need to mount a struggle in the ideological realm to prevent the spread of subversive ideas. The main thrust of this tendency has been the critique of nationalism that I have referred to as 'revisionism'.

Unfortunately, this project of modernisation was undertaken at a time, at the end of the great modernising wave that carried the industrial West from the end of the Second World War, when the chief intellectual apparatus for the elaboration of a serious intellectual critique of modernity was soon to come into crisis. By this I mean the decline in the fortunes of Western Marxism. It is true that the Anglophone Left academy was revivified in the late 1960s and early 1970s by a turn to previously neglected writers such as Gramsci and the early Lukács, and translations of more recent theorists such as Althusser, Colletti and Habermas. But it is also the case that the post-1968 period saw an increasingly powerful wave of poststructuralist thinkers, whose work, frequently dismissive of Marxism, rapidly attained a dominant position in the universities of Britain and the United States. In the Republic itself, the capacity of revolutionary nationalism to subsume all other insurrectionary projects and critiques to itself, as evidenced by the fates of James Connolly and Constance Markiewicz, and the anti-Communist character of the post-1922 Free State, made the development of a local Marxism, whether at the level of intellectual project or active practice, almost impossible. The Irish Labour Party, while anxious to pay lip service to such illustrious forbears as Connolly, had, in the wake of Independence, found itself to be in competition largely with the most traditional and irridentist of the nationalist parties, Fianna Fáil. This meant that the pragmatic politics of reformist improvements in the living conditions of workers engaged its attentions more than more ambitious projects of social revolution or the seizure of the means of production (Brown, 1985a, p. 105). This, combined with Fianna Fáil's ability to form single-party governments, also resulted in Labour's attaining power only by way of coalitions with Fine Gael, the party representing class interests most clearly in opposition to those of Labour. Labour's history has therefore been marked by a series of debates as to the efficacy of coalition. The intellectual effect of this was clear when the new industrial modernisation was initiated. All the parties of the Irish Left, including the Workers' Party, the British and Irish Communist Organisation and the Labour Party, assumed that modernisation would lead to industrialisation and the rise of working-class consciousness, leaving behind the traditional patterns of clientelism, nationalism and religious orthodoxy.[2] They thus locked their political programmes to the teleological projections of modernisation theory as much as their non-socialist rivals (Bew, Hazelkorn and Patterson, 1989, pp. 197, 155). The mediocrity and bland pragmatism of such an approach has meant that while the Lemass/Whitaker liberalisation launched an economic modernisation, the

---

2 'The Workers' Party' was the qualifying name taken on by the 'Official' arm of Sinn Féin, in the aftermath of the split between 'Officials' and 'Provisionals' in parallel with the scism between the 'Official' and 'Provisional' wings of the Irish Republican Army in 1970. In 1982, they dropped the name 'Sinn Féin', to become simply 'The Workers' Party'. In 1992, the Workers' Party split further, over allegations of involvement in paramilitary activity in Northern Ireland and internal debates in the wake of the collapse of state communism, becoming 'Democratic Left' and a rump Workers' Party.

elaboration of a concomitant intellectual critique of that process has proven difficult and confusing. Indeed, Bew, Hazelkorn and Patterson have gone so far as to argue that 'the present impasse of social democracy must therefore reside in its dogmatic embrace of modernisation theory which has left it theoretically denuded in a situation in which neither economic growth nor crisis has witnessed the working class embrace the socialist agenda' (Bew, Hazelkorn and Patterson, 1989, pp. 197–8). Thus, they argue, the Irish Labour Party has accepted a consensus model of Irish society, based on the idea of the national interest. It must be acknowledged that Bew, Peter Gibbon, Ellen Hazelkorn and Patterson have utilised modern Marxist thinking, drawn from Althusser and Poulantzas. However, it should be noted that the overwhelming focus of their work on contemporary history has been on the Northern statelet, and that it has not been beyond criticism on sectarian grounds (Stewart, 1991).

I have chosen the work examined in what follows because it seems to me that the crisis can be understood as one of *narratives*. Marxist writers such as Fredric Jameson and David Harvey agree roughly that the 1970s saw the definitive arrival of what the latter has called 'the condition of postmodernity' (Harvey, 1990; Jameson, 1991). By this I mean not merely the idea of 'consumer society' or 'post-industrial society', but what Jean-François Lyotard, writing admittedly from a sharply different perspective, has called 'incredulity toward metanarratives' (Lyotard, 1984, p. xxiv). For Lyotard, metanarratives are those great post-Enlightenment stories that Western societies have used to legitimate themselves and their activities (in almost all areas of activity, from cultural production to imperialism to research in the arts, sciences and humanities) to themselves. Progress, Enlightenment, the drive towards Freedom – these would be examples of metanarratives. In a more localised manner, the presiding Irish metanarrative since the early nineteenth century has been that of nationalism, a discourse which describes itself as the long struggle for freedom from the neighbouring island and the drive to construct a viable independent political, economic, social and cultural unit. This unit is the nation-state. As late as the Lemass/Whitaker modernisation, this grand narrative was in place. However, it has come under increasing attack since the late 1960s and early 1970s, when the island experienced the 'crisis of authority' I named and have sketched in above. This great nationalist push has been exposed as a failure, as destructive and even as a sham. Major post-Independence goals such as re-unification and the restoration of the Irish language have not been realised. Economic viability has been called into question, both at the end of the de Valera period and with the crisis that, since the 1970s, has affected the Lemass-inspired narrative of modernisation put in its place. The decision to join the EEC in 1973, and participation in the creation of a European Union since the early 1990s have raised the question as to what the worth of national sovereignty was in the first place, if it was to be so easily diluted again in inter-national political arrangements. The ongoing problem of emigration, whether that of the 1950s or of the 1980s, has raised similar questions.

Culturally, the difficulties of analysing this kind of juncture have been well described by Desmond Bell (Bell, 1988). He points out that while Ireland, in the first half of this century, produced a cluster of the greatest Modernist writ-ers (Yeats, Joyce, Beckett), the radical impact of their work was not felt here, but more often in the metropolises of Europe. Thus, Ireland has had no expe-rience of Modernist cultural internationalism, or of the avant-gardes' assaults on the institutions of high culture and on bourgeois conventions, or their cel-ebrations of mass society, the media or science. The Romanticism of the Revivalists was never systematically challenged by a socially radical indige-nous modernism. Cultural nationalism could present itself, in the context of the struggle with Britain, as the only socially radical aesthetic programme (Bell, 1988, p. 228).

Modernism, for Bell, came late to Ireland, at the end of the 1960s, and less as a result of the social ferment that afflicted Europe and the United States at the turn of the century than as a result of the Lemass/Whitaker modernisa-tion. By this time, however, modernism as an international aesthetic move-ment was already a spent political force and had indeed been recuperated by precisely the forces it had once set itself up in opposition to:

> In 1960s Ireland 'modernism' as pseudo-international style and sensi-bility was championed not by a radical avant-garde but by the purvey-ors of consumer capitalism … In Ireland this modernism degenerated into a shoddy simulation of consumer prosperity in a society undergo-ing a tawdry and shortlived experience of the global post-war capital-ist boom.
>
> (Bell, 1988, p. 229)

Now, in the 1990s, rather than a renewal of 'adversarial cultural aspirations' in the form of 'critical regionalism', we in Ireland are faced with a 'provincial flight into nostalgia in the face of the ever-present contradictions of moder-nity'. We lack a cultural avant-garde, but unfortunately we still possess a mil-itant rearguard. So, modernism in Ireland remains a largely untried project:

> *Such are the contradictions of Irish modernisation that we have prematurely entered the post-modern era.* We are experiencing for example – in the sphere of economic ideology, 'monetarism' without a prior social democracy; in politics a 'new right' without an old left, 'post-national-ism' with the national question materially unresolved; at the social level,

a return to 'family values' without the advances of feminism; at the cultural level, the nostalgia and historicist pastiche of 'post-modernism' without the astringent cultural purgative of modernism. We are entering the future, as some wag has commented, walking backwards.

(Bell, 1988, p. 229)

Jürgen Habermas may help us to understand this situation in philosophical terms. He points out how classical social theorists of the nineteenth century such as Max Weber, George Herbert Mead and Émile Durkheim described a process of 'rationalisation' that affected both cultures and societies. For Weber, the disenchantment of European world-views that caused the demise of the influence of religion, and which took place in the wake of the Reformation was 'rational'. Modernity, for Weber, was characterised by the development of separate domains of empirical science, of art, and of moral and legal theory, but all of this process could still be described under the heading of rationalisation. However, Habermas notes the usage of the term 'modernisation' since the 1950s, an approach, he suggests, 'that takes up Weber's problem but elaborates it with the tools of social-scientific functionalism' (Habermas, 1987, p. 2). This, then, is the modernisation theory that I have been describing. Habermas points out two effects of this theory of modernisation. The first of these is that it lifts 'modernity' out of its origins in modern Europe and abstracts it into a model, supposedly neutral in both geographical and historical terms, for processes of social development in general. Further, the link between Western rationalism and modernity is broken, so that modernisation processes can no longer be understood as rationalisation, 'as the historical objectification of rational structures' (Habermas, 1987, p. 2). For Habermas, the problem with this abstraction is that it removes the process of modernisation from any endpoint or goal of completion. It is becomes an autonomous self-propagating evolution. This is what Bell is alluding to when he describing the Irish slippage from modernisation to postmodernity, without a necessary culture of modernism intervening. For Habermas, it is this abstraction of modernisation from the project of modernity that permits social scientists to refer easily to 'postmodernism', as to do so is, for Habermas, to take leave of the project of rationalisation that he sees as the project of modernity. Habermas quotes Arnold Gehlen to the effect that in this situation, the motivating principles of the Enlightenment are dead, and only their consequences live on. Thus,

From this perspective, a self-sufficiently advancing modernization of society has separated itself from the impulses of a cultural modernity that has seemingly become obsolete in the meantime; it only carries out the functional laws of economy and state, technology and science, which are supposed to have amalgamated into a system that cannot be influenced.

(Habermas, 1987, p. 3)

It is in this context that the call by the critic John Wilson Foster for the 'psychological *embourgeoisement*' of liberal humanism seems at the least disappointing (Foster, 1991, p. 231), at worst intellectually inadequate and naïve. Likewise, Edna Longley notes that

Irish literary criticism can't leap from primitivism to post-modernism without an intervening period of historical, cultural and evaluative ground-clearing. We have had neither a revisionist literary criticism nor a thorough-going empiricism.

(Longley, 1992d, p. 20)

While this formulation is apparently unexceptionable (apart from the astonishingly patronising and inaccurate term 'primitivism'), it presupposes that 'primitivism' is the only phenomenon to be critically analysed, and that a 'revisionist literary criticism' or a 'thorough-going empiricism' are the only alternatives. There is no sense of the kind of project of critical modernism that Bell writes of, no sense that the bourgeois 'modernity' that has emerged as the social and cultural concomitant of the Lemass/Whitaker liberalisation in the Republic, unfinished as it may be in important respects, ought to be subjected to critical scrutiny. What Longley and Foster seem to miss is Bell's sense of the 'contradictions of modernity'. In the desire for 'psychological *embourgeoisement*' and for a 'thorough-going empiricism', we can read the signs of a seriously undialectical form of critique, that is incapable of paying attention to the underbelly of the process of modernisation. Not merely that, but a form of critique that is unable to comprehend its own historicity, its own location in the midst of the processes it is describing. As I have been arguing, this is an effect of the narrow sense in which modernisation has been imagined in Ireland. It does not seem to occur to Longley and Foster that they too, and the positions to which they adhere, may come under assault by the forces they wish to unleash on nationalism or 'primitivism'. Again, modernisation, as it is implicit in 'psychological *embourgeoisement*' or 'evaluative ground-clearing', is understood as an entirely beneficent process. What Longley and Foster fail to grasp are the full ramifications of the process of which they constitute the intellectual analogue. Berman, again, puts the case admirably. In arguing that Marx was a great modernist writer himself, Berman suggests that Marx recognised the revolutionary role of the bourgeoisie, but that he also saw that the economic and political revolution initiated by the bourgeoisie would eventually sweep it away. Thus, Berman suggests,

> The irony of bourgeois activism, as Marx sees it, is that the bourgeoisie is forced to close itself off from its richest possibilities, possibilities that can be realized only by those who break its power.
>
> (Berman, 1983, p. 93)

The 'richest possibilities' of the bourgeoisie are the brilliant generative energies which they release, the positive image they have produced of the life of action. Their problem and their weakness is that they express these energies principally in the making of money, in the accumulation of surplus value. But, as Berman asks, why should the good life of action be limited only to the making of profit? Why should people who have seen what the active energy of human beings can bring about simply accept the social arrangements into which they have been born as given and therefore immutable? If the bourgeoisie can organise and co-ordinate their actions to change the world, why should not others do so also, to change it still further?

> The 'revolutionary activity, practical-critical activity' that overthrows bourgeois rule will be an expression of the active and activistic energies that the bourgeoisie itself has set free. Marx began by praising the bourgeoisie, not by burying it; but if his dialectic works out, it will be the virtues for which he praised the bourgeoisie that will bury it in the end.
>
> (Berman, 1983, p. 94)

The kind of criticism practised by Foster and Longley is afraid to address its own conditions of possibility, as to do so would be to allude to its historical contingency. That is, they wish to produce a critique of what they see as 'tradition' – for example, nationalism – but they wish not to have that critique applied to themselves. Hence, they wish to halt the dialectic of criticism at the point of 'pyschological *embourgeoisement*' and 'evaluative ground-clearing'.

Hopefully, then, a crucial function of this book is to draw attention to the gaps and elisions, the points of hesitation in cultural production in Ireland, and also in the kind of cultural critique exemplified by Foster and Longley. It is in such gaps or at such moments of hesitation that this book tries to locate itself, drawing attention to the tensions between tradition and modernity, between national culture and modernism, between authority and critique.

In the shifts I have made so far between discussion of various kinds of (mostly academic) writer, I have been working with an idea of the writer or intellectual derived from Gramsci. I have been suggesting that Irish academics have theorised Irish modernisation and the Irish nation in ways that have been heavily influenced by modernisation theory. But Benedict Anderson's formulation of the nation as an 'imagined community' assumes that it is not merely academics who 'imagine' national communities. The value of his idea is that it makes clear that the national community is a social creation. Nevertheless, it is also vital to note that this 'imagining' of community referred to above is in various ways circumscribed. Every member of a community may be *enabled* to imagine the nation, but some imaginings are more powerful or legitimate than others. Powerful imaginings might be seen as those of *intellectuals*. 'All men are intellectuals, one could therefore say', Gramsci writes, 'but not all men have in society the function of intellectuals' (Gramsci, 1971, p. 9). For Gramsci, the role of intellectuals was crucially to provide legitimacy for the social order, whether that was the existing status quo, or for a newly emerging socio-political arrangement. The moment of such emergence is precisely such a 'crisis of authority' as described earlier. As Edward Said suggests (drawing on Gramsci), all cultural and intellectual activity in society takes place on ground demarcated by the State, and thus is crucially related to authority (Said, 1984, 168–77). For Said and Gramsci, ideas are produced in order to be effective, in order to be disseminated and to have social force. A great deal of thought elaborates on a relatively small number of principal directive ideas. Said glosses Gramsci's use of the term 'elaboration' in two ways:

> First, to elaborate means to refine, to work out (*e-laborare*) some prior or more powerful idea, to perpetuate a world view. Second, to elaborate means something more qualitatively positive, the proposition that culture itself or thought or art is a highly complex and quasi-autonomous extension of political reality and, given the extraordinary importance attached by Gramsci to intellectuals, culture and philosophy, it has a density, complexity, and historical-semantic value that is so strong as to make politics possible. Elaboration is the ensemble of patterns making it feasible for society to maintain itself.
>
> (Said, 1984, p. 171)

This work of elaboration is carried out by intellectuals, and the insight of Gramsci and Said is to realise that it can consist equally of the projection of grand programmes on the level of the nation state, or of apparently much more modest cultural production. Another way of putting this would be to say that the elaboration of the nation (a series of cultural narratives) is an essential enabling possibility of the state. But the state is itself an institution, or series of institutions, that can be understood and manipulated only in ways that are culturally mediated. This results in a national culture that is both crucial to and dependent on the state. Thus, the community tends to be imagined in ways that serve and legitimate the interests, political and economic, of certain élites within that community. These imaginings achieve social and political authority through their relationships to the dominant means of communication and cultural reproduction in the community – newspapers, publishers, the electronic media (radio, television and film), advertising, the entire system of education. So the nation tends to be imagined via the mediation of powerfully centralising forces in society, organs of civil society and of the state, that tend to have been organised in terms set by the national state. Of course, in the present era of multinational capital and communications, this situation is no longer quite as pure, in national terms, as it was in the nineteenth century. But though even state-owned or partly-owned media may be subject to controls and restrictions that are legislated for from outside the boundaries of the state, the organs of cultural production and reproduction still tend to be national in their horizons of operation. The nation, as 'imagined community', has not yet been fully transcended as a mode of social formation and identity-construction.

Homi K. Bhabha has developed the idea of the nation as a narrative that Anderson suggested. That is, Bhabha reminds us that the nation conceives of history as itself story-shaped, but that the historian or critic can read this nation-narrative as having been actively constructed (Bhabha, 1990, pp. 1–7). So one can say that the nation is a narration. With Hayden White we then realise that narrative is fundamentally related to the matter of *authority*, and that, even when it is dealing with 'real', historical events, narrative employs figurative devices that we associate with fictive discourse. So, the susceptibility of events or experiences to narrative representation is in positive proportion to their social or political authority or importance (White, 1987, pp. 11–14). To return to Said and Gramsci, everyone tells stories, but one must first have 'permission to narrate', whether the subject of this narration is an individual, a family, a local community, a social class or minority, or a nation. This is not to suggest that nations or history are fictions, but merely a reminder that part of the effect of such narrations is derived from their deployment of tropes also used in fiction or myth. White writes that

> A given culture is only as strong as its power to convince its least dedicated member that its fictions are truths. When myths are revealed for the fictions they are, then, as Hegel says, they become 'a shape of life grown old'.
>
> (White, 1978, p. 153)

What I am arguing here is that the emergence into self-conscious relief of cultural narratives, or their self-revelation as constructs, can be read as a local expression of the crisis of metanarratives. For the function of narratives is not simply to legitimise grand national or state projects, but to make sense of the quotidian activities of ordinary people. So, in what follows, I am interested in suggesting relationships between paternal, familial, authorial, cultural, discursive and political authority. I will be trying to elucidate the relationships between these forms of power, as they are manifested in moments of crisis.

Now, the Republic of Ireland and Northern Ireland are obviously not the only regions of the West to have experienced the political, social, economic and cultural upheavals associated with postmodernity. But I am interested in suggesting that the ways that these two regions have experienced these traumas have been inflected with aspects of local experience that can be understood in terms of what Seamus Deane has called our 'long colonial concussion' (Deane, 1986b, p. 58), being the crisis of Ireland's post-1922 political ideologies, state unionism and state nationalism. Consequently, Bhabha's comments, building on the work of Tom Nairn, on the 'ambivalence' of the nation seem particularly appropriate to the Irish situation:

> It is an ambivalence that emerges from a growing awareness that, despite the certainty with which historians speak of the 'origins' of nation as a sign of the 'modernity' of society, the cultural temporality of the nation inscribes a much more transitional social reality ... Tom Nairn, in naming the nation 'the modern Janus', [suggests] that the 'uneven development' of capitalism inscribes both progression and regression, political rationality and irrationality in the very genetic code of the nation. This is a structural fact to which there are no exceptions and 'in this sense, it is an exact (not a rhetorical) statement about nationalism to say that it is by nature ambivalent.
>
> (Bhabha, 1990, pp. 1–2)

The crises that built in Ireland, North and South, in the 1960s, and finally burst in the streets, in the economies and in the political systems in the period from 1969 to 1973, all partook of the character of material manifestations of the discursive ambivalence of which Bhabha writes. The point is that this period did not simply consist of atavistic cultures and ideologies coming into contact with modernity, but of national ambivalence coming into contact with, and frequently articulating with and being expressed through postmodernism (taking the latter to be indeed 'the cultural logic of late capitalism'). It is this conjunction that causes us to find in the texts here examined elements of what are often analytically separated out as 'tradition', 'modernism' and 'postmodernism'. If postmodernism nostalgically reprocesses history as 'heritage' or pastiche, it is worth remembering that history, in the form of 'tradition', is frequently already socially and politically an invention. This implies the amenability of 'tradition' and 'postmodernity' to articulation, often to anti-progressive ends; consequently also the continuing cultural, intellectual and political importance of *critical* forms of modernism in the fields of cultural production and criticism – Brechtian self-consciousness in the former, Marxism in the latter.

What I have tried to do here is to read a selection of cultural documents in their relationships to this crisis of nationalism, and its relationship to modernity and postmodernity. I have felt free to comment on other, mostly academic/intellectual trends of roughly the same period, because they seemed to me to be either illustrative of the crisis (as in the case of economics) or more directly related to cultural work of the time (as in historiography). Methodologically, such an approach is enabled and legitimised by the relationship between culture and authority, as it is described by Edward Said and David Lloyd. That is, that culture can be understood as not merely a series of texts and practices, but as a *force*, what Said calls 'a system of values saturating downwards almost everything within its purview' (Said, 1984, p. 9). What Said does here is to draw out the imbrications of power in Matthew Arnold's definition of culture as the best that is known and thought (Arnold, 1932, p. 70). He realises that Arnold's idea is related to what Gramsci was later to call 'hegemony', being the actively constructed ideological dominance of the ruling group in society, a dominance that is produced and elaborated by intellectuals, including literary artists (Gramsci, 1971, p. 12). Said continues by noting that Arnold identifies triumphant culture with the State, in that culture is man's best self and the State its materialisation. In this formulation, the power of culture is potentially the power of the State itself (Said, 1984, p. 10). So, for an intellectual to have conferred upon his or her work the honorific title of 'culture' is for him or her to be endowed with an authority that is ultimately related to that of the state. Said goes on to suggest that the coincidence of state authority and cultural legitimacy results in a sense of centrality, confidence, the sense of majority, community, belonging and 'home' in cultural production. To fall outside this legitimate culture is to be 'homeless', irrational, anarchic, beyond representation (Said, 1984, p. 11). Thus the processes by which certain practices are deemed culturally legitimate are as much a matter of exclusion as inclusion. Lloyd advances the case even more forcefully: 'To the monopoly of violence claimed by the state', he argues, 'corresponds the monopoly of representation claimed by the dominant culture' (Lloyd, 1993, p. 4). Furthermore,

> Control of narratives is a crucial function of the state apparatus since

its political and legal frameworks can only gain consent and legitimacy if the tale they tell monopolizes the field of probabilities. The state does not simply legislate and police against particular infringements, it determines the forms within which representation can take place. Access to representation is accordingly as much a question of aesthetics as of power or numbers, and not to be represented often as intrinsically a function of formal as of material causes.

(Lloyd, 1993, p. 6)

It is important to realise that this matter of narrative is not simply a matter of the grand corporate consciousness of whole communities, or of the privileged consciousness of major artists. Alan Sinfield elaborates a model of cultural production in accordance with that of Said and Lloyd, but he stresses the importance of narratives in everyday life, for ordinary people:

The point to stress here is that stories are *lived*. They are not just outside ourselves, something we hear or read about. They make sense for us – of us – because we have been and are in them. They are already proceeding when we arrive in the world, and we come to consciousness in their terms. As the world shapes itself around and through us, certain interpretations of experience strike us as plausible because they fit with what we have experienced already. They become commonsense, they 'go without saying'. Colin Sumner explains this as a 'circle of social reality': 'understanding produces its own social reality at the same time as social reality produces its own understanding'.

(Sinfield, 1989, pp. 24–5)

The series of activists chosen are writers and film-makers whose work spans the period, roughly from 1970 until 1990. I have chosen work that seems to me to pose the question of narrative, whether self-consciously or not, and the intention has been, against the grain, to produce politicised readings of works that often resist such an approach. Of course, this book cannot claim to be an exhaustive survey, but it makes a start at the writing of this crucial recent period of Irish cultural history. If the broad linkages that are made across the cultural sphere seem to amount to an unnatural and crude yoking together of disparate elements, then I make no apologies. The very separation of activities – cultural, intellectual, political – is a defining characteristic of the present moment, and therefore the duty of the critic is, precisely, to synthesise, to bring seemingly disparate materials into a single focus.

So, two of Brian Friel's most apparently 'unpolitical' plays, *Living Quarters* and *Faith Healer* are discussed by trying to reread them in the light of an earlier 'political' play, *The Freedom of the City*, by bringing out the liberal limits of their collective usage of apparently radical Brechtian techniques. John Banville's novels of the 1970s and early 1980s, his 'historical novels', are placed in relation to the philosophical and political questions that have beset Irish historiography during the period. I have discussed the 'Dublin Renaissance' of the 1980s, offering a critique of one of its most obvious manifestos, and of the novel that is often seen as its culmination, Dermot Bolger's *The Journey Home*. Two of the most interesting and experimental independent Irish films of the period, *Caoineadh Airt Uí Laoire* and *Maeve*, both of which have their roots in the Northern violence, are examined in comparison to the political and geographical tropes of the best-known Irish commercial feature films of the same time. Lastly, I have discussed the work and careers of two of the major critics of the period, Edna Longley and Seamus Deane. Overall, the aim has been to bring out the relationships traceable between these works and the narrow and abortive project of modernisation discussed above.

Some explanation is in order as to the absence here of creative writing by women. My intention has been to deal with writing that is either canonical (Friel, Banville) or counter-canonical (Bolger). I do not believe that a solid canon, or counter-canon, of recent or contemporary Irish women's writing as yet exists, and the problem with the essentially agonistic model of cultural production in use here is that it has the effect of seeking out suitable groups of opponents who can be pitched against each other. The ambition of the Raven Arts Press project initiated by Bolger makes it attractive for such criticism, for it formulates itself as a movement, on various grounds (generation, place, class, worldview). with writers in prose, poetry, drama and journalism, and these separate activities can be seen as mutually reinforcing (as in O'Toole's critical path-clearing for Bolger). Of course, *every* critical reading or selection is appropriative of the material it treats. Every critical project, however modest or ambitious, amounts to a re-narrativisation of the evidence of cultural history. But I chose at the outset to deal with figures that had achieved canonical or near-canonical status, and a serious study of contemporary female writers would seem to be as much an investigative and reconstructive task as a critical project. Having said all of this, I have not hesitated to deploy feminist criticism where it seemed useful and appropriate, since issues of cultural and political authority have been important to this project, and these are frequently understood in implicitly patriarchal terms.

The present work does not deal with poetry, for at least two reasons. Firstly, contemporary Irish poetry does not lack for serious critical attention. An impressive volume of work has been published on recent Irish poetry – by Seamus Deane (1985), Edna Longley (1986, 1994), Robert Garratt (1986), Dillon Johnston (1985), Neil Corcoran (1992) and Elmer Andrews (1992). Less work has been published on the novel – the amount of critical material published on Seamus Heaney is very considerably greater than that on John Banville, his approximate contemporary. Secondly, the focus in what follows on the debate on 'revisionism' was driven partly by a desire to study ways in which the Northern crisis could be seen as an important context or, alternatively, a denied politico-discursive space in contemporary Southern writing. At least one powerful critic, Edna Longley, has constructed an increasingly deliberate and explicit critical project out of the 'revisionary' impulse that she detects in and draws out of much contemporary Ulster poetry. Since this book is also concerned with the idea of 'revisionism', but from a different perspective from that of Longley, it has seemed suitable to pursue a critical project in a different direction. I am concerned, that is, to take issue with Edna Longley, but my argument with her is part of a wider discussion of 'revisionism'.

Fascinating as the overall lineaments and contours of the culture of Ireland over the period are, clearly, this book could not have dealt with everything. The result has been a hybrid, made up of cultural history, and formalist but politicised readings of individual texts. Such an approach may be accused of eclecticism and opportunism, but I take comfort in Said's reading of Gramsci, and also Giambattista Vico, as a methodological resolution of the difficulties of critical-intellectual work in these times:

The fundamental thing is that history and human society are made up of numerous efforts crisscrossing each other, frequently at odds with each other, always untidy in the way they involve each other ...

... A heterogeneity of human involvement is therefore equivalent to a heterogeneity of results, as well of interpretative skills and techniques.

(Said, 1985b, p. 145)

The point is to try to produce an overarching picture, without homogenising individual writers or works into some totalising system. The struggle is to move coherently between the necessary and obvious specificities of individual works, and the more difficult and obscure general trends of social and cultural history. That struggle is necessarily constitutively open-ended and unfinished, part of an ongoing dialogue. My hope is that the work undertaken here will form part of that critical and analytical conversation.

CHAPTER 1

Brian Friel: politics, authority and geography

Born in Co. Tyrone in 1929, Brian Friel is widely regarded as Ireland's greatest living playwright, the dramatic writer closest in stature to those who emerged in the Revival and its aftermath – Yeats, Synge, O'Casey and Beckett. His career as a dramatist spans three decades, and for this study he is a notable figure in that I find that his work announces matters both of form (the strengths and limitations of formal reflexiveness) and of content (representations of geography) that are worked out in the other writers that I will be looking at.

Friel's themes are various, but certain ideas and issues return repeatedly in the plays. I wish to look at the issues of authority, narrative and geography in two plays of the late 1970s, *Living Quarters* (1977) and *Faith Healer* (1979) (see Friel, 1984). I am concentrating on these plays, because they are among Friel's most apparently domestic or personal works, which seems to me to be precisely the reason to attempt to locate them in a political matrix. In this approach, I am taking my cue from Edward Said, who suggests that 'the critic is responsible to a degree for articulating those voices dominated, displaced or silenced by the textuality of texts' (Said, 1984, p. 53). My intention, therefore, is to try to flush out the implicit politics of these plays, which are read mostly as studies of familial dysfunction (*Living Quarters*) and the nature of dramatic art (*Faith Healer*). With this aim, I will approach them via a reading of Friel's most explicitly and self-consciously 'political' play, *The Freedom of the City* (1973; see Friel, 1984). I hope to demonstrate the political limits of that work, and then to show how those limits are reworked in the later apparently apolitical work.

In Friel, we see a complex working-out of the problem of artistic and political identity that Terence Brown has suggested is characteristic of much Irish writing of the 1970s (Brown, 1985a, pp. 317–23). Friel appears to have seen himself at this time as a 'bardic' artist, that is, as an exemplary spokesman, or dramatic conduit, for his nation. Indeed, looking at his entire oeuvre, one can see it as a social history, or narration, of the nation from the early 1960s until the early 1990s. Changes in the family, the social role of the writer, the yearnings, failings and disillusionment of the middle classes, emigration, the decline of the 'Big House', the demise of the Irish language, the difficulties of the intellectual, the Northern crisis and political violence, and, behind all of these, the idea of modernity itself – all of these issues emerge in Friel's plays. However, the concept of the bardic artist, and the 'nation' in question here, can also be revealed to be actively constructed ideas, that emerge from Irish literary tradition. They are, to that extent, unstable. A clear expression of this concept of the bard appears at the beginning of *The Mundy Scheme* (Friel, 1969), a corrosive satire on the rising bourgeoisie that emerged in the Republic in the wake of the Lemass/Whitaker liberalisation of the late 1950s. It is also visible in Friel's sense of himself (Hickey and Smith, 1972, pp. 221–5). *The Mundy Scheme* is subtitled *'Or May We Write Your Epitaph Now, Mr. Emmet?'*, referring to Robert Emmet's famous 'Speech from the Dock' in the aftermath of his abortive rising of 1803, when he declared: 'When my country takes her place among the nations of the earth, then and not till then, let my epitaph be written'. So Friel here sets out to question the achievements of Irish independence, particularly the 'progress' of the preceding decade. The play's Prelude gives us a strong sense of Friel's concerns, and his position, at this time:

> *Voice*: Ladies and Gentlemen: What happens when a small nation that has been manipulated and abused by a huge colonial power for hundreds of years wrests its freedom by blood and anguish? What happens to an emerging country after it has emerged? Does that transition from dependence to independence induce a fatigue, a mediocrity, an ennui? Or does the clean spirit of idealism that fired the people to freedom augment itself, grow bolder, more revolutionary, more generous?
>
> (Friel, 1969, p. 7)

Although this Prelude is staged, and to that extent self-conscious and therefore not to be taken as 'objective' or an authentic expression of authorial intent, the Swiftian ferocity of the satire that follows requires this opening framing statement to be taken as normative, stable and authoritative. So we see here a manifestation of Friel's 'post-colonial' understanding of Irish history – the evident investment in the idealistic tradition and narrative of national liberation, the sense of disappointment in the state built in the Republic since 1922, and the sense that that disappointment has been increased rather than lessened by the modernisation of the 1960s.

In 1971, Friel articulated the anger that motivated the satire of *The Mundy Scheme*:

> Ireland is becoming a shabby imitation of a third-rate American state … We are rapidly losing our identity as a people and because of this, that special quality an Irish writer should have will be lost. A writer is the voice of his people and if the people are no longer individuals I cannot see that the writer will have much currency.
>
> (Hickey and Smith, 1972, p. 224)

Friel's concern here is, of course, that of identity: that of the individual, of the writer, and of the nation. All three are rapidly losing their sovereignty: the nation-state is being prostituted (in *The Mundy Scheme* at least) to multinational capital, the Irish writer is losing his national identity, and the people are losing their identity as individuals. Interestingly, individual identity is seen as most fully realised in the 'imagined community' that constitutes the nation, and the writer is reckoned to be in danger of losing his social role if this complex of relations is disturbed. In the same interview, Friel declared that he knew 'no reason why Ireland should not be ruled by its poets and dramatists' (Hickey and Smith, 1972, pp. 224–5). However, he was gloomy about the prospects for such acknowledged legislators, paraphrasing Tyrone Guthrie to the effect that 'if Yeats and Lady Gregory were alive today, they would be unimportant people' (Hickey and Smith, 1972, p. 225). So Friel is interested in the status of the creative writer, and sees him as having a special relationship with 'the people'. In this concept we see an idea of the 'representative writer' of the nation. David Lloyd has drawn out the implications of this identitarian literary politics, demonstrating that in its most famous Irish critical exponent, Daniel Corkery, there is an insistence 'upon a continuity between individual and national identity which is borne by literature', an insistence, furthermore, that 'only a national literature can be considered literature at all, since only such a literature is representative' (Corkery, 1931; Lloyd, 1993, p. 44). According to Lloyd, Corkery's thesis was a reworking of the identity thinking that had constituted the aesthetic of Irish cultural nationalism since the Young Ireland movement, and it implied that 'a normal literature is a national literature, and the function of a national literature is normalizing' (Lloyd, 1993, p. 47).

The relationship Friel articulates can be described, as I suggested earlier, as *bardic*, and it was about to break down irretrievably in Ireland. I will be tracing, in my readings, the crisis and breakdown of this idea in Friel. It is easy to see that Friel's model here is somewhat nostalgic and sentimental, of course, in the face of 1960s modernisation, and also unhistorical in its positing an unbroken continuity in the relationship between Irish writers and their constituency since the Revival. As Terence Brown has described, the traditional roles available to the writer – either the legitimiser of the status quo, or its lonely, liberal conscience – were in the process of being swept away, and the literary intellectual marginalised, because, broadly, of the lifting of repressive censorship and the increased provision of state aid for artists, especially writers, in the form of tax breaks in the 1970s (Brown, 1985a, pp. 312–23). However, in Northern Ireland, the relationship was complicated by political violence, and the sectarian divisions of society, with the result that as social and economic forces combined to detach Friel from an obvious community in the South, political conflict put pressure on Friel to identify himself openly with his background community, that of Roman Catholicism and national-ism, in the North. In the 1980s, Friel went on to attempt to resolve this prob-lem with Field Day, with debatable results. My intention in examining *Living Quarters* and *Faith Healer* is to deal with the two plays in which the figure of the writer is most explicitly analysed, before it is reformulated in less obvious terms in later plays such as *Making History* and *Dancing at Lughnasa*.

As I pointed out above, Friel identified the artist as 'the voice of his people', as a mediator between his people and other groups and formations (such as the Church, the state, and other peoples), and between his people and themselves. This is a bardic conception. The traditional bard functioned as a mediator of language, one who from the linguistic resources of the culture to hand fashions a series of deliberately arranged messages which serve to rein-force that culture's self-image. The structure of these messages is tailored to the needs of the culture for which they are produced, not to the internal requirements of the 'text' nor of the individual artist. The final 'authority' of bardic messages is the audience in whose language they are transmitted.

The bardic communicant lies at the heart of his culture. This is not mere arrogance or self-promotion, but a response to the society's felt need for such a centre. The bardic function is generally a dynamic and positive one. It works to pull into its own core position its audience, and also the reality to which it refers. John Fiske and John Hartley call this positive role 'clawback': 'the bardic mediator constantly strives to claw back into a central focus the sub-ject of its messages' (Fiske and Hartley, 1978, p. 87). This process, often par-tial (both in the sense of being partisan, and of being not fully adequate) and selective, is one of turning the Other into the Same, of reclaiming new and unfamiliar phenomena for ideology. Equally, when this process fails, it demon-strates the need for the ideology to mutate, in order to cope with changing circumstances.

Lastly, it must be stressed that the bardic function tends towards what Fiske and Hartley call *socio-centrality*. They continue:

> The bardic mediator tends to articulate the negotiated central concerns of its culture, with only limited and often over-mediated references to the ideologies, beliefs, habits of thought and definitions of the situa-tion which obtains in groups which are for one reason or another peripheral.
>
> (Fiske and Hartley, 1978, p. 89)

This brings us back to Friel's statement in 1971, which envisages 'the writer' as the 'voice of his people', and 'the people' as being composed of 'individuals'. It is worth noting that this image supposes a *male* writer, and that the liberal-humanist notion of the 'individual' is, firstly, defined historically in specific terms (white, male, middle-class); and, secondly, is an idea that sits uncomfortably with the explicitly bardic or even shamanistic role Friel posits for the artist, both here and in later work such as *Faith Healer*.

This bardic function may not, therefore, be quite as generous or inclusive as it initially seems. As described above, it may be exclusive, on grounds of class, ethnicity or gender. When we consider Friel's relationship to his audience(s), this is not a minor matter. Returning briefly to *The Mundy Scheme*, we can see complications of this self-representation of the writer. The play is about a morally-bankrupt Irish government, which, in order to buttress an ailing economy, draws up a scheme to turn large tracts of the West of Ireland into an international graveyard, with plots being auctioned off to the highest bidder. The critique offered in the play of the new materialism, modernisation and *embourgeoisement* of the 1960s is conducted in primarily moral or ethical terms. Government and the state bureaucracy are satirised for their greed and dishonesty. The modernisation and opening-up of the economy represented by the Mundy Scheme is portrayed principally as a project of self-aggrandisement enacted by corrupt politicians and civil servants. While Friel is clearly aware of the problematising of national identity brought by the new economic policies, and the dependent relationship with foreign states and capital they produce, he can only criticise the social structures and phenomena produced in Ireland by these changes in terms of the (im)moral behaviour of bureaucrats. He offers no analysis of the fundamental economic and class dynamic at work, only a moral castigation of an epiphenomenon.

The moral/ethical critique of government and state is typical of the humanist intellectual, with its reformist implications, and failure to comprehend the full range of economic, political and social structures. This is not to suggest that such critique is unnecessary, or not useful, but rather to suggest that it is not thoroughgoing enough. In the limitedness of this critique, in its emphasis on individual morality and, implicitly, on the heroic dissenting voice of the individual artist/intellectual, and so the concomitant reciprocal relationship of intellectual and society, we see the limits to Friel's conception of the 'nation' of 'individuals'. We see also how Friel is working within the problematic of identity, separated from the 'material dimension', in exactly the manner described by O'Dowd (O'Dowd, 1988).

An excursus into the typology of intellectuals provided by Antonio Gramsci yields another framework to place around Friel, that will cut across the bardic model. Gramsci distinguished between 'traditional' and 'organic' intellectuals (Gramsci, 1971, pp. 5–7). For Gramsci, almost anyone connected with the production of knowledge is an intellectual. The former are positioned in society in such a way as to perform the role of producing, reproducing and reinforcing the ideas that underpin the existing status quo, and are therefore not linked visibly to social change. They can be teachers, priests, writers of all kinds, politicians, bureaucrats, scientists. In contrast, 'organic' intellectuals are identifiable with emergent social classes or formations, and they assist that group's insertion into and conquest of civil society. Gramsci really regarded *all* intellectuals as organic intellectuals, in the sense that traditional intellectuals, by buttressing the status quo, are consciously or unconsciously serving the interests of the social class whose hegemony enables that status quo.

Relating this set of ideas to Friel, we see that Gramsci's work permits us to see more clearly the tension that exists in Friel between nationality and class. That is, in his image of the writer as bard, and in his adumbration of the problematising of the concept of 'Irishness' by the modernisation of the 1960s, Friel appears to fit the Gramscian model of the organic intellectual, as an oppositional writer in the mould of Sean O'Faolain, raising ideas – nationality, the nationalist tradition of liberation – that the ruling élite would have preferred to remain buried. However, of course, the bardic function admits of no specific class consciousness – it appeals to what Benedict Anderson, writing of nationalism, calls a 'deep horizontal comradeship' (Anderson, 1991, p. 7). If *The Mundy Scheme* is a critique of Irish 1960s *embourgeoisement*, it is one conducted in bourgeois ethical terms. Another way to see this apparent contradiction is to realise that, if, as Terence Brown suggests, Lemass' chief ideological success lay in disassociating modernisation and Anglicisation, or in nationalising modernisation, then *The Mundy Scheme* to a great degree represents the uneasy reconciliation of this project (Brown, 1985a, pp. 246–7). Looking back at the conception of society Friel hinted at in 1971, we realise that he saw society as made up of 'individuals' whose identity was threatened by the tide of modernisation. This identity was composed equally of nationality and humanity, and both were at risk. So, in the same passage that he conceives of the writer as bard, Friel also appeals to the bourgeois-liberal notion of the individual, and, hence, appears more in the nature of a traditional intellectual. This individual is incomplete or damaged if without a clear national self-consciousness. This confusion also applies to the bardic conception of the writer, who is, for Friel, somehow of the world, but not in it. What Gramsci's typology of intellectuals provides us with in this context is a model that demonstrates that the identity of even the 'traditional' intellectual is determined by overlapping factors. It is a construct partly of the individual will but also inescapably of the social, economic and political forces that surround it.

The explosion of the Northern crisis in the summer of 1968, with the heavy-handed repression of Civil Rights marches, brought Friel to a point where he had to confront his political position directly. Having been involved in the Civil Rights movement, he was living in Derry at the time of Bloody Sunday (30 January 1972), and for some time he had discounted the likelihood of his, or anyone else's, writing a play concerned with the 'Troubles'. In 1971, he said: 'I have no objectivity in this situation; I am too involved emotionally to view it with calm' (Hickey and Smith, 1972, p. 222). He also believed that for a conflict to have dramatic possibilities, 'you must have a conflict of equals or at least near equals. There is no drama in Rhodesia or South Africa, and similarly there is no drama in Northern Ireland' (Hickey and Smith, 1972, p. 222). This reflects Friel's understanding of the Northern problem as a colonial one, and his belief in the illegitimacy of the Northern state. It also exposes his assumption in the 'objectivity' of the aesthetic act, and, linked to this, a mimetic concept of the literary work – a play is only drama if it consists of the actions of equal but opposite antagonists; conversely, reality is amenable to dramatic representation if it contains the preconditions for a kind of aesthetic objectivity. Thus, at this time, the idea of political drama appeared to Friel to be an oxymoron, though it might be argued that certain political plays, as various as *Antigone* and *An Ideal Husband* fulfil his dramatic criteria.

So *The Freedom of the City* appeared as a radical departure for Friel, and the critical reception the play was afforded seemed to bear out this assessment. This play, based on the events of Bloody Sunday in Derry in 1972, when thirteen Civil Rights marchers were shot dead by British Army paratroopers, was first performed in 1973. During the previous five years, Friel had been accused of near-complicit silence on the subject of the 'Troubles', and the plight of the minority community (Pine, 1990, p. 105). But *The Freedom of the City* was a clear and deliberate intervention into Northern politics. What must be clarified is the nature of that intervention. This will also help us to understand the strain that the political breakdown had put on Friel's bardic self-image. We will find that there is a close relationship between Friel's concept of artistic identity, and the identity he ascribes to his characters.

To Richard Pine, Friel makes a distinction between his position as *artist*, and as *citizen*. The former attempts, indeed feels obliged, to maintain a certain distance from events, and from his material. The latter, compelled by political, social and economic developments, speaks out:

> In *The Freedom* we can detect a controlled rage which is utterly characteristic of Friel's confluence with those events [i.e. political and social events], and yet it further indicates the control he exercises over that part of him which is more citizen than artist.
>
> (Pine, 1990, p. 105)

For Pine, Friel's position as spokesman for the minority community is one thrust upon him, one he disowns; Friel disclaims loyalties, denies himself the 'succour' of community. According to Pine, Friel does this to achieve artistic distance, or objectivity. He is also wary of seeming to write *agitprop* for the Provisional IRA, of condoning violence, of contributing to the mariolatry of Republicanism (dying for Ireland or for Cathleen ni Houlihan) by portraying 'terrorism'.

But Pine's view goes against Friel's bardic conception of the artist. Friel is no less a 'spokesman', for all his silence in openly polemical terms. Friel does participate in the 'cultural war' in Northern Ireland, and his apparent disavowal of 'tribalism', and of the 'armed struggle' is no less a political position for its lack of a weapon. Pine takes Friel's disavowals at face value, forgetting the bardic idea, and consequently masks a politics with a rhetoric of artistic distance or 'balance'. Pine concedes that Friel's politics is cultural, that his culture is political, but he is disingenuous in his refusal to name that politics.

The point about *The Freedom of the City* is that it is 'political' depending on where the viewer stands amidst the array of discourses the play deploys. To reviewers in metropolitan London and New York, the play was an apology for 'terrorism'.[1] But to argue this is to ignore the humanist ideological point that is being made, which is ultimately none too radical.

The play dramatises events very similar to those of Bloody Sunday, in retrospect, when the three innocent civilians whose deaths are portrayed are already dead. It moves between scenes depicting the tribunal of inquiry into the deaths (a reference to the discredited Widgery Report), with reports by soldiers, officers, policemen, a sociologist, a pathologist, a forensic scientist; and scenes of the three, Michael, Skinner and Lily, sheltering in the city's Guildhall. We also see and hear briefer discursive contributions on the events – journalists' reports, a priest's sermons, the songs of a balladeer. So the actual actions of the three are dramatically juxtaposed with the various discursive constructions placed upon them.

What becomes immediately apparent, through a deployment of the Brechtian devices of irony and narrative discontinuity, is the failure of any of these discourses to adequately grasp, describe or understand what 'really' happened. The abstract theorising of Dodds, the sociologist, about poverty, the clinical explanation of the deaths by the pathologist, the euphemistic rationalisations offered by the military, the journalist's platitudes, the priest's moralising – none of these provides a full 'human' understanding of the characters,

---

1 Christopher Murray points out that Clive Barnes, a New York critic, found the indictment of the tribunal in the play 'far-fetched, indeed impossible'. See Murray, p. 71. See also the synopsis of British press reaction in Dantanus, p. 140.

motivations, aspirations, social, economic or political backgrounds of Lily, Skinner and Michael. Friel's point is that each of these discourses, in their attempts to grasp what 'really' happened, are as answerable to their own internal rules as they are to the data before them. To that extent, theirs are foregone conclusions. The strength and the weakness of this approach is its levelling capacity. The play displays the way that each of the various discourses seeks to recuperate the histories of Lily, Skinner and Michael in ways that validate that discourse's claim to 'truth'. This applies as much to the official state discourse of the tribunal as to the balladeer. Each of these discourses attempts to narrate the hours and minutes leading up to the deaths, in its own terms. So the tribunal can only understand the actions of the three by inserting them in a narrative of 'terrorism'. The priest can only render them as Civil Rights idealists duped by 'Godless communism' (Friel, 1984, 156). Dodds is interested in Lily, Michael and Skinner as representatives of what he calls 'the culture of poverty', as part of a wider argument. The balladeer constructs the three as insurrectionary heroes in the line of 'Tone, Pearce and Connolly' (Friel, 1984, p.118). What the play fails to provide is the sense that, in the real social and political world, these narratives are not relativistically equal; that the discourse of the tribunal, or of Dodds, would have what Michel Foucault called greater 'effect[s] of power' (Foucault, 1980, p. 131). They would be backed by the authority of the state, or of the university. Likewise, the priest and the journalist possess spiritual and social authority, respectively, derived from the Church and the role of the media. The interesting, because marginal, figure in this hierarchy is the balladeer. Any authority he possesses is derived from his closeness to 'the street'. The balladeer is, in fact, an illegitimate version of Friel himself. He is the sentimental and bellicose nationalist artist that Friel refuses to be. As rendered by the balladeer, the Enlightenment bourgeois revolutionism of Tone, the Gaelic nationalism of Pearse, and the working-class Marxism of Connolly are demoted and discredited.

The problem with this links us back to my remarks earlier about Friel's bourgeois (or constitutional) nationalism. The partial images provided by the various colliding discourses of the play suggest that Friel is interested in his characters in the aggregate, as fully 'human'. The play points out the innocence of Michael, Skinner and Lily, but it can deal with them basically only as victims. This is inscribed in the very staging of the play, with the space outside the Guildhall either that of riot and death, or of discursive misrepresentation. Only inside the relatively intimate space of the Mayor's Parlour can 'true' feelings, motivations, aspirations be explored. Here is a space beyond politics. Here we learn that Lily was not really marching for 'Wan man, wan vote' (a right which had already been won), but for her mentally-handicapped son. Michael, who actually believes in the ideals of the Civil Rights movement at the moment of his death (which he sees only as a terrible error), is constantly the butt of Lily's and Skinner's humour. In his earnestness and naiveté, the Civil Rights movement itself is shown to be of limited value. In Skinner, we find the closest approximation of the true militant, but his constant ironising and anarchic humour, while often genuinely funny, also serves to weaken his potential for real resistance. Political powerlessness can only be compensated for by the putting on of what Seamus Deane calls, after Hamlet, an 'antic disposition' (Deane, 1985, p. 169). Skinner is too deprecating of himself and of others ever to be an effective revolutionary agent. The implication here is that resistance necessitates a repression of some part of one's humanity. The only political space left at the end of this relentless process of depoliticisation is that which it is not necessary to represent in the play, because it is, for Friel, 'natural'. This is, unsurprisingly, bourgeois or 'constitutional' nationalism.

The conservative nature of Friel's politics is matched by aesthetic caution. He uses, as I said earlier, Brechtian techniques to present his self-conscious narration of the 'events' of the play, breaking up the plot with the interpolations of Dodds and the balladeer's songs, and using ironic juxtaposition to display the inadequacy of the various accounts presented. However, his presentation of his three main 'characters' contradicts this. He retains, in ironic but authoritative contrast to the various discourses that the play stages, the authorial and dramatic authority to show us Lily, Michael and Skinner as they 'really are'. The play's irony only works if this central humanist trope is retained. The sovereignty of the author or the central characters is never in doubt. The domination of audience by the stage or the actors is not questioned, since the authority of the author remains necessary to convince us of the 'innocence' of the three. At the beginning of the second Act, the actors playing Lily, Michael and Skinner describe their deaths, in advance of the 'facts', and 'calmly, without emotion, in neutral accents' (Friel, 1984, p. 149). But even this moment of apparently Brechtian 'alienation' is contained, and only makes sense, within a conventional relationship between audience, stage and author, where the latter is seen as the origin of authenticity and meaning. Therefore the imbrication of author, text and institutional theatre with a wider social, political and economic structure cannot be raised, as this would deprive the play of its political force and effectivity.

A radical view of this political effect is offered by Lionel Pilkington, who draws on Brecht, Augusto Boal and David Lloyd to show that if a homology exists between the monopoly of violence claimed by the state and the monopoly of representation claimed by dominant culture, then the institutional theatre can be expected to contribute to the discrediting of militant forms of resistance. Pilkington's examples are Friel's *The Freedom of the City*, *Volunteers* and *Translations*. He writes that

in each instance Friel's anti-republican tendency is based, tautologically, on the ultimate passivity of the spectator. As in the case of the
final moments of *The Freedom of the City* and *Volunteers*, for example, it
is the spectator's inability to do anything, except watch passively the
action on stage, that serves as the proof that nothing, in fact, can be
done ... All that the theatre can do in the face of political resistance is
re-confirm an identity which is recognizable as 'true'. In doing so, however, the bourgeois theatre reveals (at least to criticism) its implicit
counter-insurgency function. To adapt the definition of counter-insurgency that appears in a British Army manual of 1971, the theatre functions – like censorship or the imposition of a military curfew – as a
means of isolating an anti-colonial politics 'physically and psychologically from [its] civilian support'.

(Pilkington, 1994, pp. 134–5)

It is worth adding to this that the play's construction of Lily, Skinner and
Michael as 'innocent' and 'human', and hence representable, is predicated on
the existence of persons who might be 'guilty', 'inhuman' and hence unrep-
resentable. These latter are, of course, republican militants, as against the
security forces. I think this distinction between the guilt of the IRA and that
of the security forces (in the play and in the real events responsible for the
deaths of innocents) is allowable, in that the play's system of representation
retains a space for the security forces to speak, even if that discourse is ironically shown to be a self-protecting lie. But republican insurgents are not
afforded what Said has called 'permission to narrate' (Said, 1994, pp. 247–68),
and the implication is that such people have no history, no context and no
legitimate political motivation. The irony of this is that it is precisely such a
discursive practice that the play implicitly condemns when it is applied by the
tribunal to Lily, Michael and Skinner.

Pilkington neatly sums up what I have elaborated in some detail about *The
Freedom of the City* above. Pilkington's analysis is politically aggressive, of
course, but it thereby helps us to see aesthetic as well as political contradictions in *The Freedom of the City* and other, less obviously political, plays, as we
shall see below. This analysis also serves to show the severe strain that Friel's
bardic self-conception had come under from a concatenation of phenomena,
events and experiences. Through it all, however, is maintained the sovereign
integrity of the writer, and, necessarily, his characters.

In *Living Quarters* (originally performed in 1977), a contemporary retelling
of Euripides' *Hippolytus*, and *Faith Healer* (originally performed in 1979), we
find apparently more domestic or personal explorations of this theme of the
rôle of the artist, and his interaction with society. These issues are explored

at the levels of both form and content. As I suggested earlier, the crisis of authority is one visible at the level of the writer and the literary work, but is not unrelated to the instability of the state and the nation.

In *Beginnings*, Edward Said has teased out the etymology of the term *authority* at some length, notably linking writing to power, to the ability to inspire belief, to the concept of the *author* as father or ancestor as well as writer; and, via the Latin terms *auctor* and *auctoritas* to increase, production, invention, possession and continuance. He concludes:

> Taken together these meanings are all grounded in the following notions: (1) that of the power of an individual to initiate, institute, establish – in short to begin; (2) that this power and its product are an increase over what had been there previously; (3) that the individual wielding this power controls its issue and what is derived therefrom; (4) that authority maintains the continuity of its course.
>
> (Said, 1985a, p. 83)

In *Orientalism*, Said refers to authority, but in more explicitly worldly terms:

> There is nothing mysterious or natural about authority. It is formed, irradiated, disseminated; it is instrumental, it is persuasive; it has status, it establishes canons of taste and value; it is virtually indistinguishable from certain ideas it dignifies as true, and from traditions, perceptions, and judgements it forms, transmits and reproduces.
>
> (Said, 1979, pp. 19–20)

In these remarks on authority, we see a tension in Said's own work between theorising literary production in Nietzschean terms of the will; and in Marxian terms of cultural production, with meaning being produced in relation to economic, social and political processes. This tension can be seen as contradictory, but it may also be productive, for if in *Orientalism* Said's interest was to point out the ways that discursive formations both enable and represent real power (economic, political, military) in the world, then his meditation on authority in *Beginnings*, while obviously concerned with authorial power over textual content and form, reminds us also that texts are willed interventions into the world of discourse.

Sandra Gilbert and Susan Gubar draw on Said's meditation on authority, in order to point out that he theorises writing as explicitly a male act, where the author has power over his text, his characters, the scenarios he creates and the commentary he offers. To write, according to this formulation, is to claim a power of creativity analogous to the fathering of children. Conversely, however, 'paternity is itself, as Stephen Dedalus puts it in Ulysses, a "legal fiction", a story requiring imagination if not faith' (Gilbert and Gubar, 1979, pp. 4–5). Fatherhood is not something to be proven logically for a man, but rather it is a story, a narrative he devises to make sense of his circumstances, to explain and domesticate his partner's child's existence to himself, and so to ease his anxiety.

Of course, this linkage of literary production and paternity, even as it is used as technique of self-affirmation, is tautological and circular. It is a theory that would appeal to Borges, who actually wrote out the implications of such thinking in his short story 'The Circular Ruins' and in the parable 'Borges and I' (Borges, 1970, pp. 72–7, 282–3). Pierre Bourdieu has demonstrated that what he calls the 'charismatic ideology', which is exemplified by Said's meditation above, 'directs attention to the *apparent producer* ... the 'author', suppressing the question of what authorises the author, what creates the authority with which authors authorise'. Bourdieu continues:

> The question can be asked in its most concrete form (which it sometimes assumes in the eyes of the agents): who is the true producer of the value of the work – the painter or the dealer, the writer or the publisher, the playwright or the theatre manager? The ideology of creation, which makes the author the first and last source of the value of his work, conceals the fact that the cultural businessman (art dealer, publisher etc.) is at one and the same time the person who exploits the labour of the 'creator' by trading in the 'sacred' and the person who, by putting it on the market, by exhibiting, publishing or staging it, consecrates a product which he has discovered and which would otherwise remain a mere natural resource; and the more consecrated he personally is, the more strongly he consecrates the work.
>
> (Bourdieu, 1993, pp. 76–7)

What Bourdieu is doing here is disseminating the meaning of 'authority' to an array of sources and processes. He also usefully reinserts the literary intellectual into the wider grouping of organic intellectuals upon whom he depends to win consent for his work. In this, he usefully enlarges on Said's remarks about authority in *Orientalism*.

Michel Foucault pointed out the historically recent provenance of the modern idea of authorship, and suggested that the 'author' is in fact a social function to police and limit meaning-production. He wrote:

> First of all, discourses are objects of appropriation. The form of ownership from which they spring is of rather a particular type ... [which]

> ... historically ... has always been subsequent to what one might call penal appropriation. Texts, books and discourses really began to have authors ... to the extent that authors became subject to punishment ...
>
> Once a system of ownership for texts came into being ... at the end of the eighteenth and the beginning of the nineteenth centuries – the possibility of transgression attached to the act of writing took on, more and more, the form of an imperative peculiar to literature.
>
> (Foucault, 1984, p. 108)

This metamorphosis of the authorial name took place in Britain in 1709, with the English Copyright Act. Previous to the Act, copyright had been perpetual; after its enactment, it was limited to twenty-one years, after which the author's name became a market commodity (During, 1992, p. 124). Foucault went on to suggest that 'if we are accustomed to presenting the author as a genius, as a perpetual surging of invention, it is because, in reality, we make him function in exactly the opposite fashion' (Foucault, 1984, p. 119). In fact, the author-function allows a limitation of the production of significations in a world of market-based capitalist thrift.

With Gilbert and Gubar, Bourdieu and Foucault, we see that authorial authority, as it is conventionally understood, is both a powerful mode of textual and discursive understanding, and also an ideology of relatively recent historical provenance. Perhaps the best-known attempt to subvert this ideology in the field of literary, and more particularly dramatic, production remains that of Bertolt Brecht. We have already seen Brechtian influences in Friel's *The Freedom of the City*; in *Living Quarters* and *Faith Healer*, they are much more clearly in evidence. However, in these plays, as in *The Freedom of the City*, Brechtian formal experiment is allowed only a circumscribed freedom. Ultimately, metadramatic form is not permitted to erode the authority of the author or of the institutional and political setting in which his work is 'consecrated'.

In *Living Quarters* and *Faith Healer*, we find extensive meditations on authority. Both plays are, among other things, about the writer, the nature of the act of writing, resistances which that process seeks to overcome, and its effects in and relations with the world. Both plays, like *The Freedom of the City*, deal in memory and recollection, with the action being over at the opening. *Living Quarters* is about a contemporary middle-class Irish family, the Butlers, living in Friel's fictional locale of Ballybeg, in Donegal. The play is about the events leading to the suicide of Commandant (the rank in the Irish Army that approximates to major) Frank Butler. The play takes its title from the fact that, as a soldier, Butler, and his family with him, has had to accept postings wherever in the country the Army chooses to place him. Ballybeg, then, is not the ancestral home of the family – Butler is, in fact, a name associated with the south-east of Ireland rather than the north-west. The social status of the Butlers, as internal exiles, is indicated further by their obsessive hankering for Dublin; by the gulf between them and the local population (most clear in the contempt in which Charlie Donnelly, the local husband of the middle Butler daughter, is held) and also by the class snobbery that destroyed the eldest daughter's relationship with her young husband, Gerry Kelly. This class-inflected provinciality is a recurrent theme of Friel's, especially in those plays such as *Aristocrats* (originally performed in 1979) but also in his adaptations of Russian writers such as Chekhov, whose *Three Sisters* was performed by Field Day in 1981, and Turgenev, whose novel *Fathers and Sons* he adapted for the stage in 1987 and whose play *A Month in the Country* he translated in 1992.

Seamus Deane has suggested that Friel's plays are marked by 'the pursuit of one elusive theme, the link between authority and love' (Deane, 1985, p. 166). The prospects for both in *Living Quarters* are bleak. Patriarchal authority is seen to be flawed, love is tainted with its relationship to power. In aligning itself with public, hierarchical structures (the Army), it has distanced itself from the private sphere which nurtures it. Frank muses:

> … what has a lifetime in the army done to me? … have I carried over into this life the too rigid military discipline that – that the domestic life must have been bruised, damaged, by the stern attitudes that are necessary over – I suppose what I'm saying is that I am not unaware of certain shortcomings in my relationships …
>
> (Friel, 1984, p. 194)

In this *milieu*, all relationships fail, whether between Frank and his first wife (his love for her 'withered into duty' when she became ill) or between him and his second wife, Anna who, lonely in his absence on duty, has an affair with his son, Ben. Conversely, as Miriam reveals, the health of Louise, the first wife, had been impaired by Frank's egoistic and monomaniacal refusal to countenance any transfer save to Dublin (Friel, 1984, p. 189). Helen's marriage was ruined by her mother's class snobbery, with the connivance of Ben, and she is an emigrant. Miriam has married 'down', to Charlie Donnelly, a local court clerk; she has internalised her mother's insults ('Miriam, you're neither a Butler nor a Hogan. I'm afraid you're just – pure Ballybeg'), resulting in a sense of self-loathing ('I'm a coarse bitch': Friel, 1984, p. 190). Ben, following his mother's wishes, had begun to study medicine, thwarting his father's ambitions for him as a soldier, and contributing to the souring of their relationship. However, he quit college, suffering a breakdown, after his mother's death. His future lies in shifting employment and petty breaches of the law.

If Tina, the youngest child, has, up to the events the play reviews, led a sheltered life, then she shares a bleak future with Helen in London, where the latter suffers a breakdown and has to quit work, while Tina works as a waitress in an all-night cafe. Father Tom, Army chaplain and friend of Frank, undergoes an acute crisis of self-belief and faith during the play. Drunken and unable to prevent his friend's suicide or mobilise others to help him, Tom retires, almost physically immobile. Anna, Frank's betrayer, survives with some hope for the future, but it is a hope dearly purchased. She emigrates to California, and there finds social and economic independence, but at the expense of her sense of place. She lives in Los Angeles, the deracinated city *par excellence*, a place without a centre, populated by people with self-constructed identities. In Deane's terms, she may have broken free of authority, but she may also have lost love – perhaps this is the absence she wonders about in Sir's ledger at the very end of the play.

The Butlers, then, are revealed to be an acutely dysfunctional family, broken by pressures of repressed sexuality, class interests, egoism. As was made clear by the account given above, these pressures are very frequently linked to social space, as well as physical geography and 'place'.

It is difficult not to relate this familial dysfunctionality to Friel's very full deployment here of Brechtian techniques. That is, Friel seeks to use Brecht's 'alienation effect' to anatomise an alienated family by placing them in an alienated stage space. Most obviously, this is done through the figure of Sir, who is a metadramatical surrogate of the author or the director, who moves characters around, speeds time up or slows it down or cuts out swathes of it, provides ironic or glancing commentary on the action ('There's always a gaiety at this stage': Friel, 1984, p. 225). Sir reminds us of the play's mediated nature, of its being staged, and of its temporality. He reminds us that the action we see is in fact a *re*-staging of past events, a series of memories. But it is also more than that. In his introduction, Sir tells us that what we are about to see on stage is a rehearsal, *after the fact*, of the day of Frank's reception in Ballybeg, the family reunion and his suicide. The characters 'reconvene here to reconstruct it'. Further,

> But reverie alone isn't adequate for them. And in their imagination, out of some deep psychic necessity, they have conceived this (*ledger*) – a complete and detailed record of everything that was said and done that day, as if its very existence must afford them their justification, as if in some tiny, forgotten detail buried here – a smile, a hesitation, a tentative gesture – if only it could be found and recalled – in it must lie the key to an understanding of *all* that happened. And in their imagination, out of some deep psychic necessity, they have conceived me – the ulti-

mate arbiter, the powerful and impartial referee, the final adjudicator, a kind of human Hansard who knows those tiny little details and interprets them accurately. And yet no sooner do they conceive me with my authority and my knowledge than they begin flirting with the idea of circumventing me, of foxing me, of outwitting me. Curious, isn't it?

(Friel, 1984, pp. 177–8)

So Sir lays bare the main premise of the play at its start. He undermines the drama and the suspense. All that we see is already written out, in his ledger. The characters know this too. We will see Sir redirect characters when they try to go against the temporal structure of the play (as when Charlie tries to enter the action early: Friel, 1984, p. 181), or against its spatial arrangement (as when Tom exits on the wrong side of the stage (Friel, 1984, pp. 227–9)). But above all, in his introduction above, Sir makes the audience reflexively aware that the stage is an imagined space, the product of an 'imagined community', whose members still recognise its contours even from the grave. Of course, Sir also functions to remind the audience of other spaces, such as the theatre. When he addresses the audience in his introduction, and when he announces the interval, and when he tells Charlie that 'There are no spectators, only participants' (Friel, 1984, pp. 177–8, 215, 181), Sir draws attention to the fact that we are an audience, sitting in the architectural space of the auditorium, watching action on stage. Alluding to the distance between audience and action in seeking to bridge or deny it, Sir brings that distance into relief.

As I said earlier, there is a close link here between alienation and geography. This is perhaps most obvious in Frank, who yearns for the staff appointment he believes he deserves in Dublin, and who finds that UN service in the Middle East is more desirable than staying in a backwater posting in Ballybeg. Such service also has causal effects – it is because he is the 'Hero of Hari' that Frank is slated for promotion and transfer to Dublin. The opposite of this are the conditions of Ben and Miriam. Miriam has become 'pure Ballybeg' – that is, identified with place – but in the context of her family this is an insult, and thus she is ambivalent about it. Ben, in his isolation on the dunes, has achieved a kind of lyrical identification with the local landscape – illustrated by the way that his description to Helen and Tina of the route to his caravan blends into generalised nostalgic memories of childhood by all three (Friel, 1984, pp. 209–11). This identification, however, is achieved only at the expense of isolation – illustrated by the way that nostalgia and temporary empathic unity give way to isolation once again when Ben tries to share his 'confidence' with Helen. She rejects this, Tina is excluded from the argument and they are all separated once again. But Ben's isolation is also what permits his identification, which is with an empty landscape. No local people intrude on his aestheticised communion with Nature. At the play's ending, the exiles of Tina, Helen and Anna represent alienation in geographical terms. The social structure of home, the family, has imploded under the force of its own authoritarianism and the only alternative is the inauthentic autonomy of exile in London or Los Angeles.

This geographical aspect of the play also affiliates it to a wider context. Frank is an officer of the army of the Republic in the middle 1970s. His vision is set either on Hari, an exotic locale suited to heroic action, or Dublin, site of the bourgeois comforts he yearns for. Yet just across the Border, which is never mentioned in the play, the Northern crisis is at its height. At the same time as Commandant Butler is undergoing his crisis of patriarchal authority, then, the Southern state is facing its greatest crisis since 1945. Political leadership in Ireland in the early 1970s was confused, though so also was popular thinking. According to J.J. Lee,

> The Northern virus inevitably infected the Southern body politic. The wonder is that it infected it so little for so long. This was partly due to the quarantine measures adopted by Jack Lynch. His own instinct was against involvement. But he had to tread carefully. 'Re-unification' held ritualistic pride of place not only on the agenda of 'national aims' but in Fianna Fáil rhetoric. Public opinion, as far as one can tell in the absence of specific surveys, had subscribed overwhelmingly to the aspiration of a united Ireland since partition, at least as long as nothing need be done about it. In 1969 the majority seemed to be mainly concerned to prevent the problem spilling over into the South, while at the same time being anxious to protect Catholics in the North from feared Protestant pogroms.
>
> Lynch thus found himself confronting a confused popular instinct, searching for a way to do nothing while persuading itself of its anxiety to do something. How to disengage from the implications of the rhetoric without affronting self-respect required a sustained mastery of shuffle techniques.
>
> (Lee, 1989, p. 458)

However, Lynch was also under pressure from within his own cabinet. Three senior ministers, Charles Haughey, Neil Blaney and Kevin Boland advocated that the Irish Army move into Northern Ireland, taking control of the towns of Derry and Newry, and of the Roman Catholic-dominated areas west of the Bann. Haughey and Blaney were later dismissed from the government because, according to Lynch, they did 'not subscribe to government policy in relation to the present situation in the Six Counties'. This came in the midst of rumours of an imminent *coup d'état*, and Haughey and Blaney, with others, were charged with attempting to import weapons into the Republic illegally. Both were acquitted. So the Northern crisis had penetrated to the heart of the Southern state, revealing the ambivalences of Southern state nationalism. The actual policies enacted illustrate this. The Army was deployed to the Border, with the objective of setting up field hospitals for the care of wounded, Catholic refugees, and the Government called for a United Nations peace-keeping force to be deployed in the North. It also called for negotiations with Britain about the future of Northern Ireland, 'recognising that the re-unification of the national territory can provide the only permanent solution for the problem' (Farrell, 1980, p. 261).

Living Quarters sets up an array of geographical references, as I said ear-lier, that signify the alienation of the Butler family from itself and its environs. It also sets up a series of spatial oppositions – the private (the general series of repressed memories that organise and separate the characters) versus the public (the heroism of Frank, the ceremony of his return and promotion, the exterior personae of characters); the near (Ballybeg, the Army camp, Ben's refuge in the dunes) versus the far-away (Hari, Dublin). 'Place' is invested emotionally – the Hari of heroic action, the Dublin of future yearning, the Army camp of familial repression and failure, the environs of Ballybeg (the pier at Portnoo, Ben's caravan in the dunes, the coastguard station) associated with nostalgia. The family itself consists of 'insiders' and 'outsiders' (and these positions shift through the play), as well as being 'outside' the local commu-nity itself. Outside the family also lies the affiliative order of the Army. Frank's authority and ascendency in the latter order is set off against and undermined by his failure in the other. However, this geographical and spatial alienation also takes place within a society and a polity that was experiencing an acute crisis, or alienation, in its ideology of national and state geography. The medi-ating structure is the Army. An army is an organisation whose function is the control of space, of land and territory. It is the most obvious spatial expres-sion of the coercive power of the state. It is assigned offensive or defensive roles that are defined in spatial terms. While organised hierarchically, it also disposes itself operationally in spatial terms – different units are assigned dif-ferent areas to hold, or corridors to advance in; these will be allotted accord-ing to geographical compatibility – armour to operate in open country, light infantry in cities, mountains, woods. It is significant, therefore, that Frank Butler's service has been in the Middle East, and not on the Border, which can only be a few miles from Ballybeg. The Irish Army has an established and well-regarded history of UN peace-keeping, in the Congo, Sinai, Cyprus, South Lebanon and elsewhere. But it is first and foremost intended, in theory, to defend the territory of the state. That in its historical existence it would have great difficulty in doing so is beside the point. The Southern state defines itself as 'Ireland', and claims the island as the national territory, while acknowledging that its legal limits are those of the 'Free State', that is, the twenty-six county entity. Thus, it is ideologically contradictory. For while the Republic may assert its right to represent the entire nation, it also, in the exercise of that right, is compelled to recognise the Border, militarily, diplomatically, legally, in defence of its own sovereignty. So, the state that claims the right to speak for the whole island and its people, must, by the same token, defend and assert the Border. This is the dilemma that made 'shuffle techniques' the order of the day for Lynch in 1969–70.

The Irish Army, the military expression of the Southern state, is similarly ideologically hobbled. If the Constitution lays a claim to the Six Counties, the Army is associated with such a claim, even if it never tries to exercise it. But it is also committed to the maintenance of the Border. In the 1970s, both impulses were strong.

Frank's UN service and heroism come into a particular relief in this light, and make it possible to bring back into the play much that had seemed shut out, that is, a political context. In retrospect, it seems extraordinary that Northern Ireland is not mentioned in the play *at all*. Its location, its time and conditions of production as a cultural artifact (Friel was living in Muff, Co. Donegal by this time), its choice of the Army as a social location for its protagonists – all of these factors make the absence of the North from the play almost perverse. We note, then, with Hayden White that it is the 'need or impulse to rank events with respect to their significance for the culture or group that is writing its own history that makes a narrative representation of real events possible'. Further,

> Every narrative, however seemingly 'full', is constructed on the basis of a set of events that might have been included but were left out; this is as true of imaginary narratives as it is of realistic ones. And this consideration permits us to ask what kind notion of reality authorises construction of a narrative account of reality in which continuity rather than discontinuity governs the articulation of the discourse.
>
> (White, 1987, p. 10)

In relation to Friel's work, insofar as this amounts to a narrativising of Irish contemporary history, the North represents discontinuous experience to the South. It offends and complicates the developmental narrative of Southern modernisation. Therefore it is to be repressed. The North is the 'event' that might have been included in *Living Quarters* but was left out. This contrasts with Friel's previous two plays, *The Freedom of the City* and *Volunteers* (performed in 1975) both of which dealt with the North directly. It is as if, in the face of the negative reactions these plays received (especially the former), Friel tried to write a private familial drama, but the political pressures found their way into the work in displaced and sublimated form. Frank's story then becomes an allegory of the ambivalence of the Southern state in the face of the Northern crisis – the outward success of the 1960s subverted by the domestic crisis initiated by a younger generation. More specifically, his UN mission is precisely analogical to the UN mission that the Southern government called for in Northern Ireland. His rescue of nine of his injured men, while under fire from hostile 'guerillas', is exactly the task Southern nationalists projected for the Irish Army in the Six Counties. Hari, then, is not merely a place for heroic and decisive action on a personal basis for Frank, compared to the failures of domesticity in Ballybeg; it is also a site for the projection of the wishful fantasies of Southern state nationalism in relation to the North.

To return to the issues of authority and authorship, *Living Quarters* sits rather unhappily between the Romantic model implied in Said's consideration of authority in *Beginnings* and the Brechtian tropes Friel uses. Sir is the most obvious of such tropes, but his identity is uncertain. He may be a director-surrogate, since he works with a pre-existent script and marshalls characters. But he also may be a figure of the author, as he not only manipulates stage time, as a director might, but in a sense produces it, since he is the narrator the play must retroject to give itself coherence and meaning. In this uncertainty, we have a metaphor of Friel's own ambivalence about being an activist artist and intellectual, actually moulding society, and the neutral observer of events.

But Sir is also related to Frank, having after all the appellation the latter would have in his work. Sir is a figure or name of authority, one to whom even Frank is subservient. Further, there is an unstable network of nomenclature between Sir, Frank and Tom, the shifts occurring as authority in these figures fails or succeeds. This shifting of names ('Sir' and 'Father') between the author-figure, the figure of familial and state authority and the figure of Church authority demonstrates a linkage between authorial uncertainty, the instability of the state and the diminishing importance of the Church in a society which was divesting itself of the old deference before institutions without developing a European secular humanism. Tom is mercilessly stripped of his illusions of importance in the course of the play, reduced finally to a drunken, empty figure chanting 'We're here because we're here because we're here' (Friel, 1984, p. 230). Both his pastoral efficacy and his own faith are deeply shaken by the family's revealed contempt for him, Frank's suicide and his inability to persuade them to do anything to prevent it (Friel, 1984, pp. 241–2). Bearing in mind the link of paternity and authorship, we can see Frank as a failed author-father, who cannot control his character-children. The logical extreme of this breakdown of authority is the affair of Anna and Ben. But the parallels with authorship go further, since Frank's greatest failure is one of imagination, shown by his inability to empathise with Anna, and his tendency to see her only as a decoration of himself. This imaginative failure links him to the author-figure, who tries to achieve an imaginative ordering of the world, only to find it resistant to his designs.

Ultimately, however, the Saidian model wins out over the Brechtian, for though Friel stages authorial anxiety in both Frank (the author as father) and Sir (the author as a bardic projection of a community seeking to narrate itself, his 'Ledger' being the raw facts of history requiring the shaping and editing of the author to allow it to function as a 'true' representation), the authority of the stage and the actors, *vis-à-vis* the audience, is never broken down. Friel's most Brechtian play remains firmly in the hands of the institutional theatre, and as such remains in accordance with the model of the dominative theatre explained by Boal (Boal, 1979, Chs. 1 and 2). The play's status as a contemporary re-writing of Euripedes' *Hippolytus* perhaps makes this inevitable. The most un-Brechtian fatalism of the play is revealed most clearly in the way that Sir's ledger seems to contain even the resistance that is manifested towards it, as in the case of Anna's attempt to talk to Frank during the photo session (Friel, 1984, pp. 201–2). A degree of pseudo-Brechtian leash ('openness') is given to the play, only to have it drawn in ('closed') by the ledger. The play never comes near the analysis of the institution of the theatre (which, as Bourdieu indicated, is centrally involved in authorising the author) attempted by Brecht.

In *Faith Healer* the stress on authority and on narration as legitimised by authority is even more explicit. It is a play of four monologues. The first and last are delivered by Frank Hardy, the faith healer of the title. The second is given by a woman, Grace, who may be his wife or his mistress. The third is delivered by his manager. Loose similarities obtain with *Living Quarters*: here we have another Frank, another 'author', another triumphant homecoming turned sour. The 'events' the play deals in are already over; Frank and Grace are actually dead. Ulf Dantanus suggests that *Faith Healer* is partially derived from the Gaelic tradition of storytelling, that of the seanchaí (Dantanus, 1988, p. 172). This is, of course, a bardic tradition, with its stress on the ritualistic and communal aspects of storytelling. However, the practice of storytelling is put in doubt here, as the three narratives contradict each other in regard to fundamental details. Unlike *Living Quarters*, the play contains no autocritique, no already-incorporated and also-staged commentary on itself. But the nakedness of its total reliance on the charisma of its character-actors (that is, the characters are themselves performing for the audience, to try to win their assent) and its eschewing of naturalistic or realistic conventions displays the contingency of the authority of the narratives.

The three speakers, whose monologues narrate different versions of their life together travelling around Wales and Scotland from one shabby venue for Frank's 'performances' to the next, require an audience. To this extent, the audience produces the play, by providing a communal consciousness to link the three narratives. In this sense, in its exposure of the audience-actor relationship, the play might be called Brechtian. But in fact the opposite is the case. For the play confidently and coherently to stage the contest of the characters' narratives, it must first assume domination of the audience, or, in Lionel Pilkington's phrase, the 'passivity of the spectator'. This is achieved by the charisma of the characters, their 'performances', and the performances of the actors playing them – Frank's enigmatic presence and his extraordinary description of his approach to his own death, Teddy's humour and the mystery of his intimacy with Grace, Grace's trembling, near-suicidal pathos. Frank's 'gift' is the equivalent of a tragic flaw; it is the cause of both his charisma and success, and his downfall. The three narratives spiral inwards, from divergent origins, to the stunning conclusion of Frank's murder at the hands of the wedding-guests, with tragic inevitability. Boal points out how for Hegel, drama was driven essentially by 'The Character as Subject', not 'the Character as Object'. Drama is not constituted by plot or narrative, or material conditions, rather drama is a conflict that arises out of the clash of opposed free subjectivities. For Boal, this is one of the central characteristics of bourgeois drama. It also is reminiscent of Friel's comment on the impossibility of drama being written about a situation of political inequality, and goes some way to explain Friel's difficulty with writing drama about obviously political topics. But this leads, in Hegel, to what Boal calls the 'aristocratising' of the dramatic character, especially the hero, since only someone unshackled by worldly contingencies such as the law, work or civic obligations can have the freedom to exteriorise their spirit so fully. The only limitation is the will of another character (Boal, 1979, pp. 88–9). This is precisely what we see in *Faith Healer*. The drama lies in the performances of the characters, and in the contradictions and tensions in their narratives. All else is stripped away. There is no apparent social setting; all we are left with is the authority of the individual narrator, or 'author'. In Boal's terms, and remembering Foucault, this reveals the bourgeois assumptions underlying the play, of the centrality of the individual and the author as both the source and limit of meaning, and also the absence of the social. The performances of the three characters may be self-conscious to the extent that they are 'theatrical', but this involves the audience *only* as a theatrical audience. The theatrical claim on audience attention that Frank, Teddy and Grace in their turn make is such that they arrogate to themselves the sovereign power of representation in the theatre, and nothing exists outside the tight circle they draw between themselves and the audience. Consequently, nothing exists outside the theatre.

Writing of musical performance, Said has drawn on Richard Poirier's essay 'The Performing Self' where Poirier describes performance as

> … an exercise of power, a very anxious one. Curious because it is at first so furiously self-consultative, so even narcissistic, and later so eager for publicity, love and historical dimensions. Out of an accumulation of secretive acts emerges at last a form that presumes to compete with reality itself for control of the mind exposed to it.
>
> (Said, 1991, p. 1)

Further, performance is not simply a happening, but 'an action which must go through passages that both impede the action and give it form' (Said, 1991, p. 2). This describes the verbal strategies of Frank, Grace and Teddy with regard to their narrations of each other, but also it reminds us of the massive effort they, and, through them, Friel, expend to win the audience's assent, to attain hegemony in the theatre. So the play is constituted, as a play, in the collective consciousness of the audience, but this presupposes the total colonisation of that consciousness by the three 'author-characters' on stage.

This is what we find to be the internal formal struggle of the play. It is a play about the radical undecidability of 'truth', as it is striven for by memory, recollection, history. In its staging of narration, the play is reminiscent of *The Freedom of the City*, and also looks forward to later works such as *Making History* (Friel, 1989) and *Dancing at Lughnasa* (Friel, 1990). However, in *Faith Healer*, we seem to find this concentration in its purest form. The issue is stated at its clearest by Grace, with her suggestion that, for Frank, people were fictions:

> It wasn't that he was simply a liar … it was some compulsion he had to adjust, to refashion, to re-create everything around him. Even the people who came to him … yes, they were real enough, but not real as persons, real as fictions, his fictions, extensions of himself that came into being only because of him. And if he cured a man, that man became for him a successful fiction and therefore actually real, and he'd say to me afterwards, 'Quite an interesting character that, wasn't he? I knew that would work'. But if he didn't cure him, that man was forgotten immediately, allowed to dissolve and vanish as if he had never existed.
>
> (Friel, 1984, p. 345)

Finally, at the end of her monologue, she breaks down:

> O my God I'm one of his fictions too, but I need him to sustain me in
> that existence – O my God I don't know if I can go on without his sus-
> tenance.

(Friel, 1984, p. 353)

But we know from Frank's and Teddy's narratives that Grace had reason to
feel at least ambivalent about Frank. Causes for this would include, on his own
account, his 'bitterness', 'deliberate neglect' and 'blatant unfaithfulness' (Friel,
1984, p. 335); his repeated appropriation and alteration of her biography when
introducing her; his apparent callousness in leaving her while she was giving
birth to their still-born child. As she appears on stage, Grace is clearly undergoing an emotional breakdown. Later, Teddy tells us that she has committed
suicide. Clearly, she is not a reliable witness.

The climactic events in all three narratives are those in, firstly,
Kinlochbervie, and secondly, in Ballybeg. The first of these, the still-birth, is
notable both in itself and for the references that circulate about it. Both Frank
and Grace, in the incantatory recitations of the names of obscure and remote
Welsh and Scottish villages that punctuate their narratives, gradually return
obsessively to the name of Kinlochbervie. But Frank never mentions the
events that Teddy and Grace maintain took place there. He tells us that he
and Grace were holidaying there, when word came that his mother had had
a heart attack. But Grace and Teddy describe being there in the course of a
(faith-healing) tour. Grace is adamant that Frank's mother had been dead for
years before she met him, and that the sick relative was his father. Teddy is
sure that the front axle of the van was broken, so he could not have driven
Frank to Glasgow as the latter describes. Frank would like to have had a child,
significantly a son, but informs us that Grace was 'barren' (Friel, 1984, p. 372).
But from Grace's and Teddy's narratives, we are led to believe that a child was
born at the roadside outside Kinlochbervie, and, according to Grace it was
the result of repeated attempts to have a child (Friel, 1984, p. 346). (It is interesting to remember here Gilbert and Gubar's use of Joyce's idea of paternity
being only a patriarchal or legal fiction 'requiring imagination if not faith':
Gilbert and Gubar, 1979, p. 4.) Here we have a father, whose self-proclaimed
vocation is the imagining of people to make them whole, retrojecting a possible fiction of his wife/mistress' infertility to blot out his paternity). But
Teddy's and Grace's narratives conflict in the details of the birth. Teddy tells
us that Frank deliberately left Grace when he knew she was in labour, to walk
in the hills. He, Teddy, delivered the dead child, buried it, prayed over it and
erected a cross over the grave (Friel, 1984, pp. 363–4). Grace, however, reports

that Frank was with her and Teddy at the birth, and that it was Frank who exe-cuted the burial, spoke the prayers and set up the cross (Friel, 1984, pp. 344–5). Teddy's repeated assertion at the end of his account that his relation-ship with Grace was

> 'a professional relationship going back over twenty-odd years'. 'Cause that's what it was, wasn't it, a professional relationship? Well, it cer-tainly wasn't nothing more than that, I mean, was it?
>
> (Friel, 1984, p. 369)

leads us to suppose that, at least on Teddy's part, the relationship may in fact have been more than merely professional. Teddy may have wished to project himself in the role of surrogate father to Grace's child. Alternatively, Grace may not have been able to come to terms with the idea that Frank had been other than a loyal father to her child. Of course, we cannot know. But here, as in *Living Quarters*, we have an imploding family unit, an egotistical father, a possible triangular relationship, and the investment of paternal or familial energies in an alternative form of authority, faith healing in this case.

It is clear that in these plays there is a linkage between exile and familial reproduction. Both Franks return 'home' in the hope of regeneration, only to have those hopes dashed. 'Home' is the place of stunted familial and social relations. In Friel's oeuvre, the theme of exile is a crucial one – it is present in *Philadelphia, Here I Come!*, *The Enemy Within*, *The Gentle Island*, *The Loves of Cass Maguire*, *Aristocrats*, *Making History* and *Dancing at Lughnasa*. The fre-quency of exile among Irish writers is frequently commented upon. Friel him-self, with his moves from Omagh to Derry, and then to Muff, Co. Donegal, is an exile, not only in the Republic (since as Richard Pine tells us, he regards himself as a citizen of Derry), but in Northern Ireland as well, to the extent that there he was an internal exile because he did not identify with the insti-tutions of the British state (Pine, 1990, p. 16).

So, Frank Hardy has led his career as 'artist' in exile, yet all the while edging towards his home, Ireland, in that he only practices his 'art' in Scotland and Wales, the so-called 'Celtic fringe' of the United Kingdom. He imputes this to Teddy's and Grace's belief, being English, that the 'Celtic temperament was more receptive to us' (Friel, 1984, p. 332) because of his being Irish. Grace says that neither she nor Teddy wanted to return to Ireland, but that Frank overruled them (Friel, 1984, p. 351). Frank implies that the decision was made consensually, because they were all 'heartsick' of Wales and Scotland (Friel, 1984, p. 338). This brings us to the only description, in fact the only sentence, that is identical in all three narratives:

... we crossed from Stranraer to Larne and drove through the night to County Donegal. And there we got lodgings in a pub, a lounge bar, really, outside a village called Ballybeg, not far from Donegal Town.

(Friel, 1984, pp. 338, 351, 367)

The Border, and the political fact of Northern Ireland, are elided here, sub-sumed in the phrase 'drove through the night'. It seems that, in fact, Frank has been treading a 'border' elsewhere. For if Wales and Scotland constitute the 'Celtic fringe', they are also a kind of border. In his restless prowling of Scotland and Wales, in his ambivalence about Ireland, Frank wishes to stay away but cannot resist coming back. He works in Wales and Scotland, not only because of the alleged receptiveness of the 'Celtic temperament', but also as a rejection of England. Northern Ireland itself is not seen as an intermedi-ate zone, or a site of ambivalence when it comes to ethnicity; this troubled condition is displaced to Scotland and Wales. In the context of a play which culminates in the return home of an exiled 'artist' and his murder by some of his compatriots, this is not a minor point – Northern Ireland, the site of the most troubled intersection of Britain and Ireland, is passed over entirely, and is therefore both repressed and absorbed. Conflict in Ireland is not repre-sented as having anything to do with the relationship with Britain.

To an extent, the relationship of Frank, Teddy and Grace mirrors this. In the light of the suggestion by Richard Kearney that the relationships in the play amount to an allegory of Anglo-Irish relations (Kearney, 1988, p. 131), and of the work of writers such as Said and Homi Bhabha, we can recognise that frequently the descriptions given by Frank and Grace of each other deploy metaphors and tropes frequently used by the coloniser of the colonised. In *Orientalism*, Said suggested that the stereotype is a form of knowledge, which is characterised by a kind of 'vacillation' (Said, 1979, p. 58). It enables the experience of something foreign to be understood in terms of the famil-iar or the domestic. Thus, 'such a category is not so much a way of receiving new information as it is a method of controlling what seems to be a threat to some established view of things' (Said, 1979, p. 59). Said, then, stresses the element of power that inheres in the discursive deployment of stereotype. Bhabha, writing in Said's wake and drawing on the resources of psychoanaly-sis, seeks to complicate that formulation. He suggests that the authority of colonial discourse insofar as it operates through the stereotype is fundamen-tally *ambivalent*, that power is accompanied and undermined, even at the moment of its articulation, by anxiety. He argues that colonial discourse is dependent on the concept of 'fixity' in its ideological construction of other-ness, and that the stereotype, 'its major discursive strategy', 'is a form of knowledge and identification that vacillates between what is always "in place", already known, and something that must be anxiously repeated' (Bhabha, 1994, p. 66). Further, he notes that it 'is recognizably true that the chain of stereotypical signification is curiously mixed and split, polymorphous and perverse, an articulation of multiple belief':

> The black is both savage (cannibal) and yet the most obedient and dignified of servants (the bearer of food); he is the embodiment of rampant sexuality and yet innocent as a child; he is mystical, primitive, simple-minded and yet the most worldly and accomplished liar, and manipulator of social forces.
>
> (Bhabha, 1994, p. 82)

Now, it must be admitted that, for Frank, Teddy is unthreatening. He is the comical, loyal working-class Londoner. He has no authority over Frank, he is often bewildered by the conflict between Frank and Grace ('citizens of Ireland' as he calls them: Friel, 1984, p. 364). There is little in Teddy's cultural identity that impinges on Frank. Grace, however, is different, and her difference lies in the fact that she is intimate with Frank and also in the fact that her identity and nationality are ambiguous. Frank tells us she is from Yorkshire, and that her name is Dodsmith. After that, he is unsure, and xenophobically dismissive: 'Grace Dodsmith from Scarborough – or was it Knaresborough? I don't remember, they all sound so alike, it doesn't matter' (Friel, 1984, p. 335). This is, of course, an ironic inversion of the Englishman's geographical vagueness about what lies beyond the Channel. Grace says that Frank used to change her name and place of origin to hurt her, and that he used to suggest that she came from places in the Republic, Northern Ireland or England. By her own account, she is from Tyrone (Friel, 1984, p. 347). Frank's inability or unwillingness to allow Grace a stable patrimony is part of his fictionalising power over her, though it also reveals the extent to which she troubles him. If her account is true, then Frank is, among other things, displaying the ambivalence of the South towards the population of the North, unable to decide if 'they' are truly 'Irish', or 'British', or some kind of hybrid, and if the latter, then whether they are assimilable, if they want to be assimilated, or if they are to be eliminated from the national narrative.

Frank's efforts to assert narrative authority over Grace's identity and origins bespeak an unease about her that is related to his own unease about his 'art' and about Ireland. As he obsessively traverses the 'Celtic fringe', ambivalent about his own position, so he constantly reasserts his authority to 'fix' Grace, to reassure himself. This desire to place, and to that extent control her is definitively evidenced in his descriptions of her personality as 'Controlled, correct, methodical, orderly', as his saviour from drink, of her 'mulish' loyalty (Friel, 1984, p. 335); in his dismissal of her miscarriages, labour and delivery in Kinlochbervie, in calling her 'barren'. He describes her mother's description of herself as being afflicted with 'nerves' and of her father being 'obsessed with order' and of Grace as wanting 'devotion' (Friel, 1984, p. 373). All of these descriptions are characterised by being cast in pathological terms, of neurosis. The story that Grace tells of leaving the byre in Norfolk, asking Frank not to follow her, Frank re-tells, not referring to her leaving, thus:

> ... and what she said was: 'If you leave me, Frank, I'll kill myself.' And it wasn't that she was demented – in fact she was almost calm, and smiling. But whatever way she looked straight at me, without fully facing me, I recognized then for the first time that there was more of her mother than her father in her; and I realised that I would have to be with her until the very end.
>
> (Friel, 1984, p. 374)

In this portrayal, a number of interesting features stand out. Frank describes Grace as *irredeemably female* (she partakes more of her mother's neurosis than of her father's obsessive rationality), as a child (Frank would have to be with her 'until the very end'), as neurotic if not insane, and as in some way deceitful (her way of looking at him).

Equally, Grace's narrative displays the same impulse to grasp, contain and finally describe Frank, often in terms of colonial stereotype. He is 'convoluted', a liar, 'sly', alcoholic. Sometimes he is violent, sometimes passively hostile. Finally he is elusive and enigmatic. She portrays him as 'watching me warily – nothing was simple for him – he's watching me and testing me with his sly questions and making his own devious deductions ... drawing sustenance from me ... finally he drained me' (Friel, 1984, p. 342). So Frank is 'devious' but also parasitic. Grace is envious of the 'completion', 'private power' and 'certainty' he attained before a performance. She resents his privacy and the fact of his being 'in such complete mastery that everything is harmonized for him, in such mastery that anything is possible' (Friel, 1984, p. 343). Trained in the rationalities of the law, Grace has tried to apprehend Frank's 'gift' of faith healing, which she describes as having 'defined him', as being 'essentially him' (Friel, 1984, p. 349), but it has eluded her. So she is wary of it, and of him. But she also concedes that 'if by some miracle Frank could have been the same Frank without it, I would happily have robbed him of it' (Friel, 1984, p. 349). This struggle over Frank's essence or meaning is composed, then, of Frank's attempted rejection of Grace's 'devotion', which is born of incomprehension; and her initial attempts to understand his essence by applying her legalistic 'rigour' to it. She is envious of his capacity for a kind of pure subjective sovereignty, which enables him to elude her entirely, and, in Grace's terms, turn against her and erase her.

Frank's and Grace's struggle is a one that takes place in language, just as onstage their narratives are in competition. Seamus Deane has suggested that Friel is demonstrating here that 'there is an inescapable link between art and politics, the Irish equivalent of which is the closeness of eloquence and violence'. The link is disappointment, here 'a disappointment all the more profound because it is haunted by the possibility of miracle and Utopia' (Deane, 1984, p. 20). In the relationship of Grace and Frank, eloquence precisely is violence. Grace formulates Frank's power in verbal terms:

> God, how I resented that privacy! And he's reciting the names of all those dying Welsh villages ... releasing them from his mouth in that special voice he used only then, as if he were blessing them or consecrating himself. And then, for him, I didn't exist.
>
> (Friel, 1984, pp. 343–4)

Frank achieves this rhetorical power, plenitude and self-presence by denying Grace. He achieves full subjectivity only by denying hers. Equally, Frank contains an element – his 'gift' – which Grace finds irreducible to the terms of her own understanding, and, in that sense, 'other'. If Frank's fictionalising is a discursive attempt to 'fix' Grace and reassure himself, her attempts to grasp his 'essence', her jealousy of his sovereignty, represent a counter-discourse.

The two sides of this struggle are nevertheless mutually dependent. Grace describes peace between herself and Frank in terms of 'the neutrality of the ground between us' (Friel, 1984, p. 349). If Grace tells us that Frank 'drained' her, she also concedes that she is one of his fictions, that she needed him to narrativise her experience to give her life meaning and that therefore she was psychically dependent on him. If Frank has rhetorical authority, indeed authorial authority, over Grace, he also admits he was physically dependent on her. Their relationship is symbiotic, and mutually defining. Not only does each seek to define and therefore establish discursive control over the other, but for each of them, this activity is one conducted with some anxiety, and in the interest of self-definition. Frank constitutes his identity by negating Grace's. She strives to apprehend and represent him to herself, and in so doing constitutes herself.

Grace and Frank approximate to Arnoldian images of the dull, rational Anglo-Saxon, and the flamboyant, poetic Celt. But, as I suggested earlier, one of the issues on which they disagree most clearly, and which is therefore troubling for their relationship, is Grace's assertion of her Irishness. On her own account, her family is from Tyrone, while Frank describes her to us as a

Yorkshirewoman. But Teddy also states that Grace is Irish. Her description of her family home, outside Omagh, with its avenue and 'formal Japanese gardens' and servants; and also of her father ('patrician') and the 'professional' family's 'long and worthy record of public service' (Friel, 1984, p. 348), point to an upper-middle-class, probably Protestant Unionist background. So it is possible that Frank's narrative strategy is to locate Grace as safely 'English', in order to cope with her troubling, ambiguous Northern Protestant provenance. This latter is unsettling because it is both Irish and not-Irish, especially in the discourse of Irish nationalism.

The conflict of Frank and Grace, then, is fought out in the terms of cultural struggle. Declan Kiberd has argued, in a Foucauldian mode, that:

> The notion 'Ireland' is largely a fiction created by the rulers of England in response to specific needs at a precise moment in British history. The English have always presented themselves to the world as a cold, refined and urbane race, so it suited them to see the Irish as hot-headed, rude and garrulous – the perfect foil to set off British virtues. The corollary of this is also true. The Irish notion of 'England' is a fiction created and inhabited by the Irish for their own pragmatic purposes. Coming from an almost neolithic community on wind-swept seashores, the Irish immigrants in British cities had no understanding of life in the anonymous workplaces into which they were plunged. They found it easier to don the mask of the garrulous Paddy than to reshape a complex urban identity of their own.
>
> (Kiberd, 1986, p. 83)

So the discursive war between coloniser and colonised takes the form of mutually serviceable, but also mutually reductive fictions. Kiberd's argument is that the coloniser always achieves a position of superiority in such conflicts, no matter what his relationship with the colonised. Such superiority enables the production of a discourse sufficiently totalising that no element of the identity of the colonised is safe from its grasp. Drawing on psychoanalysis, Bhabha and Ashis Nandy suggest that colonial discourse 'fixes' the colonised as the repressed and rejected, but also necessary, 'other', over against which the coloniser defines a unitary and coherent subjectivity for himself. The coloniser is thus also able to use the colonised as the repository onto which potentially upsetting or fragmenting psychological or sexual impulses can be projected. In the face of this, the colonised is forced to assert a respectable and sovereign identity, as a reply to a discourse that defines him as barbarian, childish, feminine, incompetent, treacherous and irrational. But these are precisely the characteristics that we have found Frank and Grace attributing to each other.

Returning to the idea of the 'bardic' artist that I suggested Friel subscribed to at the beginning of the 1970s, we see at the end of *Faith Healer* both its apotheosis and final failure. Frank's inscription of that idea in the play is made clear in various ways. The stress on Frank's mastery of words and voices, his image of himself as a performer, even his 'maddening questions' of self-doubt presuppose his bardic function in the manner in which they take form: 'Did it [the healing gift] reside in my ability to invest someone with faith in me or did I evoke from him a healing faith in himself? Could my healing be effected without faith?' (Friel, 1984, pp. 333–4). Frank's power is meaningful only in the context of a relation, a performance with or before another person. It is communal, as is the play. The bard's function is to reinforce the cultural self-image of his audience, to 'make them whole'. He reproduces the ideology that constitutes them as subjects, in the Althusserian sense (Althusser, 1984). This is figured in Frank's 'healing'. The bard also serves to domesticate the foreign; this is also part of the process of self-fashioning of the culture the bard speaks of and for. In Frank, we see this in what he calls his 'exultation' and 'consummation' when he succeeds in healing someone, which results in the sense that

> the questions that undermined my life then became meaningless and because I knew that for those few hours I had become whole in myself, and perfect in myself, ...
>
> (Friel, 1984, p. 333)

We also see it in Grace's description of him and his subjects:

> Even the people who came to him – they weren't just sick people ... yes, they were real enough, but not real as persons, real as fictions, his fictions, extensions of himself that came into being only because of him.
>
> (Friel, 1984, p. 345)

That is, Grace sees Frank's activity as both curative and intensely selfish, self-confirming, even self-curing.

In bardic terms, however, the problem with this is that Frank does his healing in Wales and Scotland, a community and constituency not fully his own. When he does come home, he does not experience any sense of homecoming. The welcome given him by the wedding-guests, however, convinces him, and he attains a sense of plenitude: 'All irony was suspended' (Friel, 1984, p. 339). The injured finger of Donal, one of the wedding-guests, Frank sees as a challenge or a threat. Grace, however, describes Frank approaching the guests, offering to heal the finger (Friel, 1984, p. 352). Teddy fails to mention the wedding-guests specifically or the finger at all. So even here, when Frank finally embraces or is embraced by his community, we cannot be sure whether they challenge and welcome him, or he foists himself upon and challenges them. It is only when the wedding-guests, in Frank's account, return with McGarvey, the paraplegic, and Frank, realising that they will attack him if he fails (as he knows he will) to heal McGarvey, offers himself to them, that he feels 'for the first time … a simple and genuine sense of homecoming' (Friel, 1984, p. 376). Not merely that, but he also attains that sense of self-sufficiency that he had previously only felt when he had healed someone:

> Then for the first time there was no atrophying terror; and the mad-dening questions were silent.
> At long last I was renouncing chance.
>
> (Friel, 1984, p. 376)

Here, Friel seems to be taking the bardic imagery to an exceptional extreme. The artist's final fiction, which is also true, is his own willed annihilation. This annihilation is a self-sacrifice. He cannot heal McGarvey, cannot make him whole, so he allows himself to be dismembered. In this act of self-abnegation, he finds himself, he finds his community and he surrenders his body to it. It is as if he has been a product or projection of that community, bodied forth to act back upon it and heal it, and when he finally fails in that task, he must dissolve and be submerged again in that community. This would suggest that his role and actions are not to be understood as entirely voluntary, and indeed Frank calls faith healing 'a ministry without responsibility, a vocation without a ministry' (Friel, 1984, p. 333). Frank is never quite sure if he is in posses-sion of his 'gift' or if it possesses him; whether he, the bard, speaks the lan-guage of his community, or it speaks him. But the bardic artist's messages are designed to cater to the needs of the culture or community for which they are produced, not to those of the individual artist. The ultimate 'authority' of the bardic message is the audience in whose language it is mediated. The wed-ding-guests, therefore, are figures of something much wider, as is their vio-lence. They are metaphors for the condition of Irish society. Seamus Deane writes:

> … the return to home and death out of exile … reinstitutes the social and political dimension which had been otherwise so subdued. Home is the place of the deformed in spirit. The violent men who kill the faith healer are intimate with him, for their savage violence and his miracu-lous gift are no more than obverse versions of one another. Once again, Friel is intimating to his audience that there is an inescapable link between art and politics, the Irish version of which is the closeness

> between eloquence and violence. The mediating agency is … disap-
> pointment, but it is a disappointment all the more profound because it
> is haunted by the possibility of miracle and Utopia.
>
> (Deane, 1984, p. 20)

Yet even at the point of death, Frank's fictionalising impulse is active. He has
known the scene of his murder, he knows he will fail to heal McGarvey and
be killed. Yet the scene, in its ritualistic and scrupulous arrangement, is also
beautiful: '… everything glowed with a soft radiance – as if each detail of the
scene had its own self-awareness and was satisfied with itself' (Friel, 1984, p.
375). The scene, therefore, is commensurate with the kind of self-present sovereignty that Grace had described in Frank when he was about to heal someone, and, indeed, that Frank described in himself at such moments: '… I had
become whole in myself and perfect in myself …' (Friel, 1984, p. 333). In this
way, his violent death is transformed into a natural, organic process, an aesthetic object. The situation again recalls Borges, with the writer's subjectivity
disappearing into his text, the artist narrating his own death. Yet unlike
Borges, Friel portrays this as part of a communal ritual. He imbues it with a
social intimacy and a performative aspect very far from the esoteric closeted
worlds of Borges. Frank's position is similar to that of Scheherezade, in the
Thousand and One Nights, but his is the opposite strategy. His narration, rather
than holding night, or death, or the world, at bay, wills it on. A progressive
reading of this can be produced by comparison with Gabriel García Márquez'
One Hundred Years of Solitude, where the novel adopts the Borgesian trope of
self-dissolution to end its narrative, and, implicitly, to begin true History, with
the reader compelled to abandon the world of text for the real world. In a
comparable way, Frank's narrative works to draw the audience closer and
closer to his death, drawing near it at the end of his first monologue, and then
circling closer and closer to it in the second. Not merely this, but the audience is specifically implicated in that death, by Frank's movements on-stage.
These move from his crumpling up the newspaper cutting about his healing
nine people in Llanblethian, as he describes doing so the night of his death in
Ballybeg (Friel, 1984, p. 371), through his buttoning up his coat and putting
on his hat as he describes being called outside by Donal (Friel, 1984, p. 374),
to his presenting himself to the audience, downstage, as he describes walking
across the yard to confront McGarvey (Friel, 1984, p. 376). The audience,
that is, are the wedding-guests, and Frank is offering himself to them, to be
killed. As in Márquez, this ends the play, and returns the audience to the real
world. The allusion to the gap between stage and audience, that both bridges
the gap and yet forces the audience to acknowledge its existence, is another
Brechtian trope. Again, however, it is deployed in such a way as to negate its

radical potential. The text is opened to audience involvement, but this involvement is only that of subjects of Frank's, and therefore Friel's, narrative authority, which is not challenged. Frank offers himself to the audience as a sacrificial victim to a guilty audience, but it is they who have been interpellated into the subject-position of killers by the ideology of authorial and stage authority. So story-telling is socially cohesive or 'healing', but also narcissistic, and inclined to draw attention away from the world, and the imbrication of the theatre in that world. Even at the moment of its greatest apparent crisis, Friel's (self-)understanding of authority remains firmly rooted in the bourgeois conventions identified by Boal. The fierceness with which they are asserted is the sign of that crisis.

What I have attempted here has been to examine the self-representation of authorial crisis in these two plays, by relating it to the earlier *Freedom of the City*, which stages the crisis of representation in clearly socio-political terms. The result is a vindication of Deane's suggestion of the Irish literary-cultural relationship between eloquence and violence, but also an extension of that notion into the realm of the social, in that eloquence is the analogue at the level of the individual of the monopoly of representation claimed by the dominant culture. In this way, we return to Said's articulation of the state, culture and the intellectual: the state is the political-institutional manifestation of the best that has been thought and done, the culture is the elaboration and refinement of those ideas, and the intellectual is the individual socially sanctioned to engage in such elaboration. The crisis of authorial authority is clearly related to the crisis of state authority. It has been in these plays of the 1970s that Friel has most radically explored the crisis of authority of both state and author.

CHAPTER 2

Irish metahistories: John Banville and the revisionist debate

Born in Wexford in 1945, John Banville is separated from Brian Friel by a generation, and by the Border. Therefore, one can say that his writing and publishing history has been traced against the changes in the Republic since the late 1960s – the Northern crisis and its echoes in the South, economic stagnation, membership of the EEC. So we do not find in Banville the same portrayal of the transition from a traditional society to modernity that we find in Friel. Partly because of this, and partly also because he has not had the political burdens placed upon him that Friel has, Banville does not write for or about a community in the way that I have suggested that Friel does. Where Friel could be placed in the line of the Revivalists, Banville's aesthetic locates him in a very different position:

> I don't really think that specifically 'national' literatures are of terribly great significance … We go on and on about our great writers but we have very few great writers, perhaps two. Two great writers or even ten great writers don't really make a literature … The fact that Joyce and Beckett were born in Ireland or even wrote about Ireland is not really important … There is an Irish *writing*, but there isn't an Irish *literature* … We can't continue to write in the old way … Most of Irish writing is within a nineteenth-century tradition where the world is regarded as given … But the modern writer cannot take the world for granted any longer … I've never felt a part of any (national) tradition, any culture even … I feel a part of a purely personal culture gleaned from bits and pieces of European culture of four thousand years. It's purely something I have manufactured.
>
> (Sheehan, 1979, pp. 76–80)

Elsewhere, Banville has suggested that 'We're part of a tradition, a European tradition; why not acknowledge it?' (Imhof, 1987, p. 13). So we find that Banville clearly has a very different sense of cultural geography and reference from that of Friel.

Unlike Friel, then, Banville seems to have turned his back resolutely on the nation, at least in any sense of his writing supporting or reflecting it directly. Though he has famously and crucially appropriated the best-known Irish 'nineteenth-century tradition' (the 'Big House' genre) for the purposes of his own novelistic project, he has brought to that tradition a deliberately eclectic European culture. In the novels I will refer to here – *Birchwood* (originally published in 1973), *Dr Copernicus* (originally published in 1976), *Kepler* (originally published in 1981) and *The Newton Letter* (originally published in 1982) – Banville deploys a determinedly cosmopolitan geographical and historical range of reference. Even, however, as he refers to the canon of high European culture, Banville's emphasis is personal and self-conscious. His culture is 'purely personal'; tradition is something separate from him that he can lift elements from and produce something 'manufactured'. Banville sees himself as an inheritor of European Modernism, but unlike Yeats or Eliot, he does not systematise. He works with a bricolage of 'bits and pieces'. This ambivalent attitude to the inheritance of Modernism and European culture, regarded at once as a treasury and a junkyard, a repository simultaneously to be revered and plundered, appears to place Banville in the category of postmodernism.

His sense of artistic individualism is, of course, in accordance with Terence Brown's remarks about the emphasis in Irish writing of the 1970s being on subjectivity. Brian Friel, for example, began his career as a short story writer at a time when the genre was dominated by O'Faolain, O'Connor and Lavin, and when it was often used by them as a tool of 'surgical analysis of an apparently diseased Irish reality' (Brown, 1985a, p. 318). Banville, however, has not felt bound to the tradition of realism, and the aesthetic politics of social or political dissent of the earlier generation has held no attraction for him. He has been a beneficiary of 1960s modernisation and liberalisation, to the extent that, unlike earlier Modernists such as Joyce and Beckett, he has not suffered censorship or felt the necessary linkage of artistic integrity and intellectual exile. He has been able to carry on the Joycean project of the Hibernicisation of Europe and the Europeanisation of Ireland, from Ireland itself. Indeed, for Banville, the realism of the counter-Revivalists named above has itself seemed an orthodoxy, and his espousal of reflexive experiment must be seen in that light as much as in that of his relationship to European Modernism. For him, post-Independence writers had mostly ignored the lessons of Joyce, Beckett and Flann O'Brien, as much as they failed to respond to Kafka, Proust or Nabokov. However, Banville is not merely a formalist: with regard to the opposition of art and action, he confesses:

> ... I shall, I suppose, appear simple-minded if I say straight away that I have never been able to understand why it must always be one or the other that one must plump for, since, frivolous creature that I am, I cannot rid myself of the quaint conviction that art *is* action.
>
> (Banville, 1977, p. 20)

So, polemical or openly tendentious literature hobbles itself, but form can constitute a realm of activism itself. However, this aestheticism also leads Banville away from any sense of writing of or for a community, unless it be one of brilliant and erudite readers like himself. In fact, in spite of his metafictional experiments, Banville's work is marked by an underlying individualist humanist impulse, that separates him from more obviously political experimentalists such as Gabriel García Márquez or Salman Rushdie.

Richard Kearney places Banville in what he calls the 'counter-tradition'. This, for Kearney, is a group of Irish writers including Flann O'Brien, Aidan Higgins and the later Francis Stuart, who have taken up the challenge of Joyce and Beckett, and who continue the exploration initiated by them into literature as the possibility of writing, of representation and of knowledge. For Kearney, the work of this group shares the modernist shift of narrative from *quest* to *self-questioning* (Kearney, 1988a, p. 83). This inward, metafictional turn again is in accordance with Brown's comments about the subjective cast of Irish writing of the 1970s. But Banville's work can be placed in a broader historical and political context also. The tension in his work between realism and modernism, between Irish and European issues of both content and form, marks him out as a writer absorbing both the optimism of 1960s modernisation, convergence with Europe, prosperity and liberalism (signalled in Banville by his lack of interest in political dissent), and the nascent pessimism of the 1970s, economic stagnation, the apparent atavism of the Northern crisis. Banville writes at the moment that modernism elsewhere in the West appeared to have run into the sand, and at the moment in Ireland that it had finally arrived only to be put in crisis, as a socio-political project. He writes at a moment of metanarrative crisis, when nationalism as a project of state legitimisation has been replaced by modernisation and the movement into Europe, but that modernisation suddenly appears challenged by instability in the state, brought on by the re-appearance of nationalism in the North, and economic slowdown. He writes, in other words, at a moment that elsewhere in the West appeared to be characterised by capitalist crisis and radically new forms of politics. But in Ireland, the situation was complicated by the intertwining of apparently atavistic social and political forces, with their new opponents. This is exemplified in the way, in Northern Ireland, that the Civil Rights movement and the People's Democracy contained within them segments of traditional nationalism and republicanism; and in the co-existence of Paisleyism and the reformism of Terence O'Neill. Modernity in Ireland appeared threatened not only by elements of 'postmodernity', such as the new student and feminist politics, the oil crises or the supranational structures of Europe, but also by traditional forces that the self-conscious modernisers of the 1960s thought that they had left behind. But as

Jürgen Habermas has pointed out, one must distinguish between social modernisation and cultural modernism (Habermas, 1985, pp. 6–8). Habermas
shows that neoconservatives such as Daniel Bell tax modernist culture with
the dissemination of the kind of negative values – chiefly a selfish and irresponsible individualism – which would be better attributed to the effects of
societal modernisation. Thus, for Habermas, *contra* the claims of French poststructuralism, the project of modernity is not finished or dead. In spite of the
recuperation of the antiaesthetic revolts of earlier avant-gardes such as the
Surrealists, projects of resistance to societal modernisation and cultural reification are still possible. Habermas writes about how the deliberate articulation of aesthetic experience with what he calls 'life-history' actually serves to
move that aesthetic back out of its putatively autonomous sphere, and reaffil-
iate it with matters of 'truth and justice' (Habermas, 1985, pp. 12–13). This
formulation allows us to give a wider social and political context and content
to Banville's apparently aestheticist work, for he is by his own account something of a 'bricoleur', that is, a borrower from the traditions of European culture. But he also writes about individuals whose life-experiences impinge on
their intellectual or aesthetic theories in such a way as to radically alter them,
or to show up their ethical contradictions.

Banville is deeply concerned with the related issues of narrative and history, both at the micro- and macro-levels, and with the epistemological questions they raise. It is this concern that has shaped my selection of his novels
examined here – it seems to me that in the novels named above, these issues
are studied most sharply, whereas in the more recent work – *Mephisto* (1986),
The Book of Evidence (1989), *Ghosts* (1993) and *Athena* (1995) and *The
Untouchable* (1997) – the concentration has been more on matters of subjective psychology, guilt and redemption, even if filtered through analogous
epistemological examination. But Banville has not been alone in this historical discussion, as the discipline of history writing in Ireland has been in ferment over a period that almost precisely matches Banville's literary career.
Therefore, I propose to provide a context for Banville's writing by placing it
next to a discussion of Irish historiographical debate. In so doing, I hope to
illuminate the relevance to Irish cultural and intellectual development of
Banville's *oeuvre*, and, to this extent, to read him 'against the grain' (Benjamin,
1992, p. 248). For the difficulty is that the novels by Banville that I am examining appear often to have no links with Ireland at all. This can lead a critic
such as Rudiger Imhof to suggest that Banville's quality is in direct proportion to his cultural self-distancing from Ireland and the Irish literary tradition
(Imhof, 1989, pp. 7–13).

A CONTEXT FOR BANVILLE:
THE IRISH HISTORIOGRAPHIC REVOLUTION

In 1938, Theodore William Moody and Robert Dudley Edwards, both of them research students at the Institute of Historical Research of the University of London, founded the journal *Irish Historical Studies*. This was the shared organ of the Ulster Society for Irish Historical Studies and the Irish Historical Society, founded in 1936 and 1937 by Moody and Edwards, respectively. Their aims, as co-editors, were, as they put it in the first edition of *IHS*, 'constructive' and 'instrumental'. By the first of these terms, they meant the publication of the results of original research and of 'Historical Revisions', being articles offering re-interpretations of historical phases or events 'in the light of new facts'. By the second, they meant an array of articles on

> the scope and the teaching of Irish history; articles on research methods and problems; select documents, with editorial comment; select and critical bibliographies and guides to sources, manuscript and printed; annual lists of writings on Irish history including articles in periodicals; annual lists of theses on Irish history completed and in progress in the universities of Ireland; reviews of books and periodicals dealing with, or having a bearing on, Irish history.
>
> (Moody and Edwards, 1994, pp. 36–7)

Further,

> In our review section, we are anxious to include a complete record, with explanatory comments, of the work in Irish history contained in current periodicals. We aim at co-ordination and co-relation of historical work, and we hope to be a means of avoiding duplication.
>
> (Moody and Edwards, 1994, p. 37)

Clearly, Moody and Edwards had very considerable ambitions in their field, and intended nothing less than the total reconstitution of the historical discipline in Ireland. Not merely did they intend to set history writing on a professional footing, but they also aspired to set the agenda for the discipline decisively for many years to come. This is evident in the desire to centralise, regulate, organise and filter historical discourse; to establish methodological procedures and protocols; to mediate documentary evidence and bibliographical materials; to establish protocols of historical pedagogy. The fourth edition of the journal saw the publication of 'Rules for Contributors', with the implication that the editors sought to create and enforce a code for recognisably scholarly production.

Moody and Edwards modelled their efforts on such major Western jour-nals as the *Historische Zeitschrift, Revue Historique, American Historical Review* and *English Historical Review*, and understood themselves as striving to bring Irish historiography up to international standards. But, according to Ciaran Brady, they also sought to achieve

> the propagation of both the methods and the results of the academic historians' work to the widest possible audience in the shortest possi-ble time.
>
> (Brady, 1994b, p. 4)

This project was effected in various ways: the Thomas Davis Lectures on RTE radio, initiated in 1953; the 1966 television series, 'The Course of Irish History', organised by Moody and F.X. Martin; and the 1977 television series 'The Heritage of Ireland'. More removed from the immediate public sphere, but significant to the overall task of consolidation has been the *New History of Ireland*, a gigantic nine-volume project of synthesis begun in 1968. According to Brady, the intention of this was to

> commence a second, highly accelerated phase of the programme launched in the 1930s by which the entire course of Irish history would be reconstructed, by chronological and thematic syntheses to be produced by a generation of experienced scholars trained in the meth-ods of the professional academic historian.
>
> (Brady, 1994b, p. 6)

Though Moody, who announced this programme, admitted that much of the primary research necessary for it had yet to be done, nevertheless it was reck-oned that the existence of the *New History* would act as an incentive to such research. If this was not enough, *IHS* was given to the production of agendas for future research, most notably that of Edwards, 'An Agenda for Irish History, 1978–2018' (Edwards, 1994).

It is clear, then, that Edwards and Moody, with associates including D.B. Quinn, R.B. McDowell and Aubrey Gwynn, sought to mould Irish historio-graphical discourse and to define the limits of debate both for their own time, and for long after it. This is arguable especially in the light of the political context in which they were operating. *IHS* was founded sixteen years after the foundation of the Free State, and only one year after that state had given itself a Constitution of its own making. Civil war, and great political instability marked the early years of that State. However, stability was gradually developed in the 1930s, as Fianna Fáil entered the Dáil in 1927, won the 1932 general election in coalition with Labour, secured an overall majority in 1933, put in place the 1937 Constitution and won another overall majority in 1938. That year also saw the end of the 'economic war' with Britain, and the Anglo-Irish Agreement. It was only at this time that the state became fully legitimate, and capable of claiming the consent of republicans. But, as is well known, this period of state consolidation was also marked by the construction of a powerfully conservative political and cultural hegemony, expressed and supported by draconian censorship and emergency legislation.

In this context, it was perhaps not altogether surprising that *Irish Historical Studies*, in its constitution, should have included a ban on articles dealing in Irish politics after 1900. In fact, the ban was not strictly necessary, since the British governmental records of the period were still closed and the political collections were then still in private hands, and not deposited in libraries or archives, so serious political history could not be written. According to Ronan Fanning, this ban was placed because Moody and Edward were 'sensitive to the imperatives of Irish history as revolutionary propaganda' (Fanning, 1988, p. 18). Accounts given by Oliver MacDonagh and Roy Foster of the political uses to which Irish history has been put suggest that Moody and Edwards had reason to be concerned (MacDonagh, 1983, pp. 1–6; Foster, 1994). Terence Brown has called the movement and practice initiated by Moody and Edwards a 'revolution' (Brown, 1985a, p. 292). Desmond Fennell has called it 'the historiography of the Irish counter-revolution' (Fennell, 1994, p. 186). Whatever the virtues of the ban, the revolutionary context appears to be beyond dispute.

The new history sought to establish its objectivity by adopting methods it described as 'scientific'. An empirical approach would enable it to extract the 'facts' from the historical record, and allow it thus to distinguish itself from variously fictional, mythic or ideological discourses. Therefore, it would be 'value-free' and 'truthful'. The *locus classicus* of this approach is Moody's valedictory lecture of 1977, 'Irish History and Irish Mythology', where he asserts that

> History is a matter of facing the facts of the Irish past, however painful they may be; mythology is a way of refusing to face the historical facts. The study of history not only enlarges truth about our past, but also opens the mind to the reception of ever new accessions of truth. On the other hand, the obsession with myths, and especially the more destructive myths, perpetuates the closed mind.
>
> (Moody, 1994, p. 86)

The rhetoric here is that of hardheaded realism that is also moralising. History and myth are unambiguously separable; one is a positive discourse of truth, moral courage, honesty and sanity, the other is a negative discourse of untruth, evasiveness and irrationality. There is no sense that myth might provide access to a 'truth' that 'facing the facts' could never reach. Exactly what is meant by 'myth' is unclear – is it a matter of non-existent events and unsustainable causations, or is it a matter of incorrect conclusions being attributed to historical processes? Access to the facts is unproblematic and direct. It does not seem to occur to Moody that 'history' or 'facts' or 'truth' might be discursively constituted, or that in the process of extracting the facts, the historian might be affected by subjective, textual, institutional, economic or political factors. 'History' for Moody is a unitary discourse of truth. Writing it is simply a matter of laying bare the 'facts', which will then speak their own story. But Hayden White, drawing on Northrop Frye, has suggested that 'every history has its myth', and different historiographical modes exist, just as there are different fictional modes based on different identifiable mythic archetypes (White, 1978, p. 127). These historical modes consist of different ways of ordering the 'facts' so as to produce different meanings, be they cognitive, moral or aesthetic. The notion of such an interpenetration of myth, fiction and history would have appeared as so much moral and epistemological anarchy to Moody, who expresses here a deep faith in the 'facts' and the transparency and modesty of the historian.

This may seem harsh, but the point is not so much that Moody, personally, was especially conservative, but rather to suggest that he, and *Irish Historical Studies* with him, partook of the conservatism of their founding moment. This, then, cuts somewhat against the putative independence and autonomy of the historians and of the discipline of history. More accurately, study of the historical and political context helps us to realise that the historians' putative independence was one that had to be *made*. *IHS* constituted a form of public sphere that had to be cleared in the space of Irish civil society. My allusions to the rules and regulations, the codes and protocols, including the ban on articles on contemporary politics, that accompanied the foundation of that journal are an attempt to describe the exterior, or exoskeleton, of that discourse, in the Foucauldian sense that discourses are composed on the basis of a series of *exclusions* (Foucault, 1981, pp. 52–3). But the acceptance of this formulation immediately implies that a discourse that purports to be autonomous in fact has a relationship, more or less mediated, with political and economic forces, not to mention the social, economic and political dynamics that may be taking place within the discourse. The difficulty arises when that autonomy is raised to the status of a Platonic ideal.

White, of course, has pointed out that history, as it was written in Europe, underwent a profound change at the time of the French Revolution. Before

1789, historiography was seen as a literary activity and its 'fictional' aspect was acknowledged openly. But in the early nineteenth century, historians came to identify 'truth' with 'fact', and to see fiction as impeding the understanding of reality rather than as another way of apprehending it. Fiction was denigrated as the representation of the merely 'possible' or 'imaginable'. In White's account, historiography established itself as an academic discipline at the time of the consolidation of the nation-state in Europe, and also in a context of deep hostility to myth. The Left blamed myth for the failures of the Revolution, while the Right blamed myth for the Revolution's excesses. Incorrect readings of history, mistaken notions about the nature of the historical process, overoptimism about the possibility of change in societies were held to have produced the Revolution, influenced its course, and led to the effects it produced in the longer term. Therefore, White says,

> It became imperative to rise above any impulse to interpret the historical record in the light of party prejudices, utopian expectations, or sentimental attachments to traditional institutions. In order to find one's way among the conflicting claims of the parties, which took shape during and after the Revolution, it was necessary to locate some standpoint that was truly 'objective', truly 'realistic'.
>
> (White, 1978, p. 124)

What was necessary, therefore, was the 'disciplinisation' of history, that is, the creation of a properly rigorous, academically recognisable and professional 'discipline'. At a time marked by clashes of various political ideologies, each presupposing a particular philosophy of history or master narrative of the historical process, which legitimated their claims to realism, it was logical to attempt to constitute a specifically historical discipline that would determine the 'facts' of history, and against which the objectivity, realism and truth of the philosophies of the various political ideologies could be judged. As White puts it,

> Under the auspices of the philosophy of history, programs of social and political reconstruction shared an ideology with utopian visions of man, culture and society. This linkage justified both and made a study of history, considered as a recovery of the facts of the past, a social desideratum at once epistemologically necessary and politically relevant.
>
> (White, 1987, p. 61)

The epistemological analysis of the elements of this linkage consisted, according to White, in opposing a disciplined historical method, understood as empirical, to a philosophy of history understood as metaphysical. The political analysis consisted in turn in opposing utopian thinking in all its forms, but most especially political, with a disciplined historical consciousness. Thus, a disciplined history could be held to produce historical knowledge that would serve as the standard of realism in political thinking and action.

However, White goes on to suggest that

> The politicalization of historical thinking was virtually a prerequisite of its own professionalization, the basis of its promotion to the status of a discipline worthy of being taught in the universities, and a pre-requisite of whatever 'constructive' social function historical knowledge was thought to serve.
>
> (White, 1987, p. 62)

Most particularly, this was true of professional, academic, institutionalised or incorporated historical studies, which defined the aims of such study as opposed to the philosophy of history, that restricted itself to the extraction of the facts pertinent to delimited areas of the past and that saw its role as simply the narration of 'true' stories. Such studies also explicitly refused the construction of grand theories of the historical process, and therefore resisted what were seen as the temptations of prophecy of the future and of direct advocacy in the present.

But the politics of this disciplinisation, conceived, as disciplinisation is, as a system of negations, consisted in what it marked out for repression in those wishing to attain the authority of discipline itself for their work. What was thus set aside was utopian thinking, the kind of thinking without which revolution, of Left or of Right, would be untheorisable (to the extent that it claimed authority on the basis of historical knowledge). The problem, therefore, with this version of historical study, as White points out, is that it purports to be above politics, and yet claims the authority to deem 'unrealistic' any remotely utopian political programme. 'Realism' is identified with antiutopianism.

The resonances of White's remarks with conditions in the Irish Free State in the 1930s, but also the Irish Republic in the 1970s are clear. The differences between these two periods are important, however. Moody and Edwards began their project of the professionalisation and disciplinisation of Irish history in the aftermath of revolution, and, anxious to make their neutrality obvious, instituted in *Irish Historical Studies* their unnecessary (to professional historians, anyway) ban on articles on politics after 1900, that is, on revolutionary politics. Their empiricist approach, demonstrated in Moody's strictures on 'myth', was explicitly anti-teleological, anti-theoretical and determined to separate itself from myth or fiction.

This 'revisionist' history has been the subject of intense intellectual debate in Ireland, especially since the recrudescence of violence in the North. This has been the case, because the revolution in Ulster brought forth a new wave of much more assertive, activist and public pronouncements from a new generation of historians, many of them former students of Edwards, Moody and their associates. The most famous of these was F.S.L. Lyons. In a 1971 lecture, Lyons issued the following anguished call:

> In the present situation, with the dire past still overhanging the dire present, the need to go back to fundamentals and consider once more the meaning of independence, asserts itself with almost intolerable urgency. The theories of revolution, the theories of history, which have brought Ireland to its present pass, cry out for re-examination and the time is ripe to try to break the great enchantment which has for too long made myth so much more congenial than reality.
>
> (Lyons, 1973a, p. 223)

Despite the explicitly public and interventionist nature of this lecture (part of the Thomas Davis series), methodologically it is very similar to Moody's more academic attack on myth, and it accords with the model of disciplinisation outlined above – the emphasis on 'fundamentals', implying a stress on facts, the attack on theory, the lament for the persistence of 'myth'. The context is, of course, in some ways similar to that of the 1930s: a recent revolutionary social and political upheaval, whose flaws and strengths were variously attributed to 'mythic' thinking, a movement that derived its legitimacy at least partly from certain interpretations of history, a nationalist teleology and utopian optimism about the possibility of social change and civil equality. The difference, however, is that in 1971, Lyons speaks from within the boundaries of, and with the implied authority of, the established Southern state. Lest this seem too conspiratorial a view that sees Lyons' call as coarsely political, it is worth noting that when this lecture was published in 1973 in Brian Farrell's *The Irish Parliamentary Tradition*, it was preceded by an introduction, by Farrell, that makes it clear that the stress on the parliamentary tradition, at a time when so-called 'physical-force' republicanism was once again making its presence felt in Ulster, was quite deliberate. In his own lecture in the volume, Farrell was fiercely critical of Pearse. (Of course, Moody's lecture cited above, also drew out what he saw as the links between historical 'myths', both Loyalist and nationalist, and the contemporary political situation: Moody, 1994, pp. 79–80, 85.) Indeed, in Lyons' idealist supposition that 'theory' is responsible for Ireland's condition, in the absence of materialist analysis of the violence in terms of the development of the two statelets, North and South, since 1922, one can discern the impulse to defend the status quo, in the manner Liam O'Dowd has suggested of post-Independence literary intellectuals (O'Dowd, 1988).

The linkage of the new history and the state is made clear by Lyons' call. He elaborated such thinking still further in his comments on the compensatory satisfactions of Ireland becoming a laboratory for international anti-terrorist techniques in Belfast in 1978 (Lyons, 1994, p. 90–1). Fanning links the confidence of Moody and Edwards to the 'partial nationalist certainty' of the consolidated Southern state in 1938 (Fanning, 1988, p. 18). But this case can be pushed further. The Free State was born of compromise, both at the level of *Realpolitik* (the Treaty) and of ideology (the failure of the nationalist project of unity). In the wake of Independence, and partition, the 'realistic' study of history was indeed, in White's words, a 'social desideratum'. Nationalist rhetoric notwithstanding, there was also a need for an intellectual analogue and justification for this pragmatic status quo precisely as 'realistic'. So we find that the new Irish historical 'realism' only embarked on its 'value-free', putatively non-ideological project at precisely the moment, after the 1937 Constitution and the Anglo-Irish Treaty of 1938, that nationalism appeared to have coincided with and was becoming naturalised in, the state; in other words, when a compromise was being achieved between the unfinished ideological narrative of nationalism, and the bureaucratic, geopolitical (but also compromised) entity that was the state. 'Realism' was only possible *after* the point that the new political reality finally seemed permanent and natural. Even so, Moody and Edwards censored the anti-narrative, anti-metaphysical, anti-nationalist impulse of their movement in a strategic act of self-preservation: the ban.

The disjunction between nation and state is important, here. Accepting with Homi Bhabha and Benedict Anderson that nations are 'imagined communities' but can also be understood as narratives that such communities tell to justify themselves to themselves (Bhabha, 1990; Anderson, 1991), it would seem reasonable to see a homology between the vision of history retrojected by an emergent nation, and historicism, viewing the latter as a kind of presentist history. Indeed, John Breuilly draws attention to this linkage of nationalism and historicism (Breuilly, 1993, pp. 56–64). But the Ulster Loyalist Rebellion of 1912, the Treaty, partition and the Civil War had fractured that imagined community, and that imagination, indubitably. So, the historicist narrative of nationalism had been refused the kind of closure and moral resolution that it sought. White has pointed out how, for Hegel, historical narrative requires a subject that would provide the reason to record its activities. In Hegel's account, this subject is the state: '… it is only the state which first presents subject-matter that is not only *adapted* to the prose of History, but involves the production of such history in the very progress of its own being'

(White, 1987, p. 12). This suggests an intimate linkage of narrativity, historicality and the law or legal system, which the agents of a narrative may militate for or against. White continues:

> Interest in the social system, which is nothing other than a system of human relationships governed by law, creates the possibility of conceiving the kinds of tensions, conflicts, struggles, and their various kinds of resolutions that we are accustomed to find in any representation of reality presenting itself to us as a history. This permits us to speculate that the growth and development of historical consciousness, which is attended by a concomitant growth and development of narrative capability … has something to do with the extent to which the legal system functions as a subject of concern. If every fully realized story, … is a kind of allegory, points to a moral, or endows events, whether real or imaginary, with a significance that they do not possess as a mere sequence, then it seems possible to conclude that every historical narrative has as its latent or manifest purpose the desire to moralize the events of which it treats. Where there is ambiguity or ambivalence regarding the status of the legal system, which is the form in which the subject encounters most immediately the social system in which he is enjoined to achieve a full humanity, the ground on which any closure of a story one might wish to tell about a past, whether it be a public or a private past, is lacking.
>
> (White, 1987, p. 14)

But this serves to remind us that the founding moment of Edwards' and Moody's project was a time of consolidation of a very recently disputed legitimacy. For these men, the legal-political system had only *just reached* legitimacy in the Constitution in the Free State, while it was necessarily bifurcated by Partition. Further, the 'narrative' with which they were concerned had been precisely refused closure, because of political division and compromise. It is not surprising, then, that they should react against a grand narrative of Irish history, and turn instead to an empirical mode that was in accordance with the untotalised, unfinished, split political dispensation that was composed of the Free State and the new Northern sub-state. Hegelian narrativity was impossible for them, precisely because of the complex, contradictory and debatable character of the legal-political arrangements on the island. For the founding fathers of modern Irish history-writing, the nation and the state were neither singular nor coincident, nor were they beyond dispute. But this does not necessarily preclude the moralising (and hence legitimising) function of the narratives actually provided.

One of the best-known and most important critiques of revisionism, made by Brendan Bradshaw, bears out this conclusion (Bradshaw, 1994a). Bradshaw argues that the new historians were heavily influenced in their approach by Herbert Butterfield's *The Whig Interpretation of History* (1931), which was a highly-regarded work at the time that Edwards, Moody, Quinn and, later, T.D. Williams did their postgraduate research in England (Bradshaw, 1994a, pp. 197–8). Butterfield was critical of teleological, or present-centred, historiography that might seek, not merely in historical terms to explain, but also to justify a social or political dispensation in the present – the so-called 'Whig interpretation'. To Butterfield, it is perhaps worth adding his rival, but methodological ally, Lewis Namier, the other dominant figure in British historiography in the 1930s. Perry Anderson has famously demonstrated how Namier and other central European intellectuals emigrated to Britain between the wars, attracted by British tradition and stability (in comparison to the revolutionary turmoil then sweeping their own countries), and its empiricist intellectual heritage (Anderson, 1992). Britain, Anderson suggests, also attracted, or was vulnerable to, this 'white emigration' because of its lack, alone among major European industrialised countries, of either a national Marxism or a classical sociology. Thus, it lacked the intellectual means to comprehend itself as a social totality. But the very lack of such 'general ideas' was what attracted Namier. Anderson shows that Namier reckoned that the English 'perceive and accept facts without anxiously enquiring into their reasons and meaning' (Namier, 1961, p. 13). Namier disdained narrative, and regarded nationalism and democracy as the great damaging forces in Europe in the period 1789–1945. But he also refused to produce an explanatory history. He removed what his critics called 'mind' from historical evolution; he demoted the influence of ideas in historical change. Ultimately, he went so far as to question the intelligibility of the historical process: 'Possibly there is no more sense in human history than in the changes of the seasons … or if sense there be, it escapes our perception' (Anderson, 1992, p. 76). So history has no meaning, least of all in the purposive actions, governed by ideas, of human collectivities. This assessment of Namier is to some extent supported by Linda Colley, writing of Namier much more recently. She observes the tendencies that Anderson enumerates, though she places them more sympathetically in the context of Namier's own biography and career (Colley, 1989). The force of Anderson's critique remains, however, when she notes how Namier's disciples 'emulated his empiricism, but not the profound sense of engagement behind it' (Colley, 1989, p. 45). Colley in fact usefully points out how Butterfield and Namier were part of a much wider anti-Whiggish revisionist movement in British historiography since the 1880s (Colley, 1989, pp. 46–8).

This description of Butterfield and Namier explains much of what Bradshaw finds unpalatable in the new Irish history. For Bradshaw, it could not cope, rhetorically or methodologically, with what he calls the 'catastrophic' element in Irish history. By the use of an austerely clinical vocabulary, attempts are made to normalise, relativise or evade by neglect or euphemism traumatic events such as the massacres perpetrated by the Cromwellians at Drogheda and Wexford in 1649, and the Famine in the 1840s. Clearly, the idea of a 'value-free' revisionism is, for Bradshaw, oxymoronic, as revisionism evolved as a reaction to the excesses of romantic nationalist history-writing during the nationalist and Literary revivals in the nineteenth and early twentieth centuries. It achieved this end by seeking to extrude, play down or deny the existence of any Irish national consciousness before the nineteenth century. For Bradshaw, Irish revisionism is inherently negative, and breaks up the national narrative. But in these features, it is wholly analogous to the description of Namier's approach given by Anderson: the empiricism, the distaste for nationalism, the assault on 'mind' or consciousness. There is little difference between Namier's belief that 'there is no free will in the thinking of the masses', and Moody's myth-critique (Namier, 1961, p. 41). In a later version of these ideas, Bradshaw suggests an explicitly presentist historicism as a more 'sympathetic' alternative to the 'value-free' approach to Irish history (Bradshaw, 1994b, p. 40). Thus, history is employed as a means of explaining the present, a short step away from the Whig interpretation. But this presupposes the possibility of a Hegelian subject of historical narrative as explained by White, which we have seen was rendered impossible by partition. Interestingly, historicism is precisely what Brady, in his account of the Edwards/Moody initiative, suggests they were trying to avoid (Brady, 1994b, pp. 18–19).

At this point, then, it is legitimate to ask whether or not Moody and Edwards were ignoring an alternative historiography that was current when they were engaged in constructing their project. Brady demonstrates, however, that it is impossible to know exactly the degree to which they were aware of or interested in international debates. There seems little evidence, for example, that they were interested in the efforts of Henri Berr with his *Revue de synthese historique*, founded in 1900, or his followers, Marc Bloch and Lucien Febvre, who founded their famous journal, *Annales d'histoire economique et sociale*, in 1929. The post-war years saw a surge of interest in economic and social history in Ireland, as noted by Fanning (Fanning, 1994, pp. 152–3), though even that had to wait until the 1970s for institutional expression. Moreover, as suggested in the Introduction, there is strong evidence of the hegemony in Irish economics of neo-liberalism and of accounts of social change couched predominantly in terms of modernisation theory.

The space available for a radical or Marxist historiography seems, on this front, to have been negligible.

It is, therefore, interesting to compare accounts of the origins of the new Irish history with E.J. Hobsbawm's moving description of how he came to espouse a specifically Marxist history, at about the same time as the foundation of *Irish Historical Studies*, and then to remember that Hobsbawm is only the most famous living representative of an illustrious group of British radical historians including Christopher Hill, E.P. Thompson, Dorothy Thompson, George Rudé, Rodney Hilton and V.G. Kiernan (Hobsbawm, 1994, pp. 250–2). As both Hobsbawm himself and Harvey Kaye make clear, the political context of 1930s Britain, and of Europe more widely, was crucial in determining the intellectual and ideological course taken by this group of historians, who were mostly approximately a decade younger than Moody and Edwards. Faced with a collapsing liberalism and the rise of fascism, they became Communists, beginning their academic careers on the cusp of what they sincerely supposed would be a revolutionary period (Kaye, 1991, p. 59). Moody and Edwards, however, had lived through the Irish national revolution, and began their work in a period of reconstruction and consolidation. It also must be admitted that, as various writers have pointed out, the political atmosphere of the Free State was not hospitable to a socialist, let alone Marxist, politics. The significant class element of nationalist struggle – the quarrel over land between Roman Catholic tenants and Protestant landlords – had been resolved by the Westminster government in the late nineteenth century (Hazelkorn and Patterson, 1994, pp. 50–2). The economic depression of the 1920s, in-fighting in the labour movement and the naivety of the Irish Labour Party in not contesting the elections of 1918 and 1921 put the cause of organised labour at a severe disadvantage in the early years of the Southern state (Brown, 1985, pp. 102–4). The intellectuals of post-Independence Ireland were mostly beneficiaries of the new dispensation, and hence were unlikely to produce a radical materialist critique of it. Radical intellectual positions consisted precisely in debunking the dominant strain of identity politics (O'Dowd, 1988, pp. 11–12). It is no surprise, therefore, to find Brady aligning Moody and Edwards with the polemics of Sean O Faolain and *The Bell* (Brady, 1994b, pp. 20–2). It is difficult, also, not to suppose that the reaction against historicism cited by Brady operated against Marxist historiography. Thus, the example of the British Marxist historians only casts into White's remarks above about the equation of realism with antiutopianism into further relief.

Brady's suggestion is that, faced with what he calls 'the sceptical, relativising challenge of philosophical historicism', the Irish new historians sought to tread a middle path between the acceptance by historians like G.M. Trevelyan that history-writing was simply a literary activity, and the efforts of the Annalistes to find processes that lay beyond the mere events of history (Brady, 1994b, p. 24). In the manner of the American 'new historians' Carl Becker and Charles Beard, and more specifically of A.F. Pollard and other writers for the journal *History* at the University of London, the Irish historians sought refuge in the analytical rigour of the social sciences. Economics, sociology, clinical psychology and political science offered, in Brady's words,

> some logically defensible *modi operandi* which reduced the area of caprice and personal bias in historical writing and rendered historical judgements and interpretations available to more external assessment and evaluation than had been the case in the past.
>
> (Brady, 1994b, p. 19)

Certainly, Pollard was writing as early as 1916 of the need for a humanist historiography, while retaining a definition of scientificity as 'accurate reasoning', or checking one's facts (Pollard, 1916, p. 28). Nevertheless, Pollard was keen to make clear the separation of history and natural science, seeing in the former an ethical mission absent in the latter (Pollard, 1916, p. 34). Later, in 1920, Pollard suggested that history was both an art and a science, a discipline necessarily probabilistic, that contained an irreducible literary element and that could never deliver final judgements (Pollard, 1920, pp. 25, 28). At around the same time, however, Pollard could write 'An Apology for Historical Research', in defence of historical method, and was happy to defend the empirical focus of much historical work (Pollard, 1922, p. 177). So, in Pollard, we find an attempt to negotiate between definitions of history-writing as science and as art, between empirical authority and probabilistic modesty, that accords well with the self-consciousness that Brady is keen to ascribe to Edwards and Moody. The difficulty remains in proving the specific influence of Pollard on them.

Brady detects, in Moody's lecture cited above, hints of the influence of the critiques of historicism mounted by Karl Mannheim and Karl Popper; he also notes the influence of Michael Oakeshott on Edwards (Brady, 1994b, p. 7). But he does not elaborate on these possible discoveries, and his essay is hampered on this front by being restricted to circumstantial evidence. In fairness, the rather different conclusions of Bradshaw, and of the present work, are similarly primarily speculative. Even so, it seems important to register some of the weaknesses of Brady's meditations. He suggests that Edwards and Moody, rather than being moved by a 'crude unreflective empiricism' in their project for the new history, were chiefly interested in establishing the sovereignty of method in Irish historical studies (Brady, 1994b, pp. 7, 24). The formal and procedural codes and protocols governing articles for *IHS* constitute ample evidence of this. Brady also suggests that they were seeking to purge the language of historical writing of grandiosely rhetorical styles associated with nineteenth-century history. For Brady,

> ... their mistrust of a self-conscious or literary style was the product of no pedantic delight in unashamed dullness, but rather of an acute awareness of the slippery nature of historical discourse, and a determination to prevent the deceptive rhetorics of the romantics or the scientists from creeping back in unnoticed.
>
> (Brady, 1994b, p. 24)

The problem with this formulation is that a 'plain' or 'unadorned' style is still a style, deliberately adopted. To this extent, Brady seems to contradict himself. For he also tells us that Moody and Edwards, in the entire course of their project, never sought to defend it on either ideological or rhetorical grounds (Brady, 1994b, p. 7). This suggests that the strength of the new history was to come through the severely policed methodological standards of *IHS*. Nevertheless, Brady goes on to suggest that the linguistic strategy most suited to Moody and Edwards' purposes, of providing them with 'argumentative tissue' while not diluting the purity of their faith to the facts, was *irony*. Therefore, according to Brady, the relationship of the facts generated by new research to existing information was not necessarily true in any 'philosophical sense'; nor did it claim any lasting authority: the relationship of fact *a* to fact *b* was not necessarily right or wrong, true or untrue, but ironic (Brady, 1994b, p. 25). Brady's argument continues to the effect that irony is an inevitably and progressively élitist style, depending as it does on an ongoing relationship between author and reader if it is to be effective, or if it is not to fall into obscurantism. This is how Brady accounts for the alienation that he detects between the academic historians of the post-Moody/Edwards generation, and their readership in the wider public.

Brady's solution to the problem thus created is not to call, as Bradshaw does, for a more 'sympathetic' history or the celebration of tradition, or for new evidence to be adduced to refute the 'revisionists', or for what he terms the 'radical deconstructionist' approach of Roland Barthes and Hayden White, deployed in Ireland by Seamus Deane (Brady, 1994b, pp. 27–8). Rather, he suggests a greater modesty on the behalf of the historians, a greater willingness to admit the provisional, 'partial and imperfect' nature of their judgements and interpretations (Brady, 1994b, p. 29).

As I pointed out above, Brady's argument is vitiated by the way, firstly, he admits the lack of evidence of self-conscious metahistorical reflection by

Moody and Edwards, but, secondly, tries retrospectively to construct a rhetorical position for them. This seems to risk the attribution of a linguistic sophistication to Moody and Edwards that they gave no explicit evidence of, in spite of their *methodological* and *institutional* self-consciousness. Not merely that, but the focus on irony leads to a position of interpretative, if not episte-mological, indeterminacy considerably at variance with the authoritative rhetoric deployed in the essays by Moody and Lyons quoted above. In other words, while the present work may be vulnerable to the charge of using, say, Hayden White *against* Moody and Edwards, Brady seems to risk contradict-ing himself by using White's tropological analysis in their *favour*. In its ideal-ism and linguistic basis, Brady's argument also seems strangely ahistorical and formalist. It seems excessive to explain the entire debate in such narrowly academic terms. Such an explanation disappointingly pays no attention to the historical, institutional or political context in which the debate has taken place. What is needed is not simply a rhetorical modesty (which could easily become a new rhetorical Trojan horse, tactically disarming the reader), but a serious autocritique of the historical profession, that is attentive to material, economic, institutional and political factors as they have affected the produc-tion of historical knowledge.

What must be said about the focus on 'myth-criticism' by both Moody and Lyons, however, is that these writers appeared, in the 1970s, not to have absorbed the debates about the nature of myth that had occupied notable French structuralist writers, such as Roland Barthes and Claude Lévi-Strauss. Barthes published his *Mythologies* in 1957; it was published in English trans-lation in 1972. Levi-Strauss published his *Anthropologie structurale* in 1958; it was published in English in 1963. Other challenges to historical method were similarly ignored. These would include Louis Althusser's 'structuralist Marxism', with its anti-humanist and anti-empiricist stress on history as a process driven by structure rather than the efforts of human subjects (Althusser, 1984). Michel Foucault's emphasis, in *Les mots et les choses* (1966; published in English as *The Order of Things* in 1970) on historical discontinu-ity and the deep structures that underlie and organise knowledge during a given epoch, similarly threw down a challenge that few Irish historians appear to have taken up (Foucault, 1972, 1974). Hayden White published his major work of tropological analysis, *Metahistory: The Historical Imagination in Nineteenth-century Europe*, in 1973. Nevertheless, Tom Dunne, Brady and M.A.G. Ó Tuathaigh write of White's work in the tones of cautious gate-keepers, fully two decades later (Dunne, 1992, p. 5; Brady, 1994b, pp. 24, 28, 30; Ó Tuathaigh, 1994, p. 325). Brady concedes that the lack of influence on Irish historical debate of its Marxist tradition, from James Connolly to Paul Bew, as well as international scholars such as Perry Anderson (raised in

Waterford) and Immanuel Wallerstein, stems from 'the relative insularity of the Irish debate' as much as from ambivalence about Marxist attitudes to nationalism (Brady, 1994b, pp. 15–16).

Another point that must be made, if only briefly, is that a myth-critique of the kind apparently promoted by Moody, Lyons and also by Ronan Fanning (1994; see below) risks, in asserting too literal a distinction between 'historical' and 'mythical' discourses, simply dismissing 'history' as it is popularly experienced. That is, within the domain that is described simply as 'myth' lies a whole array of popular tales, traditions, practices, orally-transmitted stories. That these may contain political elements is undeniable, most especially in the areas where political tension is the highest and where it remains unresolved, that is, Northern Ireland. But the difficulty lies in the fact that such stories and traditions are not simply reducible to their political content, and also in the way that in politically contested areas, 'history' is not simply an archive waiting textual organisation, but is an ongoing experience. In areas of intercommunal tension, even small events are rendered intelligible by ideological narratives – 'myths' – of nationalist struggle or of loyalist resistance, as the work of Oliver MacDonagh attests (MacDonagh, 1983, pp. 1–6). In this context, Moody's or Fanning's calls for myth-criticism, or those of Lyons (who demonstrated, most clearly in *Culture and Anarchy in Ireland* [Lyons, 1979] a more nuanced understanding of culture) betray a lack of the influence of the other human sciences cited by Brady. For simply to dismiss 'myths' as morally dangerous tales told to manipulate their audiences politically may also be to dismiss the discursive communities in which they circulate. Seen in this light, such pronouncements also arrogate to historians the moral, professional and epistemological 'high ground', for they contain within themselves the suggestion that the historian has attained a position of neutrality from which to arbitrate in disputes concerning the prejudices of others. Such statements suggest that the historian lives and works in a Platonic space, that he lies outside of the process he is trying to describe. This leads one to the conclusion that while reading Moody after reading White may be condescending, so also is trying to understand popular history after reading Moody.

So the *Irish Historical Studies* ban on articles on politics after 1900, and Lyons' activist rhetoric of 1971 (re-echoed by Fanning in 1986: see Fanning, 1994), are inverse, mirror images of each other. They express the relation of the production of historical knowledge to the stability and authority of the state. In the first case, when that stability is just established, history-writing must gain its credentials as 'realistic' and 'objective'. Moody and Edwards were trying to create a stable consensus, in a political situation that seemed to militate strongly against such an ambition. They needed to create a powerful

'regime of truth', in Foucault's words (Foucault, 1980, p. 131). But such con-
sensus-building inevitably serves politically and socially centralising forces.
Writing of the politics of interpretation that in the context of recent struggle
enjoins its readers to recognise that the 'war is over' and to forego revenge,
White writes that

> such instruction is the kind that always emanates from centres of estab-
> lished political power and social authority and ... this kind of tolerance
> is a luxury only devotees of dominant groups can afford. For subordi-
> nant, emergent, or resistant social groups, this recommendation – that
> they view history with the kind of 'objectivity', 'modesty', 'realism' and
> 'social responsibility' that has characterized historical studies since
> their establishment as a professional discipline – can only appear as
> another aspect of the ideology they are indentured to oppose. They
> cannot effectively oppose such an ideology while only offering their
> own versions, Marxist or otherwise, of this 'objectivity' and so forth
> that the established discipline claims. This opposition can be carried
> forward only on the basis of a conception of the historical record as
> being not a window through which the past 'as it really was' can be
> apprehended but rather a wall that must be broken through if the
> 'terror of history' is to be directly confronted and the fear it induces
> dispelled.
>
> (White, 1987, pp. 81–2)

But this is precisely analogous to the Irish case, both in the immediate post-
Independence period, and in the early 1970s. The effort to present a historical
discourse that was purged of ideology or myth or utopian narratives of historical
destiny operates against those social and political groups for whom the new dispensation is not satisfactory. For such groups, the stability of the academic discourse of history is a blockage that must be overcome; history for such groups
(radicals of all kinds, women, religious or regional minorities) continues to be an
arena of contest, irreducible to text, still painfully attached to experience.

   In the Irish case, then, disciplinary consensus is achieved by means of the
formidable apparatus described earlier, as well as with an (arguably) unnecessary political ban, and a methodology that, in its refusal of totality and of
grand narratives or explanatory systems, does not call the new geopolitical
arrangements into question, even implicitly. But it is also clear that the construction of consensus is intimately and in an instrumental way related to the
institution of an orthodoxy (the ultimate expression of this in the Irish case
would be the state-assisted *New History of Ireland*) and that this in turn leads
to a resistance to methodological and disciplinary self-questioning. The 'real-

ism' and 'objectivity' of the historians, and their ability to defend, or disciplinise, their discipline (amply realised in the rules and protocols of *Irish Historical Studies*) are the marks of their scholarly purity and hence authority. But these are also the signs of their acceptance of the principle of non-interference, in the fields of other disciplines and in politics. This principle of non-interference is an implicit acknowledgement of the right of the state, or political society, to organise the division of intellectual labour, and thus to map and regulate the social and political landscape, though it is also the means by which the historians, and humanists generally, assert their independence of the state. In the 1970s, in the attacks on 'myth' by Moody and Lyons, we see a new variation on what took place in the 1930s. Consensus has now been achieved, among the academic historians, but now in a period of fresh political instability, it must be defended from pernicious outside influences, principally popular history emanating from Northern Ireland that seeks, on the basis of historical arguments, the dissolution of the existing constitutional arrangements in both polities on the island. Hence, as we shall see below, Fanning's counter-attacks on non-professionals who seek to invade the invade the territory of history (Fanning, 1994). For the idea of non-interference moves in two directions simultaneously, on the one hand protecting the disciplinary field from unwanted outside influences, but on the other discouraging methodological or theoretical self-examination within the field, especially where that is seen to expose the boundaries of the field itself.

The claim of the linkage of professional history and the state is a very grand one, but I think that it may be substantiated by at least two arguments. Firstly, in the way that disciplinary authority is an inherent component of the production of legitimate knowledge, in this case, legitimate historical knowledge. As Jim Merod suggests, intellectual authority is always to an extent tautological or self-confirming:

> Intellectual authority and the authority of scholars and critics are first of all guild creations, products of the credentials conferred by schools that exercise their norms of judgement in order to reproduce themselves. The first rule of professional institutions is to maintain their own stability, to perpetuate themselves and recreate the maximum circumstances for survival and legitimacy. This makes all professional organizations procedurally conservative if not necessarily politically conservative.
>
> (Merod, 1989, p. 65)

Merod continues by suggesting that this authority is an expression of ideology, not of independence:

> The unexamined consensus by which the professionalization and rar-
> efication of knowledge are reproduced by (in terms of) predictable
> habits of authority, in which the generation of authority is the essen-
> tial 'natural' result of institutional constancy, can be looked at as the
> primary ideological component of a culture devoted to transforming
> information while obscuring the institutional ground, the material and
> economic interests, shared by universities and the state and corporate
> network that defines a major part of the general context of national
> and international power.
>
> (Merod, 1989, pp. 103–4)

So the ideology of authority that permeates intellectual activity, in the hierarchically organised university department as much as in the state bureaucracy, is
the ideological sign of the imbrication of the academy with the chief source of
social and political power: the state.

But this also issues in powerfully material ways, not merely in the realm
of ideological abstraction or influence. One must remember that the great
bulk of funding of third-level education comes not from students' fees, or (as
yet) the private sector, but from the state. Not merely this, however, but
grant-aid for research students, sabbatical leaves for study overseas or book
completion, research fellowships and scholarships are regulated in such a way
as to redound not only to the prestige of the individual student or researcher
but to that of the department or university to which that individual is affiliated. In other words, winning rewards that fund the production and elaboration of knowledge is a matter that has much to do with codes of professional
or guild or institutional responsibility. If a university wishes to gain more
research funding, it must maintain a respectable profile with the potential
sources of that funding, be they the state or the free market, while also exert-
ing a degree of pressure on students to work within certain professional parameters, to complete research within certain time periods, to mould that
research to be recognisable in the terms of certain discursive boundaries.
Overall, then, we see a competitive system, that rewards conformity, specialisation, professionalism, most clearly in its junior members (graduate students), and thereby reproduces itself. The wider point is that disciplinary self-
reproduction is possible only in conditions of institutional stability, and that
such institutional stability and consensus is not isolatable from political and
social stability outside the academy, but is in fact crucially dependent upon it.

The idea that power or authority is *productive* as much as coercive, imagined by Gramsci decades before Foucault, is further elaborated in the wider
society that the intellectual (in the broader sense, as a member of the intelligentsia) operates in. Merod once again:

The fact that intellectual authority is derived in a very real way from its institutional affiliation with the state can be seen as soon as we recognize that society (any nation, every government, each cultural system) is the construction of human choice and judgement. The crucial decisions that perpetuate social order are, as Raymond Williams says, beneath awareness in the incorporating energies of a 'selective' tradition that appears as the only set of viable terms and cultural practices. Thus it is that decisions that mold and reproduce society are influenced by the way people who hold power at important moments of social formation (or reformulation) 'read' the world, make sense of their cultural heritage, and finally legislate laws and policies that shape behavior. The role of the intellectual is never wholly visible in that work, nor is it ever suspended. It is exercised in the classroom, where students learn what educators and politicians deem desirable and necessary knowledge. It is exercised in the training of lawyers and clergymen and bureaucrats, all of whom exert pressure on political judgement and political activity. In other words, the intellectual's role is derived from the state because the position of intellectual work is inserted well within the cultural and institutional system of state power. The intellectual articulates values by interpreting texts, framing questions, and choosing a perspective from which to define the way those questions and interpretations fit into reality. But most of all, the political impact of intellectual work shows up in assumptions about the kind of world we are to address in the first place.

(Merod, 1989, pp. 237–8, n. 24)

So the intellectual performs the crucial role of imagining the forms of possibility of the society in which she or he is working.

Alongside this argument, there is the radical view offered by Richard Ohmann, who argues (in the case of literary study in the United States) that

To stand apart from the industrial system ... universities would have to be much *more* political – less pure – than they are. They would have to relinquish the flattering ideology of the ivory tower, the dodge of academic freedom, the false security of professionalism, and all the trappings of neutrality, which conceal a subtler partisanship. They would have to shape academic policy to expressly political ends, asking not 'how can we best transmit and improve the knowledge that exists?' but 'what knowledge do we and our students most need for liberation?'

(Ohmann, 1976, p. 332)

So, in other words, the universities' most effective way of asserting their independence of the state would be for them actually to politically align themselves in opposition to it. This is, of course, precisely what was not seen to happen in Ireland in either the 1930s or the 1970s. In the earlier time, the impulse was to guild self-construction and self-purification, and to the institution(alising) of a method. In the more recent period, the move was a more self-confident one to purge the public sphere of 'mythic' versions of history. The point then, for Ohmann, is that humanists generally, and historians as much as any other group, if they are to lay claim to neutrality and freedom, need to demonstrate how their neutrality and freedom have been attained. Method, and guild self-purification are not enough. If the historians are not organic intellectuals, in the sense of being affiliated to a group or class that is openly contesting, on cultural or political ground, the prevailing hegemony, then it follows that they can be understood as traditional intellectuals, whose role, according to Gramsci, was to be experts in legitimisation (Gramsci, 1971, p. 12). In this view, the historians seek, by their scrupulous methodological rigour and disciplinary control, to avoid accusations of partisanship or ideological bias, but in so doing, they provide a legitimacy for the status quo in a more subtle way. That is, by operating in a rational and normal manner within the established social and political order, they implicitly rationalise and normalise that order. They rationalise the state and its dominant culture by supporting assumptions and values that delimit the boundaries of debate. They reproduce standards of conceptual thinking, they provide information that, whatever about the ideology of its production, is not necessarily 'neutral' in its uses, they provide the categories by which analyses are carried out in certain areas of political or cultural action.

Most of this intellectual work manifests itself in texts, of course. Drawing on Gramsci, Edward Said argues that all intellectual production aspires to the consent of its consumers, and since 'texts are facts of power, not of democratic exchange', they are either part of a dominant consensus or of efforts to dislodge such a consensus (Said, 1984, p. 45; 1985b, pp. 143–6). This leads Said to suggest that one 'can interpret the meaning of a text by virtue of what in its mode of social presence enables its consent of by either a small or a wide group of people' (Said, 1985b, p. 144). Most clearly, historical narratives that unselfconsciously aspire to realism, or to making the events of history speak themselves as if reality was story-shaped, offer their readers a position as reading-subject from which the events of the past thereby represented are comprehensible and intelligible. To do this, they assume and project an ideal reader whose rationality and self-knowledge is beyond question. This means that the reader is interpellated into a position of benign, Olympian contemplation of the past. One could say that the reader-subject is constituted at the expense of the past. The greater the panorama surveyed, or the anatomical detail provided, the loftier the transcendence of the sovereign reader. To this extent, historical accounts that are purportedly neutral and value-free presume, and hope to produce, a readership that is similarly neutral and value-free.

Further, we must take cognisance of David Lloyd's point when he writes about the understandings of violence of nationalist and revisionist historiographies. He points out that nationalist historiography has tended to view violence in somewhat Whiggish terms. That is, that it provides a view of the overall course of Irish history whereby successive violent uprisings of the Irish people against British rule have culminated in the independent nation-state. Such a view has regarded the Northern crisis as evidence of the so-called 'unfinished business' of nationalism. But this attitude has little time for violence or militancy that seems to run athwart its project. To revisionist historiography, violence is a backward and irrational phenomenon that runs counter to constitutionalism and the law. It is seen, as Said has argued in a different context, as 'anti-narrative', meaningless, futile (Said, 1994a, p. 257). In this view, it is radically tautological and has no legitimate history, but its outrages have called up the modern state apparatus in Ireland: a national police force, modern administrative, legal, educational and legislative institutions. Seamus Deane and Declan Kiberd have demonstrated the degree to which nineteenth-century Ireland functioned, in spite of its putative status as a co-equal part of the United Kingdom, as a kind of colonial laboratory for these modernising innovations (Deane, 1986; Kiberd, 1986). The point, as Lloyd writes, is that for both modes of history-writing, 'the end of violence is the legititmate state formation ... the end of history is the emergence of the state' (Lloyd, 1993, p. 125).

Lloyd's remarks are part of an essay, 'Violence and the constitution of the novel', dealing with the conditions of possibility of the novel form in nineteenth-century Ireland (Lloyd, 1993, pp. 125–62). He concludes this essay with a discussion of the respective theories of the novel of Mikhail Bakhtin and Benedict Anderson, noting that they both see the novel in somewhat benign terms. He shrewdly focuses on the way that while the novel allows the emergence of a variety of social voices or discourses (Bakhtin's 'heteroglossia') and the 'imagining' of an emergent national community (Anderson), neither writer pays suffficient attention to the ways that the same form can also *exclude* or de-legitimate certain sociolects, and hence can make certain voices, narratives, modes of sociality or political practices literally unimaginable. Lloyd is interested, then, in the socially regulative function of the novel, and the way that that function is made especially clear at moments of its failure. He terms such moments 'crises of representation', and discusses these moments in relation to the novelistic rendering of Ireland's long nineteenth century. But the same term is useful to us when we try to understand the moment of crisis in Ireland at the beginning of the 1970s in the work of historians.

Underlying Lloyd's remarks on Bakhtin and Anderson is his deployment of Althusser's celebrated theory of ideology and its role in the constitution of the subject. That is, for Lloyd, the novel, as an institution, creates a certain kind of reading subject. White uses the same idea in an essay on J.G. Droysen, to show the function of the historical text in the service of a similar project (White, 1987, pp. 83–103). As he makes clear, for Althusser, ideology is most of all a system of representation which enables the individual subject to recognise himself, his social, political and ethical co-ordinates, within the socio-political system as he finds it. Ideology, in this sense, is not a system of purposely conceived and perpetrated mind-control. It is, rather, the mode of representation that produces a reading or viewing subject who identifies with the ethical system that legitimises the practices of the given society. As White suggests, the ideological component of a work of art, or of literature, or of history-writing, consists in its offering to the reader, as a position from which it is intelligible, the position of the law-abiding citizen. But White argues that historiography is the mode of representation which is most effective in this task. The reason for this is not that it may adopt a specifically moral or political position,

> ... but because in its featuring of narrativity as a favoured representational practice, it is especially well-suited to the production of notions of continuity, wholeness, closure, and individuality that every 'civilized' society wishes to see itself as incarnating, against the chaos of a merely 'natural' way of life.
>
> (White, 1987, p. 87)

To comprehend modern histories, one must adopt a subject position that recognises these values most appropriate to thinking about the 'reality' one inhabits. At this point, such 'values' cease to be mere values among others, and are naturalised, and become, to the individual subject, 'objective'. For Althusser, when such 'values' are identified with the actual practices of the society of which the reader-subject is a member, then they and the representational practices that produce them constitute 'ideology'. Therefore, to accept a particular mode of representing 'reality' is always already to acquiesce, by implication, to a certain way of determining the meaning and value of the 'reality' thus represented. This, then, takes its form in the system of symbolic relationships which governs the manner 'legitimate' forms of authority are offered for the subject. So, as White puts it,

> The purpose of the canonical representational practices of a given society, then, is to produce a subjectivity that will take this symbolic structure as the sole criterion for assessing the "realism" of any recommendation to act or think one way and not another.
>
> (White, 1987, p. 88)

As White argues, historical representation does this especially well, since it deals with the 'real' as against the simply 'imaginary', but it places this 'reality' at a certain distance by 'construing it under the modality of a "pastness" both distinct from and continuous with the "present" ' (White, 1987, pp. 88–9). The past is different from the present, in that it can be seen as 'another country', strange or foreign. But it is also and at the same time continuous with the present, in its familiarity and availability to knowledge. So the past is, in this sense, 'uncanny'; it oscillates constantly on the shadowy border of what is knowable and unknowable, absent and present. White in this way relates the historical past to the Freudian category of the 'imaginary', the realm of narcissistic and infantile fantasies driven by dreams of total control. In this realm, problems of knowledge are postponed, the past is here 'fixed' as a frozen spectacle of completed acts. The character of these completed acts is inseparable from their locations in the spectacle, which in turn are moral locations, defined by the symbolic system with which they are identified. So the contemplation of the past allows the speaking subject to exercise what White calls 'fantasies of freedom under the aspect of a fixed order, or conflict under the aspect of resolution, of violence under the aspect of achieved peace' (White, 1987, p. 89). The representation of history lets the reader 'imagine' freely, while still constrained by a 'symbolic system'. But it lets him do so in such a way as to give him a more coherent or intelligible sense of 'reality' than he may derive from his quotidian existence. Not only this, but historiography produces a sense of the 'real' that can help the reader determine what is to be deemed 'realistic' in his own present.

The argument, therefore, has been that of the alignment of the historians with the state. If this link was hidden and implicit in the 1930s, it became much more obvious in the early 1970s. It is clear in Lyons' hopeful remarks about the historical consciousness of the new 'intellectual élite, both inside and outside the universities' of the late 1960s being shaped by the new historiography (Lyons, 1973b, p. 693). It is clear in the agonised call for renewed myth-criticism made by Lyons already cited, and in the account of the new history given by Ronan Fanning, a leading practitioner, which ends with a call to his fellow historians to write contemporary history, lest the task be monopolised by the 'ideologists' and 'mythologists' (Fanning, 1994, p. 157). Yet the confidence in sovereign method remains unshaken, as we see in Fanning's quotation of another essay by Lyons. Writing in 1973, Lyons saw the writing of contemporary history as a 'plain duty', the main aspect of which would be 'simply to elicit the facts' and 'to set out those facts in the clearest and least sensational prose we can achieve'. Analysis and synthesis could be left until later. The hope was that 'by patient excavation and resolute refusal to study the recent on any but the terms dictated by our discipline …[to] contribute a little towards the restoration of sanity in this island' (Fanning, 1994, p. 159). The contemporary history at issue here is obviously that of Northern Ireland, and the confidence is that adherence to empirical historiographic method and unadorned prose will preserve the neutrality of the historians. The paradox is that this quotation comes at the end of an essay which explicitly links the confidence of the revisionist enterprise to that of the state, which acknowledges the adoption by 'the Irish political establishment after 1969' of 'that interpretation of modern Irish history commonly described as "revisionist"', and which openly admits the contemporary history it calls for will be dependent on potentially unreliable government leaks, press releases and favoured journalists (Fanning, 1994, pp. 147, 157, 159). Fanning is inclined to relate the possibility of the writing of history to the availability of official records, and in this he betrays his view of history as consisting in the actions and statements of privileged elites of politicians and the journalists and biographers who chronicle them. Obviously, this also links the production of historical knowledge to official sources, and results in a narrowly political history, with little or no space left for subaltern groups such as women, religious, ethnic or racial minorities, or regional identities, and little interest in the realm of social history also, which is the space in which the mythologies with which he is concerned find their origins and their effectivity. The point is, then, that such a history, linked to the pedagogical mission of myth-criticism, leads to a discursive situation where 'history' is conceived as the official record, or, at best, the 'reality' that lies behind the official record, while 'unofficial history' is either ignored or, if it takes a political hue, it is criticised and de-legitimised as 'mythology'. The most obvious evidence of such linkage comes when Fanning writes of how the writing of twentieth-century Irish history demands a constant 'confrontation with mythologies designed to legitimise violence as a political weapon in a bid to overthrow the state' (Fanning, 1994, p. 156). This implies not only the defence of the state, but its defence from Northern Republican violence specifically, since Fanning makes no reference to Loyalist violence, which has been dedicated to the upkeep of the Northern state, or to the abuses of power of the Northern state, a major cause of Republican violence. So Fanning's conception of contemporary history is clearly one of counter-insurgency, though it still cloaks itself in the rhetoric of empirical neutrality. Indeed, when Lyons writes of 'the dire past still overhanging the dire present' in the context of the Northern conflict, it appears that the myths that are being inveighed against are timeless, *ahistorical* constructs, untouched by the fifty years' development of the two statelets, North and South. Little attention is paid to the social, political or economic reasons for the persistent *effectivity* of such myths, as against their actual truth. Therefore, the critique operates on two levels: firstly, that of simply pointing out the untruths of such myths; secondly, of detaching them and their adherents from history. The reaction, thus, of dominant figures in the historical discipline in Ireland to the crisis years of the late 1960s and early 1970s has been an entrenchment of political position and of methodological dogma. The crisis served to expose what had only been implicit previously: the relationship of historiographic authority and political authority. The crisis has provided an illustration of traditional intellectuals struggling to maintain their control of the discursive field that is Irish history, as it has been invaded by politicians, journalists, writers, and revolutionaries. They have recognised that control of discourse makes for and enables real power in the world, but the result has been a kind of history-writing that is philosophically and epistemologically naïve, at the same time that it partakes of authorial authoritarianism. The argument therefore is that the crisis of stability in the state could be expected to produce a crisis of intellectual authority in university-based historians, who could then react in one of two ways. As I argued in my Introduction, the control of narratives and of representations is a crucial matter for the state, most especially at times of crisis. For the Gramscian 'crisis of authority' can be described as precisely a crisis in the ability of the hegemonic class to control the dominant social and political conception of the future, and hence of its ability to control historical narratives, used as these are both to understand the present and to legitimate images of the future. Thus the 'crisis of authority' is characterised by the emergence of new narratives of social and political aspiration, or the re-emergence of old ones, or both, as appeared to be the case in Ireland in the late 1960s and early 1970s. Either the crisis of the state could induce a discursive and disciplinary modesty and reflexiveness, or it could induce a lapse into discursive and disciplinary defensiveness, arrogance and dogma. I suggest that the evidence examined and discussed above points towards the latter.

The novels of John Banville offer a salutary alternative. In both his explicitly 'Irish' works – *Birchwood* (Banville, 1992a), *The Newton Letter* (Banville, 1992b) – and his 'European' novels – *Dr Copernicus* (Banville, 1990) and *Kepler* (Banville, 1983) – Banville has written a kind of metahistory that has been almost entirely absent from Irish historical debate. As a literary intellectual writing about the writing of history, he has not been entirely alone. Brian Friel's plays *Translations* (Friel, 1984) and *Making History* (Friel, 1989)

have treated of themes, some of which I dealt with earlier – authority (authorial, communal, political), narrative, the transition from tradition to modernity – but in the context of a deep past inaccessible to us now save through
language and intertexts. *Translations* is 'set' in 1824, at the time of a radical
new state-sponsored textualisation of the landscape – the first Ordnance
Survey. It explores the relationships between political and linguistic change,
between English and Irish, between the English colonising power and the
Irish colonised subject. *Making History* is 'set' in the late sixteenth and early
seventeenth centuries, and is about the Nine Years' War, fought by Hugh
O'Neill against Elizabeth I, culminating in the battle of Kinsale and O'Neill's
exile in Rome. Both plays concern themselves explicitly with the yearning for
and final impossibility of an authentic history that tells us 'what really happened'. *Making History* in particular is concerned to explore this area, pos-
sessing as it does O'Neill's biographer as a major character, and depicting
O'Neill's unsuccessful efforts to exert control over the narration of his life as
his last struggle. Friel's discussion in this play of the political exigencies governing the production of history is poignant and sensitive in its pointing up
of the elements that are left out or marginalised in the production of what
becomes a heroic narrative – his happy period as a foster-child in the houses
of Henry Sidney in Shropshire and Kent, his last marriage to a sister of the
Queen's Marshal, the extent to which his final rebellion was in fact a small
element in a much grander European war of religion, the fact that the battle
of Kinsale was a rout caused by the treachery of Irish chieftains. But the irony
is that the play is nevertheless concerned with a 'great man', and to that
extent, it repeats one of the more obvious limitations of the new history – its
tendency to concentrate on a narrowly political conception of the historical
process. Nevertheless, in the Friel plays that I concentrated on in Chapter 1,
The Freedom of the City, Living Quarters and *Faith Healer*, there was extensive
evidence of the staging of the crisis of intellectual authority that I am suggesting Banville deals with, and that the historians, as professionalised and
disciplinised intellectuals, were unable to deal with. All three plays are filled
with competing, jostling narratives and discourses. My disappointment in
these plays lies in the opinion that Friel does not press home the radical critique of authorial (and hence intellectual) authority that he opens up, but
'closes' his texts again, under the pressure of the bardic role that he feels subjected to, or of the bourgeois humanist limitations of the institutional theatre
in which he displays his art.

    Banville's efforts constitute a more thoroughgoing revisionism than either
the historians' or Friel's (Tóibín, 1993, p. 3). He writes what Linda Hutcheon
has called 'historiographic metafiction', meaning that he writes fiction that

reinstalls historical contexts as significant and even determining, but in so doing, it problematizes the entire notion of historical knowledge ... the implication is that there can be no single, essentialized, transcendent concept of 'genuine historicity' ... no matter what the nostalgia (Marxist or traditionalist) for such an entity.

(Hutcheon, 1988, p. 89)

This collision of the historical novel and modernist metafictional formalism is, for Hutcheon, what characterises postmodern fiction. However, I am less interested in whether Banville's fiction is modernist or postmodernist than in the fact that it seems to me to represent a notable, if oblique, contribution to Irish historiographic debate.

Banville's engagement with Irish subject-matter does not appear to be as sustained as Friel's uneasy relationship with bourgeois nationalism, but he has in fact engaged in a critique of the grounds of revisionism and of nationalism all the more powerful for its philosophical concentration. His novels deal with language and human experience, the possibility of writing history, the relationship between subjectivity and narration, and the interrelationship of the intellectual production of representational or conceptual systems, and the world. If Hutcheon and Kearney call Banville postmodernist, this is not anomalous in a country that still seems riven with conflicts between tradition and modernity. As Desmond Bell has pointed out, the anomalous situation of Irish modernity has been due to its belatedness, both in relation to Ireland itself and in relation to the rest of the metropolitan West (Bell, 1988). But in his apparently most non-Irish material, it is a situation such as this that Banville is choosing to dramatise: he historicises, in a reflexive manner, the experiences of two Renaissance humanist intellectuals as they, the harbingers of modernity, struggle to produce their conceptual systems in the face of personal contingencies as well as powerful forces of academic orthodoxy, religious conflict and absolutist state power. So Banville, through the lives of Nicolas Koppernigk and Johannes Kepler, is addressing the issue of the arrival of intellectual modernity in premodern societies, but he is doing so in a manner characterised by some as typical of literary postmodernism. He brings to a kind of historical writing what Seamus Deane has called a 'high state of anxious self-reflection' (Longley, 1992d, p. 20). To this extent, even these 'non-Irish' novels touch glancingly on the Irish condition: the conflict, which has been ongoing since the end of the 1960s, inherent in the arrival of intellectual modernity at the apparent end of that intellectual era.

Banville's novels of this period engage with this issue in various ways. The most important of these are through the intersection of *Birchwood* and *The*

Newton Letter with certain forms of Irish fiction, and the engagement of *Dr Copernicus* and *Kepler* with one of those forms. *Birchwood* and *The Newton Letter* are both examples of the 'Big House' novel. *Birchwood* also partakes of the Gothic mode. In each case, Banville uses metafictional techniques to alienate the reader from any possibility of understanding these novels as realist texts. In *Dr Copernicus* and *Kepler*, Banville writes 'historical' novels, but he metafictionally disrupts any emerging similarity between these books and those of the tradition we now trace to Sir Walter Scott. In *The Newton Letter*, the two projects come together: we read a story of a man who could be the author, in that he is trying to write a biography of another great scientist, Sir Isaac Newton. What makes the narrator of *The Newton Letter* similar to Banville is his failure, and his tendency to write about that failure. Just as the narrator of *The Newton Letter* fails to write his book in the manner he had planned, so Nicolas Koppernigk and Johannes Kepler find that their projects of astronomical representation and knowledge are compromised also. But what *The Newton Letter* suggests is that Newton's late breakdown was due to a crisis of language, and Gabriel Godkin, the narrator of *Birchwood*, spends his life dealing with epistemological and representational difficulties. Gabriel, Koppernigk, Kepler, Newton, the narrator of *The Newton Letter*, Banville's implied author: this is a list of authors in crisis. I am suggesting here that a major part of the interest of these books lies in this representation and self-representation of crisis. In it, Banville intrudes in or 'interferes' with Irish history-writing, Irish intellectuals, the historical novel, and the nineteenth-century 'Big House' mode that has been adopted by Irish novelists from Maria Edgeworth to William Trevor (Said, 1985b, p. 157). It is precisely in Banville's representation of crisis, his embrace of and play with crisis, that his difference from and rebuke to Irish historiography lies. Unlike academic historians, who unwittingly reveal their relationship to the state and to political authority in the vehemence of their defence of that state, of the political and cultural representational dispensation it underpins, and of their discipline from any who might 'interfere' with its carefully regulated economy, Banville exposes authorial authority and the conceptual apparatus upon which his books depend. Banville turns the Emperor's clothes inside-out.

Of *Birchwood*, Joseph McMinn has written that

> Banville seems to have chosen this well-known genre and its conventions for their imaginative, metaphorical possibilities, their insistent associations with decay, political crisis and, significantly, the image of a class of people increasingly out of touch with reality.
>
> (McMinn, 1991, p. 30)

But McMinn seems unwilling to draw out the wider implications of this choice in terms of contemporary Irish history. Blind formalism leads Rudiger Imhof to suggest that *Birchwood* was not written in a period of social or political upheaval. He reckons that the anachronistic elements of the novel (the presence of the telephone or the bicycle, for example, not to mention the fact that Gabriel Godkin speaks the phrases and ideas of Wittgenstein, Proust, Descartes) are signs that it is 'an allegory of art and the artistic imagination' (Imhof, 1989, p. 71). But the artistic imagination works with real material, and can make an intervention in a cultural tradition that may have political resonances. The apparent refusal of politics may itself be a political strategy, Seamus Deane has argued, reminding us that the Irish tradition of metafiction

> ... is not a political literature by any means, yet it is not a literature without politics. Its removal from the public world is contemptuous. But the removal itself expresses a deep disillusion, not only with Irish politics as such, but with the very idea basic to most politics – that the world is subject to improvement if not change or transformation. One could, I believe, argue that the degree of introversion in the major Irish fictions of this century is in exact ratio to the degree of political disillusion. Both *Nightspawn* and *Birchwood*, with their complicated political backgrounds, offer us exemplary instances of this.
>
> (Deane, 1976, p. 334)

Similarly, Kearney proposes that Banville exemplifies a turn from Revivalist cultural nationalism to cultural internationalism and an 'aesthetic revolution of the word (Kearney, 1988a, p. 13). What Kearney leaves out is the post-Independence critique of the Revival by realists such as O'Connor, O'Faolain and Lavin. In *Birchwood* Banville installs the 'Big House' novel, a form already characterised, if only thematically, by familial decline and political decay, and subverts it further, using the Gothic mode, and formal techniques such as direct address to the reader, narratorial self-deprecation, the invocation of a whole range of literary and philosophical intertexts, and historical anachronisms. This strategy has political as well as aesthetic implications.

Ernest Renan believed that 'historical error is a crucial factor in the creation of a nation' (Renan, 1990, p. 11). Homi Bhabha has shown how nations are, insofar as they are 'imagined', narratives (Bhabha, 1990, pp. 1–7). The 'Big House' novel was one of the major trends of the novel in nineteenth-century Ireland. Irish conditions were not, as Terry Eagleton has pointed out, conducive to the production of an Irish novelistic realism of the order of George Eliot (Eagleton, 1994, pp. 17–18). Realism is the form of totality and social stability, but Irish history militated against such complacent imaginings. Realism also presupposes the availability of a metalanguage, that could offer the possibility of a putatively detached, neutral omniscient narration and commentary. But Banville himself has alluded to 'something subversive, destructive even, and in a way profoundly despairing' in the uses of English in Ireland (Banville, 1981, p. 14). For him, this leads to a situation where language is seen as irreconcilable to the description of the phenomenal world. But this is only the formal analogue of Eagleton's argument that language in nineteenth-century Ireland was 'strategic for the oppressed but representational for their rulers' (Eagleton, 1994, p. 20). The point, then, is that the stability of representation, or the achieveability of versimilitude, is inevitably an issue that is at once of aesthetic, epistemological and political importance. The new Irish history both fought to achieve, and assumed, such stability, even if the kind of 'realism' it announced was reduced to what Bell has called a 'fact-grubbing empiricism' in its rejection of historicism (Bell, 1985, p. 95). Actually, its concentration on 'facts' was a reaction to the turbulence of Irish history and its tendency to stretch the boundaries of conventional realist verisimilitude. So the empiricist tendency of revisionism was partly due to the problem of representation faced by nineteenth-century novelists in Ireland, a problem that Banville returned to in the early 1970s. But it was at this moment that representation once again became problematic. In the political terms in which Ireland, North and South, represented itself, there came the parallel and equivalent crises in the North and the South: the return of violence and the Arms Trials. These were crises of narrative culture as much as they were political crises – David Lloyd suggests the linkage when he argues that 'To the monopoly of violence claimed by the state ... corresponds the monopoly of representation claimed by dominant culture' (Lloyd, 1993, p. 4). The emergence of secret, hidden or marginal voices in the political sphere, North and South, is matched by the crisis of authorial authority in narrative culture. The response to the crisis of authority is either to stage it, as Friel tries to, and as Banville does; or to restate the traditional positions. In historiographic practice, we see the recourse to authority (implied in empiricist myth-criticism, directed against marginal, insurrectionary groups in the North). Writing pastiches of the 'Big House' and the Irish Gothic, Banville attempts to subvert a literary tradition of the nineteenth century Protestant bourgeoisie, at a time when it seemed that the Roman Catholic nationalist bourgeoisie had all but absorbed or incorporated the remains of the Ascendancy. Further, by this time, this Catholic middle-class appeared, in the move into Europe, in the removal of the special constitutional position of the Catholic Church in 1972 and in its conquest of some of the former bastions of Ascendancy society (such as Trinity College and the Royal Dublin Society), to be taking on the social and cultural vestments of its erstwhile rivals. Banville's assault on realism is of a piece with Deane's critique of the 'Literary Myths of the Revival' (Deane, 1985, pp. 28–37). In this well-known essay, Deane suggests that the persistence of the 'Big House' in the Irish novel is a tribute to the influence of Yeats and a criticism of the poverty of the Irish novelistic tradition' (Deane, 1985, p. 32). He continues:

> In fact the Big House is now more concerned with tourism and tax concessions, with the preservation of the artefacts of 'culture', than with power or value. In fiction, it is an anachronism. The over-extension of the Yeatsian myth of history into fiction helps us to see what an odd and protean thing it is and how far removed it has become from contemporary reality. In seeing this, we might finally decide to seek our intellectual allegiances and our understanding of our history elsewhere.
>
> (Deane, 1985, p. 32)

In that final sentence, we see the analogy between Banville's cultural and aesthetic mining of Europe, and Deane's use of European philosophy, from the Enlightenment to Foucault, to fuel his intellectual project. We also see the turn away from and critique of revisionist historiography (Deane, 1994).

If the linkage I am suggesting between a historico-political crisis, and a novelistic one, seems forced, then that is because the separation of historiographic and fictional writing is relatively recent. Theorists of history such as White, and historians of the English novel such as Ian Watt (1987), Michael McKeon (1987) and Lennard Davis (1983) all point to its beginnings in the production of various kinds of putatively 'factual' discourse, history-writing and journalism most clear among them. Before the rise of Leopold von Ranke's idea of 'scientific history' in the nineteenth century and the disciplinization described earlier, the discourses of literature and of history were recognised as intimately-related enterprises. The apparently *necessary* relation of 'facts' and 'truth' was a product of the nineteenth century. Prior to the French Revolution, it was accepted that historiography was a literary art. This did not mean that it did not deal in the 'real', but that in its representation of the 'real', imagination and 'literary' techniques – rhetorical devices, figures, tropes – were used. But after the Revolution, as I suggested earlier, 'truth' became identified with 'fact', and history was set over against fiction, especially the novel. History became associated with the representation of the 'actual', as compared to the representation of the 'possible' or the merely 'imaginable' (White, 1978, p. 123). Nevertheless, even in the nineteenth century, as Linda Hutcheon shows, Macauley acknowledged a debt to Sir Walter

Scott, and Dickens, in his *Tale of Two Cities*, owed much to Carlyle (Hutcheon, 1988, pp. 105–6). In our own time, we see parallels between the 'historiographic metafiction' discussed by Hutcheon, and the metahistorical writing of theorists such as White, Foucault and Dominick LaCapra. What these writers share is the recognition that both the novel and history-writing are concerned with *verisimilitude* – the production of effects of truth – as much as with positive truth itself. Both novel and historical treatise are crucially dependent on narrative patterns, literary tropes and the deployment of 'interexts'. By the latter I mean historiography's dependence on archives, personal depositions, state papers, personal documents, church documents; and the novel's use of prior literary texts, forms, motifs.

The radicalism of Banville's novelistic enterprise lies in its conjoining once again (albeit in an ironic mode) of these apparently separate discourses. Banville's novels, as I have suggested, are about history and the act of writing about it. *Birchwood* and *The Newton Letter* feature first-person narrators, who recount personal or familial histories. They describe the difficulties they encounter in this task – the unreliability of memory, the fragmentary character of what can be remembered, the inadequacy of language to represent what is unearthed, the division between perception and knowledge. In these novels, such difficulties are paralleled and embodied in the ways that the narrators seek to understand the world around them and to find a unifying or organising principle that will render empirical experience meaningful. In the obviously 'historical' novels, *Dr Copernicus* and *Kepler*, the pattern is somewhat different. These novels are narrated by third-person, apparently omniscient narrators, describing the worlds of their heroes from some Archimedean perspective. However, these novels display their fictive nature in other ways: the quotation of anachronistic intertexts, the interpolation of the texts of other characters; in the actual structure of the text (the letters in the 'Harmonice Mundi' section of *Kepler*). In both of these novels, these difficulties of language or representation are paralleled in the way we also see portrayed the epistemological, intellectual, institutional problems that beset their heroes as they tried to work up their theories, as well as the social, economic and political forces that hemmed them in.

One of the most obvious links between novelistic and historiographic discourse is that both presume temporalities, or ideas of time. This is part of their respective claims to the production of a sense of reality. It must be remembered that one of the chief effects of narrative is to create 'time', to create a temporal scheme, and therefore meaning or sense, out of a raw flow of phenomena. The crudest way that this effect is achieved is by the production of a chronicle, but this form of organisation, obviously, allows for no detail and no depth of treatment. What is important, however, is that a historical narrative must, as much as any realist novel, adhere to certain conventional rhythms if it is not to lose the faith of its readers.

So, one of the crucial elements of realism is the production of a certain temporality. Part of the claim on our attention as readers that narrative makes is through the way that plot functions to create a sense of time that contributes to that narrative's internal coherence. In the realist novel, the plot must conform to a temporal rhythm that is plausible, or recognisable, to the reader: characters act, events take place in a fictional time that approximates to the *logic* of the real time of empirical experience. But, of course, fictional time is not the same as actual time: it is ordered, speeded up, slowed down by a narrator. Therefore, in a novel, when the narrator alters that sense of time, or deviates from it, we the readers become aware of it, and self-conscious of our status *as* readers. So one could say that temporal experiment helps produce a Brechtian 'alienation effect', where the reader is forced to reflect on the constructed nature of fictional temporality, and, ultimately, on the constructed nature of time in social actuality. In history-writing, while the writer is limited by what she can ascertain from the documentary record or other evidence, she is also faced with narrative or tropological decisions as to how that material is to be arranged: in chronological order; in an imputed causal order, where the historian must also decide as to the prominence to be given to certain historical actors, events, movements, themes. To the degree that the historian must 'emplot' these elements, she must fictionalise them. To give such elements narrative order, to effect an 'end' to a particular 'story' (and thus give it 'closure') is to enforce an artificial, and thus fictional pattern on what purports to be 'real material'. For historical reality to be rendered retrospectively intelligible, it must to this extent be fictionalised and given a timespan. Conventionally, of course, history-writing does not allude to this process. It seeks to let the facts 'speak for themselves'. Anything else is 'counter-factual speculation'. The closest that history-writing comes to acknowledging self-doubt, usually, is in its use of references, though the exhaustiveness of references is taken conventionally to defend the case put forward. Discursive modesty is also implied in the idea of 'revision', whereby the search never ends for new positive evidence. But re-interpretation takes place constantly also.

Both the novel and the historical narrative, then, require a plausible temporality for their readers to accept them. Banville's novels flout this convention, and this applies both in the case of his 'Big House' and his 'historical' pastiches. In *Birchwood*, the putative narrative principle is that of an autobiography. This is itself a temporal principle: the idea is that we read the narrative of the constitution of the narrating subject. We learn the story of how Gabriel got to the point of telling us the story we read. But there is more. *Birchwood* is a search for knowledge. This quest takes the form of Gabriel's

Tristram Shandy-like efforts to narrate his personal history, as suggested above, but also the history of Birchwood. It also takes the form of Gabriel's life itself. The result is that the problem of time is raised at the levels of both content and form. Gabriel refers to his problem with time, as well as having evident difficulties in achieving a confident sense of memory. Gabriel as narrator self-consciously refers to the problems he has in reconstructing his story. But these difficulties are paralleled by, firstly, the general problem of perception that he writes of – the drive he feels to find a moment or instance of 'harmony'. This can be understood in temporal terms, among others: Gabriel desires a moment of stillness in the temporal flow. Indeed at one point he discovers such a thing, in his experiment of blinking, but also realises that this is as much a product of his senses as anything else (Banville, 1992a, p. 128). Secondly, Gabriel's autobiographical narrative presupposes the reader's interest. This interest is predicated on an assumed identity between the reader's sense of time, and Gabriel's. Of course, no sooner is this assumption made than it is overturned. Gabriel's narrative is marked by anomalies and anachronisms. At times the novel appears to be set during the 'Troubles' of the 1920s, at times it seems to be set during the Famine. Telephones and bicycles appear in the narrative. The text takes as its intertexts writings of Descartes, Wittgenstein, Proust, Nabokov, reaching forwards and backwards in the European literary and philosophical tradition for the languages it uses. This, and the confusion of timescales suggested by its Gothic characteristics, where the traces of a legacy of past guilt or misdeeds returns to haunt the present, only adds to the temporal confusion of the novel. Gabriel's quest to understand his past works as an archaeological study of his family, but it only serves to reveal that his family history is one of contest. Between Gabriel's father and his 'aunt' (actually his mother), we find two competing 'histories'. Much of the confusion that Gabriel encounters is due to the fact that there is no one simple linear family narrative to be disinterred. Rather there are intertwining narrative strands. Struggling to recount his own life, Gabriel finds that a concomitant to this task is to tell the 'alternative' that others had plotted – in both senses – for him. So, the history with which the novel is concerned is also and at the same time its own negation. The result is a profoundly unsettled historical sense in the novel.

This doubled sense of Gabriel's quest, his will to describe both his own personal history and that of the Birchwood 'house' (with the dual sense of family and of physical structure) emerges, of course, also in Gabriel's wider realisation that all insights are accompanied by blindness, that things are and were never quite what we think or thought them to be, and that the processes of memory and cognition by which we try to grasp them are inherently faulty. He begins by inverting Descartes:

I am, therefore I think. That seems inescapable. In this lawless house I spend the nights poring over my memories ... Some of these memories are in a language which I do not understand ... They tell the story which I intend to copy here, all of it, if not its meaning, the story of the fall and rise of Birchwood.

(Banville, 1992a, p. 11)

Here we see the self-consciousness about memory, its partiality, and the elusive nature of its meaning. We see also a suggestion of the textuality of memory, and of the inauthenticity of 'the story I intend to *copy* here' (my emphasis). We also see, in the Cartesian inversion, the upsetting of one of the classical statements, and strategies, of Enlightenment rationalism. Descartes' original formulation privileged thought over being, ideas over objects, and assumed the impossibility of reducing consciousness to a set of determinants. Banville here turns that on its head. For Gabriel, thought is 'inescapable'; some of his memories are 'in a language which [he does] not understand'. The memories tell a story, but not necessarily its 'meaning'. This is the opposite of both conventional autobiography, and of the confidence of nineteenth-century realism in its ability to render the past accurately in narrative. Realism presupposes a metalanguage, a neutral and authoritative discourse that the narrator can arrogate to himself in order to depict the actions and ideas of his characters without challenge. Such a metalanguage assumes that its wielder is in full command of the facts of his story, and in full command of himself. Put another way, it presupposes the rationality, self-presence and centeredness of its user. It also presumes the sovereign independence of the narrating subject from the historical process. Gabriel's opening, however, suggests the opposite of these things. It supposes that for him thought consists significantly of memory, but that since thinking is involuntary, so also is remembering. So remembering takes place in a language that he does not understand. Gabriel's vulnerability before language and memory defines him as a subject of language. He is as much spoken by language, in the structuralist sense of *langue*, as it is spoken by him (*parole*). So Gabriel is not a rational self-possessed Cartesian subject, and the narrator of the novel is not fully in control of himself. The authority of the narrative has been displaced. This decentering of narrative authority has at least two repercussions. It accentuates our sense of Gabriel as an unreliable narrator – not only does he have the partiality of subjectivity, but that very subject is unsure of itself. More radically, this dissolution of the narrating subject in language disrupts the capacity of the novel to project and constitute its ideal reader. If subjectivity is constituted in and by language, then the unsettling of the field of language affected by Gabriel's inscription of his own enunciative position is ultimately unsettling for the reader. In Althusserian terms, the interpellation and hence reproduction of subjectivity in ideology requires an authoritative and stable discourse, such as literary realism. This reminds us of the relationship of 'scientific history' and literary realism traced earlier. To attack realism by denying the possibility of a novelistic metalanguage, and to do so by impugning the possibility of realistic fictional representation of the past, is an implied attack on the pretensions of conventional historiography. It is in this sense, and in this spirit, that one may begin to call Banville a 'metahistorian'.

Soon after the introduction quoted above, Gabriel tells us that

> We imagine that we remember things as they were, while in fact all we carry into the future are fragments which reconstruct a wholly illusory past.
>
> (Banville, 1992a, p. 12)

Gabriel describes his memories in textual terms, and compares himself to a historian exploring an archive. He also compares himself to 'an archaeologist mapping a buried empire' (Banville, 1992a, p. 13), an image reminiscent of Foucault's appropriation of Jorge Luis Borges at the opening of *The Order of Things* (Foucault, 1974, pp. xv–xix). Like the Irish new historians, Gabriel is moved to search for the 'thing-in-itself', Kant's *Ding-an-Sich*, the positive fact. But even when empirically confronted with what appear to be such positive facts, Gabriel finds them recalcitrant:

> I had dreamed of the house so often on my travels that it now refused to be real, even while I stood among its ruins. It was not Birchwood of which I had dreamed, but a dream of Birchwood, woven out of bits and scraps. On bright summer mornings the rooms were alive with a kind of quick silent suspense, the toys and teacups of the night before exactly as they were left and yet utterly changed.
>
> (Banville, 1992a, pp. 12–13)

This confusion of dream and reality, memory and knowledge, poetry and history, brings the deconstructive impulse exemplified by Borges' 'Circular Ruins' or 'Partial Magic in the *Quixote*' to bear on history and narration (Borges, 1970). Memory or historical consciousness obtrude between Gabriel and apprehension of the physical (historical) reality of the ruins of Birchwood. He had not dreamed of reality but of a dream (of reality). But if the past is a dream, and the present is displaced or shifted by that narrative (the past) so as to be ungraspable, what does that make of Gabriel himself? Further, since Gabriel is the centre of consciousness of the novel, the figure of readerly identification, through whom we try to make sense of what is happening (and of what has happened in the past), what are the implications for the reader? Of whose imagining is Gabriel the figment? Of whose imagining is the reader a figment? The description of 'bits and fragments' of Gabriel's dream is directly reminiscent of Banville's description of his own sense of culture, and of his sense of his own history. This brings us back to the idea of history that the novel presupposes. History here is radically perspectival, subjective, partial (that is, both biased and constitutively incomplete). Its narration is also contingent, part of the processes it seeks to describe. The accurate representation of the past is encumbered by a sense of the recalcitrance of the 'facts', and of a sense that both unconscious processes and previously-held ideas come between the narrator and those 'facts' that he wishes to grasp and to understand.

The intimations of Yeats' great poem 'Easter 1916', signalled by the phrase 'utterly changed', give us some further sense of Banville's destabilisation of history. For Yeats, the actions of the rebels constituted a kind of rupturing of secular history by the mythic forces of 'Romantic Ireland'. Hence his feeling of the transmogrification of quotidian reality: 'All changed, changed utterly' (Yeats, 1996, pp. 287–9). But in Banville, it is ordinary time that leaves the banal 'toys and teacups' 'utterly changed'. History – the linear unfolding of time – is not here a matter of great men and notable events, but of the alterations wrought by ordinary time itself on everyday objects. Thus, in such a revisionary overturning of what constitutes 'history', it is appropriate that Gabriel should invert Yeats' famous phrase.

But this phrase also allows us to examine more closely the idea of history that informs a work like *Birchwood*. It is precisely in this idea of a temporality of the ordinary that is transforming that Banville enacts an oblique quarrel with the historical novel as formulated by a critic like Georg Lukács, working as the latter was with mostly nineteenth-century models. For Lukács, there was no doubt that authors such as Sir Walter Scott, Gustave Flaubert or the Mann brothers could find a way to represent an epoch prior to their own, or that they could find a narrative form adequate to the rendering of the significance that they reckoned was expressed and worked out in the events they were describing. The difficulty lay in detail and technique. Writing in the opening chapter of *The Historical Novel* on the rise of the form, Lukács relates it in its German context to the philosophy of Herder:

> It is only during the last phase of the Enlightenment that the problem of the artistic reflection of past ages emerges as a central problem of literature … This conscious growth of historicism … receives its first theoretical expression in the writings of Herder …
>
> (Lukács, 1981, p. 18)

Herderian historicism stemmed, Lukács reminds us, from a desire to redis-cover a historical *telos*, a sense of progress in the historical process, in the face of Enlightenment scepticism. But Herder also believed in the uniqueness of cultures, events and figures. For Herder, everything in history was equal: the greatest politician or philosopher was no more worthy of historical judge-ment than the humblest slave or peasant. It followed that all historical sub-ject-matter was to be looked on with equal sympathy, be it rational or irra-tional. What mattered was particularity, and this criterion applied as much to cultures (hence Herder's importance to cultural nationalism) as to historical events or periods (hence his historicism) or to the rational or irrational char-acter of the material dealt with (hence his willingness to treat of human foibles as much as of rationally-taken decisions). This brings us back to our account of the relationship between Herderian historicism and the 'Whig nationalist' historiography opposed by Butterfield's Irish admirers.

To frame Banville's historical work, it is worth proceeding further with Lukács' formulation of the historical novel. For Lukács, the intersection of literary form and historical consciousness came in the immediate post-Revolutionary period; he notes that Scott's *Waverly* was published in 1814 (Lukács, 1981, p. 15). But Lukács also notes that eighteenth-century England was already post-revolutionary, in the political sense at least, having had its bourgeois revolution in the previous century. However, it was also undergo-ing the massive *economic* change and turbulence that would lead to the Industrial Revolution. Thus, Lukács points out, this combination of political posteriority and economic development, of stable political institutions and an emergent capitalist economy, made possible a view of society as driven by national concerns and class conflict, in short by historical processes.

Further, the French Revolution, the wars that followed it and the rise and fall of Napoleon, made history, in Lukács' view, a *mass* and a *European* expe-rience for the first time (Lukács, 1981, p. 20). This apparently general, even universal, sense of change made history seem an uninterrupted process of change, that affected every member of every society. As mediated by appara-tuses such as states and armies, and intense experiences such as wars, history was experienced as *national*. In Benedict Anderson's terms, war and its insti-tutions were powerful mechanisms for the imagining of the national com-munity. This was coupled with an economic understanding of capitalism as a dynamic, propulsive and *historical* force.

Lukács notes the rise, in the wake of the Revolution, of an anti-revolu-tionary, reactionary strain of thought – what he calls Legitimist Romanticism – which was deeply nostalgic for the stable organic world of the *ancien régime*. This was a view that linked the turbulence caused by the Revolution, to the turbulence caused by capitalism. Lukács argues that this means that the post-

Revolutionary inheritors of the Enlightenment, in opposition to this Legitimist Romanticism, could no longer afford politically to pose their central problematic – that progress evolves in non-historical terms as a contest between 'humanist reason and feudal-absolutist unreason' (Lukács, 1981, p. 25). Reminding us, as White does, that history arose as an intellectual field and scholarly discipline after the Revolution, Lukács writes:

> The defenders of progress after the French Revolution had necessarily to reach a conception which would prove the *historical necessity* of the latter, furnish evidence that it constituted a peak in a long and gradual historical development and not a sudden eclipse of human consciousness ... and that this was the only course open to the future development of mankind.
>
> (Lukács, 1981, p. 25)

In the new view, the rationality of human progress develops out of the conflictual dynamic of socio-political forces: 'history itself is the bearer and realiser of human progress' (Lukács, 1981, p. 25).

For Lukács, the philosopher of this defence of human progress was, of course, Hegel. Hegel's dialectic is the idealist expression of the struggle of classes and of the capacity of human beings to make their own history and to shape themselves in so doing. Hegel, Lukács reminds us, saw history as a process driven by both inner forces of its own, and by human activity and ideas.

Out of this historico-philosophical conjuncture, Lukács argues, a new humanism arose which sought both to preserve the positive legacy of the French Revolution and of the progressive idea of revolution generally, and to envisage the future in terms of peaceful development. The French Revolution was to be the last great upheaval necessary for positive future evolution. This new humanism was not uncritical – it was not simply a justification for the new status quo. It conducted a rigorous critique of the contradictions of progress, and for this reason, it contained a sense of foreboding, anticipating the failures of 1848.

Nevertheless, it can be seen that this new humanism described by Lukács amounts to a form of Whiggishness, the finding of a progressive telos in the historical process. Accordingly, as James Cahalan shows in his study of the Irish travails of the historical novel, *Great Hatred, Little Room*, Sir Walter Scott was a progressive thinker, convinced of the superiority of the present over the past (Cahalan, 1983, pp. 1–15). His nineteenth-century contemporaries viewed Scott as a romantic antiquarian, and there is no doubt that he was fascinated by and well-versed in myth and folklore, a collector and editor of popular poetry and ballads. He was keenly aware of the traditions of ordinary people. But along with this went an understanding that in such tales was sedimented a popular vision of the past that could not simply be dismissed. According to Cahalan, because Scott saw past and present as interrelated and informing each other, he rejected the view promulgated in Gothic fiction that the interest of the past lay in its difference from the present, its exotic nature *vis-à-vis* the present (Cahalan, p. 1983, p. 10). Cahalan shows how Coleridge in a way anticipated Lukács in his understanding of Scott. Coleridge suggested that Scott's novels' strength was their realisation in literary form of what Coleridge called

> the contest between the two great moving principles of social humanity; religious adherence to the past and the ancient, the desire and the admiration of permanence, on the one hand; and the passion for increase of knowledge, for truth, as the offspring of reason – in short, the mighty instincts of *progression* and *free agency*, on the other.
>
> (quoted in Cahalan, 1983, p. 8)

As Cahalan suggests, Coleridge appreciates Scott in almost dialectical terms, whereby past and present interact with each other, contain each other. Scott viewed history as the vital establishing framework for the present. He reckoned that the conditions of an historical epoch provided the context in which the meaning of the actions and ideas of human beings was to be understood. This does not make Scott any kind of crude determinist, but it does mean that he sought to locate his characters in a broad social and political milieu. He also wished to explain history, by using techniques taken from fiction, specifically realist fiction. So Scott believed that a language of putative objectivity, the narrative of realism, could be applied to historical events. At the same time, he saw no difficulty in weaving, albeit at some distance, the lives of actual historical personages with fictional characters. Scott used representative characters to suggest the means by which history, conceived as a progressive process, works. He used fictions to try to explain history not only in terms of Hegelian 'world-historical' figures, but also in term of how these figures and their activities became meaningful for a mass society 'below' them and usually invisible. To that extent, he practised a totalising historiographic fiction.

In other words, Scott was able to use the vocabulary of realism to describe events from the historical past. But as Cahalan, Thomas Flanagan and Terry Eagleton, with different emphases, argue, this option was not as easily available to Scott's Irish followers. These would include the Banims, Griffin, LeFanu, Carleton and Standish O'Grady. In Irish conditions, where history was conceived in cyclical terms, as explained by Oliver MacDonagh, it does not seem distant enough (MacDonagh, 1983, pp. 1–6). It is difficult to think of history, as, precisely, 'historical', if it seems constitutively unfinished. Realism is fraught with difficulties: Maria Edgeworth wrote to her father Richard, in the 1830s:

> It is impossible to draw Ireland as she now is in the book of fiction – realities are too strong, party passions too violent, to bear to see, or to care to look at their faces in a looking glass. The people would only break the glass and curse the fool who held the mirror up to nature – distorted nature in a fever.
>
> (quoted in Lloyd, 1993, p. 134)

At around the same time, Lady Morgan could write

> We are living in an era of transition. Changes moral and political are in progress. The frame of the constitution, the frame of society itself, are sustaining a shock, which occupies all minds, to avert or modify.

In such conditions, 'there is no legitimate literature, there is no legitimate drama' (quoted in Lloyd, 1993, p. 135). As Lloyd shows, writers like Edgeworth and Morgan, and also Griffin and the Banims, all accepted the Irish colonial settlement and thus assumed the possibility of reconciliation or resolution under an overarching narrative of the move from barbarity to civility. This is the metanarrative of modernity (Lloyd, 1993, p. 134). It is the underpinning of both the *Bildungsroman*, with its interest in the cultivation and social reconciliation of the individual subject; and the historical novel, where the interest lies in the recuperation of a *national* subject or community. Such gratifying or comforting narratives were troubled by an Irish situation where the Whig interpretation of English history seemed inverted:

> The era to which Englishmen point as that in which their constitution was finally established in highest perfection ... is precisely the day from whence Ireland's lowest debasement and bitterest sorrow must be dated. The 'Glorious Revolution' is to us an abomination; the 'Bill of Rights' a fraud, the 'privileges of Parliament', and the whole system of parliamentary govenrment then set up for worship and obedience, a delusion and a cruel mockery.
>
> (quoted in Lloyd, 1993, p. 135)

What this demonstrates is that the dialectic of past and present, theorised by Hegel and given literary expression by Scott, was not possible in Ireland. As we saw earlier, for Hegel the state was the proper subject of historical narrative, and dialectical progress was its content. Neither, as Lloyd shows, was available for narrative in Ireland in the nineteenth century, in the wake of the Union, in the midst of political instability, in the wake of political and sectarian traumas such as the Rising of 1798 or in the midst of a catastrophe such as the Famine. It seems clear, then, that in Banville's situation, in the early 1970s, similar conditions apply – political instability, the constitutional framework of the whole island in question, the return of the nightmare of history to disturb the narrative of modernisation (political reform in the North, economic modernisation in the South). It is unsurprising, then, that Banville should return to the failures of historical fiction, and of realism, by way of the Gothic and metafictional experiment. In this way, he both registers the Irish novel and the historical novel, and the possibility of historical narrative, and undermines them. Banville locates himself in a tradition, only to show that it is an invented one.

Eagleton suggests of Lady Morgan's texts that they tend to be inhabited by two contradictory discourses, of realism and romance, without one ever cancelling the other out (Eagleton, 1995, p. 179). One could argue in the same vein of *Birchwood*, except that Banville is aware of such failure and alludes to it. The novel embodies the realist modern narrative of *Bildung*, of reconciliation and unification, spinning out of control. The hero-narrator does indeed come into his own in the family, but only by way of a series of familial Gothic obstacles and an exotic journey. Gabriel ends up the inheritor of the family legacy, but his attainment of that endpoint is presented to the reader in terms of its failures. His 'real' family collapses under the weight of social, economic and political pressures – grasping neighbours, debt and agrarian insurgency. In the Gothic mode (the Gothic being the outrageous unconscious of the Enlightenment narrative of modernity), the family also disintegrates under the burden of its own inner biological contradictions. Gabriel's 'mother' is not his mother, his 'aunt' is his mother, his 'cousin' is his twin, his 'sister' never existed, his parents fight out their inheritance battles across a terrain constituted by Michael and Gabriel, Michael joins the agrarian insurrection and, dressed as a woman, takes part in the attack on the house and the slaughter of the Lawlesses. Gabriel's new alternative family, the circus, is both different from and similar to the old. It is different in its exoticism, its geosocial mobility, its links with magic and illusion. It is similar to the degree that, in its reflexivity, it reminds us of the presence of these traits in the Godkins anyway. For mobility is only a literal expression of the social alienation and dislocation of the Godkins *vis-à-vis* their Catholic neighbours. Furthermore, the Godkins, with their eccentricities, their deaths by spontaneous or other combustion, their degrees of insanity, and their hidden motives and drives, can be construed as being as exotic as the world of the circus.

The forms of *Birchwood* and of *The Newton Letter* are circular, in that each narrator sets off to describe how he came to arrive at the point in time and space from which he writes. So each inscribes the enunciative location of the narrator. *Birchwood*, of course, takes this process the furtherest, by alluding to the difficulty of such recollection in the first place. But this means that each novel renders itself and its discourse contingent, each is aware that, as Deane put it in his polemic against revisionism, history writes and reads us just as we write and read history (Deane, 1994, p. 244). According to Gabriel,

> I find the world always odd, but odder still, I suppose, is the fact that I find it so, for what are the eternal verities by which I measure these temporal aberrations? Intimations abound, but they are felt only, and words fail to transfix them. Anyway, some secrets are not to be disclosed under pain of who knows what retribution, and whereof I cannot speak, thereof I must be silent.
>
> (Banville, 1992a, p. 175)

Quoting Wittgenstein, Gabriel is reminding us that narrative, or history-writing, endlessly tries to project itself ahead of its subject-matter, in order to reflect authoritatively on that subject-matter. But it must haul its premises with it, and they are inevitably part of what it has left behind, that is, history. History cannot evade the conditions of its own possibility.

This is most explicitly the case in *The Newton Letter*, which is addressed to Clio, the muse of History. The narrator is a biographer of Newton, who finds the real world intruding on his work, as he tries to complete his book. The range of preconceptions that he brings to bear on his immediate surroundings (the Ascendancy Lawless family) constantly fail him, as well as marking his political and cultural preferences. His mistakes are manifold: the family's religion, Michael's origins, Edward's illness. But more importantly, as McMinn points out, the narrator is in fact trying to 'read' the Lawless family as a 'Big House' narrative (McMinn, 1991, p. 93). Assuming that reality is itself story-shaped, the narrator misses the real tragedy of the Lawlesses. So, working within a realistic narrative paradigm, where social and personal mysteries are supposed to be amenable to rational investigation, the narrator fails. In a 'Big House' novel, the genre is shown to be inadequate to itself, to be unable properly to describe its putative object. Of course, what we have been reading all along has been masquerading as a 'letter', addressed to Clio. Thus, the novel has been written in the first person, in a form that alludes explicitly to its own contingency, partiality and occasional nature.

This is why the narrator of *The Newton Letter*, a historian, gives up his book. He suddenly realises that his enterprise is one not merely of disinterring the past, but in fact is a matter of re-burying it, or, as he puts it, 'embalming' it as 'history' (Banville, 1992b, p. 21). He is realising that his work constitutes its object. Further, comparing himself to a rival biographer of Newton, he realises that 'another kind of truth has come to seem to [him] more urgent, although ... it is nothing compared to the lofty verities of science' (Banville, 1992b, p. 22). Because of his fumbling investigation of the Lawless family, the narrator goes through the crisis of knowledge that the great scientist had experienced, as evidenced in the second letter to Locke (which in fact is a borrowing by Banville from von Hofsmannsthal's *Ein Brief*). To Newton, ordinary people he met in Cambridge became suddenly 'themselves the things they might tell' (Banville, 1992b, pp. 50–1). Language failed Newton, and only a language 'none of whose words is known to me; a language in which commonplace things speak to me' would now be adequate to his purposes (Banville, 1992b, p. 51). Likewise, the narrator opens his letter to Clio by telling her 'Words fail me' and reporting a little later that he has lost his 'faith in the primacy of text' (Banville, 1992b, p. 1). This has the effect of undermining the narrator's own book-project, but also his efforts to understand, to narrate, the Lawless family. So what we have at the end of the book is a form of history-writing: it is a history of the family, and of the narrator's contact with them. But it is not a historical novel in the mode of Scott or as theorised by Lukács. Nor is it an Irish 'Big House' novel. It is a familial history that constitutes itself out of its own failures. Near its ending, the narrator writes 'I can't go on. I'm not a historian' (Banville, 1992b, p. 80). The faint echo here of the last lines of Beckett's famous trilogy – 'I can't go on, I'll go on' – serves to underline the fragmentation of the subject that Banville's project narrates. The human cannot go on, but cannot avoid narrating this condition. The implication, in the context of the writing of history, is surely that while historical consciousness is unavoidable, so also is an awareness of its crisis, its failures, its embarrassments, guilt, academic self-hatred.

What is being alluded to here, necessarily in the form and performance of these novels as much as in their content, is something usefully described by Fredric Jameson, and which stands in stark opposition to the relaunching of Irish historiography at this time:

> But historical representation is just as surely in crisis as its distant cousin, the linear novel, and for much the same reasons. The most intelligent 'solution' to such a crisis does not consist in abandoning historiography altogether, as an impossible aim and an ideological category all at once, but rather – as in the modernist aesthetic itself – in reorganizing its traditional procedures on a different level. Althusser's proposal seems the wisest in this situation: as old-fashioned narrative

or 'realistic' historiography becomes problematic, the historian should reformulate her vocation – not any longer to produce some vivid representation of History 'as it really happened,' but rather to produce the *concept* of history.

(Jameson, 1988b, p. 180)

This is the ideal that links Banville's novels about Copernicus and Kepler to the explicitly Irish work, though it is to be noted that *Dr Copernicus* and *Kepler* narrate the attempts of astronomy to ground and constitute itself as an academic discipline, in opposition to astrology, with its authority vested in its access to the 'facts'. Nicolas Koppernigk is portrayed as a man obsessed with the adequacy of systems of representation to their referents. This is clear from the opening of the novel, with its echoes of Joyce's *A Portrait of the Artist as a Young Man*, and young Nicolas' realisation that the linden tree exists independently of its naming in language, of his perception of it: 'It was the thing itself, the vivid thing' (Banville, 1990, p. 3). Nicolas begins his intellectual career with his debate with Professor Brudzewski (Banville, 1990, pp. 32–8), brusquely sweeping aside Ptolemaic theory that has served astronomy for thirteen hundred years, seeking to change knowledge to *perception*, and produce a theory that will explain the workings of the universe rather than simply 'save the phenomena' (that is, account for the observations of astronomy). Nicolas aspires to the same epistemological goal as empiricist historiography: he wishes for representation to give access to the essence of the object described, without mediation. He believes 'not in names but in things' and that 'the physical world is amenable to physical investigation' (Banville, 1990, p. 36). At the moment of his death, at the end of the novel, he hallucinates that Andreas Osiander, who has presided over the final publishing of his great masterpiece, is in fact his brother Andreas, long dead of syphilis. Andreas has been the most persistent presence in Nicolas' life reminding him of ordinary messy humanity, and of his failure to come to terms with it or transcend it. He tells Nicolas: 'I was the one absolutely necessary thing, for I was there always to remind you of what you must transcend' (Banville, 1990, p. 240). Further, in his Faustian negation of humanity and love, Nicolas denied himself

> ... the other, the thing itself, the vivid thing, which is not to be found in any book, nor in the firmament, nor in the absolute forms ... It is that thing ... fabulous and yet ordinary, that thing which is all that matters, which is the great miracle. You glimpsed it briefly in briefly in our father, in sister Barbara, in Fracastoro, in Anna Schillings, in all the others, and even, yes, in me, glimpsed it, and turned away, appalled

> and ... embarrassed. Call it acceptance, call it love if you wish, but
> these are poor words and express nothing of the enormity.
>
> (Banville, 1990, p. 241)

Andreas (or, more accurately, Nicolas, in his hallucination) has already pointed
out the hubris of Nicolas' empiricist ambitions, when he says

> It is the manner of knowing that is important. We know the meaning
> of the singular thing only so long as we content ourselves with know-
> ing it in the midst of other meanings: isolate it, and all meaning drains
> away. It is not the thing that counts, you see, only the interaction of
> things; and, of course, the names ...
>
> (Banville, 1990, p. 239)

This is Banville's humanism coming to the fore. Searching for the 'thing-in-
itself' of empiricist science, Nicolas failed to recognise the 'thing-in-itself' of
humanity and love and ordinary existence. Meaning is context-dependent. An
account of reality cannot be constructed on the basis of 'facts' alone. Such
'facts' are also available to human cognition only in and through language.
Reality is not, emphatically, to be denied, but recognition must be given to the
degree to which it is accessible to knowledge in forms always already mediated.
The methodological premiss of Nicolas' world-view permitted only a certain
understanding of his surroundings.

  Not that he had not been warned. The most sinister clue to the arrogance
and will-to-power in his enterprise, in spite of his disavowals of the world of
relationships (most poignantly with Girolamo) came in his meeting with
Albrecht, Grand Master of the Teutonic Knights. When Nicolas and his
friend Canon Giese come to him to try to protect the neutrality of Ermland
in the coming war between the Knights and the King of Poland, Albrecht
reminds the astronomer of the parallels between absolutist power and intellectual authority. To Nicolas' protest that the war will bring ruin to the
common people, Albrecht scoffs:

> Ah. The common people. But they have suffered always, and always
> will. It is in a way what they are for ... What are they to us? You and
> I ... we are lords of the earth, the great ones, the major men, the
> makers of supreme fictions ... only you and I know what true suffer-
> ing is, the lofty suffering of the hero ... The people – peasants, sol-
> diers, generals – are my tool, as mathematics is yours, by which I
> come directly at the true, the eternal, the real. Ah yes, Dr.
> Copernicus, you and I – you and I! The generations may execrate us

for what we do to their world, but we and those rare ones like us shall have made them what they are ...!

(Banville, 1990, pp. 136–7)

Here we see expressed in coldly cynical terms precisely the implication with power that Nicolas had sought to avoid, with his shunning of the world of politics (especially the revolutionary world of Novara in Bologna) and turning to a heroic, ivory-tower model of intellectual practice. Albrecht's message is that, politically and intellectually, there is no neutrality. Furthermore, political and intellectual authority are directly comparable. Both are predicated on a radical separation from everyday experience or the 'ordinary people', but this separation is enacted in order the more effectively to turn back and act on, or have influence over, those 'ordinary people'. Most tellingly, Albrecht understands his authority as giving him what Edward Said calls 'permission to narrate' (Said, 1994a, pp. 247–68), and points out to Nicolas that his narrative or discursive authority cannot be detached from political power. Albrecht tells stories about and made up of flesh and blood, armies, battles and campaigns, but the fact that Nicolas' stories are 'set' in the heavens does not diminish the earthly basis of his power to tell them. Albrecht, one might say, has a Gramscian view of intellectuals and power, four centuries ahead of the Italian revolutionary. The comparison he makes is pertinent both to the situation of historiography, and also to the discussion of authority and politics in Friel earlier.

Banville reminds us of the mediated and discursively constructed nature of systems of knowledge, and this, as I suggested above, applies as much to the 'concept' of history as it does to astronomical knowledge. Banville's text draws attention to itself as such in three obvious ways. One is the set of letters exchanged between Nicolas, Giese, Snellenburg and Dantiscus, on the subjects of Nicolas' theories and his relationship with Anna Schillings (Banville, 1990, pp. 148–55). Then there are the quotations from Søren Kierkegaard, Max Planck, Albert Einstein, Wallace Stevens and others that he actually gives endnotes for (Banville, 1990, pp. 208, 243). Most importantly, there is the long interpolated narrative of Rheticus (Banville, 1990, pp. 159–220). This is notable especially as it draws attention to its performative, strategic character. Rheticus takes pride in his telling of his tale, leaving us in no doubt as to his desire for vengeance for, as he sees it, Nicolas' part in his marginalisation and his being written out of history. But he also admits that he invents the figure of Raphael, the boy he suggests Nicolas and Giese used to work his downfall, to have some tangible reason for that wrong done him. Rheticus rubbishes *De Revolutionibus* and hopes that he will in his turn be able to make a reputation for himself on the back of his assistant, Otho, as he believes Nicolas did with him and his *Narratio Prima*. Rheticus' narrative is notable also because it tells of the struggle to get Nicolas to publish his work, and the imbrication of this textual effort with power. We are shown how texts dislodge each other, or use each other as points of departure. That *Dr Copernicus* incorporates this within itself means that while it does not meditate explicitly on the problematics of language as *Birchwood* and *The Newton Letter* do, it still can be called historiographic metafiction. Rheticus' narrative destabilises the novel as a whole, and it is in this sense that it becomes an attempt to illustrate the 'concept' of history.

This is even clearer when we come to *Kepler*. The formal organisation of this text is even more elaborate and clever than that of *Dr Copernicus*. Writing to Herwart von Hohenburg of his projected work, *Harmonice mundi*, Kepler announces that

> ... in the beginning is the shape! Hence I foresee a work divided into five parts, to correspond to the five planetary intervals, while the number of chapters in each part will be based on the signifying quantities of each of the five regular and Platonic solids which, according to my *Mysterium*, may be fitted into these intervals. Also, as a form of decoration and to pay my due respect, I intend that the initials of the chapters shall spell out acrostically the names of certain famous men.
>
> (Banville, 1983, p. 145)

This, of course, is the pattern of *Kepler* itself, as Imhof points out (Imhof, 1989, p. 132). The narrative is also arranged in circular patterns, opening and ending with dreams. Perhaps most notable is the organisation of the letters that make up the fifth chapter. Rather than following chronological order, they are presented to us in elliptical patterns, befitting the biography of the astronomer who confirmed Copernicus' speculation that the planetary orbits are not circles but ellipses, with the sun as one of the focii.

Kepler's life is a quest for harmony, in his domestic affairs, in his intellectual relationships, in his relations with worldly power, and, of course, in the heavens. For him, geometry *is* God. When he attacks the Roman Catholic doctrine of transubstantiation, declaring that God is not an alchemist, we recognise his Lutheranism, but also his struggle, like Copernicus', to set his science on a firm footing, and we remember Einstein's famous statement that God does not play dice (Banville, 1983, p. 163). Like Gabriel Godkin, and Isaac Newton, Kepler is wont to see the miraculous in the everyday, to see harmony everywhere:

> The proportions everywhere abound, in music and the movements of the planets, in human and vegetable forms, in men's fortunes even, but they are all relation merely, and inexistent without the perceiving soul.

How is such perception possible? Peasants and children, barbarians, animals even, feel the harmony of the tone. Therefore the perceiving must be instinct in the soul, based in a profound and essential geometry, that geometry which is derived from the simple divisioning of circles. All that he had for long held to be the case. Now he took the short step to the fusion of symbol and object. The circle is the bearer of pure harmonies, pure harmonies are innate in the soul, and so the soul and the circle are one.

Such simplicity, such beauty.

(Banville, 1983, p. 174)

Even politics must conform to this pattern: 'It must be all a conspiracy'. In his later years, he suspects a relationship between his inner state of mind and the religious wars raging around him (Banville, 1983, p. 178). But this is not simply a vision of heroic intellect, shot through with paranoia. Kepler's vision is an egalitarian one. He is a Renaissance humanist in the universal sense; the capacity for perception of divine harmony is in everyone.

Taken together, I consider that Banville's novels here discussed make for a considerable contribution to 'historiographic metafiction', or perhaps, fictional metahistory. What Banville demonstrates is the ineluctable imaginative component in scientific endeavour, and, hence, in systems of representation that draw their authority from their putative faith to the 'facts'. But this leads us back to the condition of historiography before the French Revolution, according to White, where 'truth' was not simply a matter of 'fact', and fiction was a discourse that was not demoted as telling of the merely 'possible' or 'imaginable'. As reflexive historical fictions that narrate failures of empiricism, at the beginning of the Enlightenment, Banville's *Dr Copernicus* and *Kepler* are both meditations on authorial authority, but also on the claims of other discourses to separate themselves from, and thereby purify themselves of, fiction and myth. Novels about the writing of texts, they, along with *Birchwood* and *The Newton Letter*, draw the reader's attention to the materiality, or, in Said's terms, 'worldliness', of texts, be they scientific or historical. They narrate the historical conditions of possibility of great scientific texts; the political, economic, social, intellectual, spiritual and emotional manoeuvres that went into the production of these works. But they do this in a provisional, self-consciously textual manner. Further, they do it in a *fictional* manner, and hence constitute themselves as historical biographies that draw upon the techniques of fiction to render their subjects as fully as possible. Their 'realism' is not dependent on the production of verisimilitude. However, conceding this point also reminds us of Borges' idea of the textuality of the 'world', and especially of history.

Banville's work, and that of mainstream Irish academic history-writing, stand as alternative responses to the cultural and political crises of the late 1960s and early 1970s. In the calls to myth-criticism of Lyons, Moody and Fanning, we see a historiography unwilling, in White's terms, to expose its 'conceptual apparatus', because to do so would have been to unsettle its authority. But the affiliation of the authority of the historians with that of the state is only made obvious in the repetition of methodological verities and disciplinary purification at a time of deep political and cultural crisis. In the face of the crisis of state nationalism, the historians' response has been to attack insurgent forms of social consciousness (mostly nationalism, but Ulster Loyalism also). Banville, in contrast, mixes history, fiction and myth up, and exposes the means by which he does so. To this extent, his intervention is not merely in the Irish novel tradition, but in Irish historiography too. His is an self-critical aesthetic of what Said has called 'interference', that openly offends disciplinary and also national boundaries, and troubles the truth-claims of both fiction and history (Said, 1985b, p. 157). It fictionalises history and historicises fiction. His writing, in Linda Hutcheon's words,

> refuses the view that only history has a truth claim, both by questioning the ground of that claim in historiography and by asserting that both history and fiction are discourses, human constructs, signifying systems, and both derive their major claim to truth from that identity. This kind of ... fiction also refuses the relegation of the extratextual past to the domain of historiography in the name of the autonomy of art.
>
> (Hutcheon, 1988, p. 93)

But there is no doubt that the past did exist. Banville merely demonstrates that it is accessible to us only in textual form, and also mediated by the sub-jectivity of the author. So he openly acknowledges his debts to Arthur Koestler's *The Sleepwalkers* and Thomas Kuhn's *The Copernican Revolution*, as well as other texts, that contribute to the 'entextualisation' of history. But this textual self-consciousness immediately begs the question: what texts, or 'evidence', were *not* referred to in the course of the production of these novels? Thus, if Banville's 'biographies' of Copernicus and Kepler are 'histories', they openly acknowledge the degree to which they construct their objects. An archaeology of the past is produced, but the materials that facilitate that production are admitted as textualised ones. So Banville's work embodies a kind of discussion and 'revisionism' of the textual and epistemological issues that Irish academic history-writing has been anxious to skirt by recourse to professional authority and putative methodological objectivity.

CHAPTER 3

Modernisation without modernism:
Dermot Bolger and the 'Dublin Renaissance'

The work of Brian Friel and John Banville that I have discussed represents alternative literary responses to the changes in Ireland since the late 1960s. However, in spite of their differences, they are both to be located in the realm of 'high culture', and they write in self-conscious reaction to a tradition, whether that is an Irish one or a European one. They write confidently for an already existent audience – basically an institutional theatre audience in Friel's case (the Abbey or Gate theatres in Dublin, for example); a more cosmopolitan readership in Banville's case. But in the 1980s, a group of younger writers coalesced around Dermot Bolger to try to produce a new writing, for a younger generation, born in the 1950s, mostly in suburban Dublin, that was reckoned to be voiceless and unrepresented in literary terms. This group felt profoundly alienated from any literary tradition, and more at home with the range of mass cultural references (television, rock music, film, Anglo-American youth culture) that the Lemass/Whitaker modernisation had brought in its wake. In 1991, the journalist and novelist Ferdia MacAnna suggested that Dublin was experiencing a 'literary renaissance'. His article, which was both historical and autobiographical, traced the rise from the late 1970s of what MacAnna considers to be a new urban literature emanating primarily from working-class Dublin. His article offers a convenient if flawed introduction to this movement, while *The Journey Home* (Bolger, 1991a), Dermot Bolger's acclaimed third novel, widely considered to be the culmination of this development, neatly sums up many of its primary concerns.

MacAnna offers an image of 1960s Dublin to set off against the new writing. This portrays the city as having been boring, provincial and culturally stagnant. He suggests that the historical vision that permeated the city was one dominated by the 1916 Rising, and the Literary and Gaelic Revivals. The city was unrepresented in the cultural life of the 'nation', which was dominated by rural values. Education was dominated by the Christian Brothers, and literature consisted in *Peig*.[1] The fiftieth anniversary of 1916 (something of a *bête noire* for MacAnna and other intellectuals of his generation) was the chief political event of the decade, and the symbolic acme of the socio-polit-

---

1   The turgid Irish Gaelic memoir of Blasket Islander Peig Sayers, published in 1936; a central and much-resented text on the secondary school curriculum in Irish.

ical culture MacAnna describes. It, along with the destruction of Nelson's Pillar on O'Connell Street by the IRA in the same year, 'was like a lunatic hangover from a remote, hysterical era' (MacAnna, 1991, p. 14). The traditional pieties of nationalism were vastly less immediate than television shows, Beatles records and the performances of George Best with Manchester United, and an interest in these was consequently reduced to the status of evidence of cultural decadence and political betrayal.

Against this monolith, MacAnna traces contemporary Dublin literature from Lee Dunne's *Goodbye to the Hill* (1965) through the rock lyrics of Phil Lynott, Heno Magee's play *Hatchet*, and the activities of Peter and Jim Sheridan, and Mannix Flynn at the Project Arts Centre. His comments on *Hatchet*, produced at the Peacock Theatre in 1972, are typical. This play dealt with the 'sordid, violent world of a Dublin hardman':

> It brought us face-to-face with a world that was never seen on Irish television, nor reflected in the cinema or other arts and only rarely mentioned in newspapers – an inner city where the characters were trapped in a never ending spiral of poverty, drink and despair ... In Heno Magee's stark vision, lyrical Dublin was dead and gone.
>
> (MacAnna, 1991, p. 17)

For MacAnna, this play's 'uncompromising realism' made O'Casey and Behan seem 'dated' and 'irrelevant'.

MacAnna constructs his historic Dublin in order to avoid the problem that the period that would really have influenced his generation (he was born in 1955) was the 1970s. This was a time of increasing liberalism in the Republic, when the benefits of the Lemass/Whitaker modernisation were felt, though only briefly. It is easier to mock the pieties of state nationalist triumphalism in 1966, than to come to terms with the messy and complicated realities of the 1970s, such as the Northern crisis, EEC membership, rising unemployment, and social and political turmoil over such issues as the Arms Trials, the rise of the Women's Movement, the non-availability of contraception and divorce, and PAYE taxation.[2] He ignores entirely, however, the work of other writers in whose work Dublin figures, and that as a place of opportunity and freedom. Writing in 1976, John Wilson Foster mentions the Dublin that is the final focus of aspiration for characters in the work of John McGahern, Edna O'Brian and Benedict Kiely (Foster, 1991, p. 36). Foster

2 'PAYE' is an acronym for Pay As You Earn, the name given to the taxation system affecting most industrial workers in the Republic. A quarter of a million people marched in Dublin in 1979 in protest at crippling levels of taxation.

points out that all too often what is discovered in the Irish city, including Dublin and Belfast, is simply urban provincialism as against rural provincialism, and he notes how in the works of Edna O'Brien, the flight from Ireland frequently only results in an obsessive remembrance of the past and the home place. This problem will be found to be repeated in Bolger.

MacAnna's history is exclusively literary, in spite of his insistence that popular culture (that is, British and American film, music, sports, television) shaped the lives of young people more than 'official culture'. He suggests that 'official culture' represented only rural life, or a myth of it, but he does not notice that Anglo-American mass culture similarly failed to represent the realities alluded to by Magee, while retaining its appeal.

MacAnna places the writers he discusses in three categories. Older writers such as James Plunkett and the playwright Hugh Leonard are seen as producing a writing characterised by the 'backward look', whether historical or nostalgic.[3] The Co-Op, an experimental press founded in the late 1970s, published writers such as Neil Jordan, Ronan Sheehan and Sebastian Barry, whom MacAnna sees as 'experimental, self-indulgent and a bit dull – in other words, irrelevant to life in modern Dublin' (MacAnna, 1991, p. 20). That is, they are not interested in 'realism' as he sees it. He suggests that they are victims of the academic canonisation of Joyce in the 1960s, and of his massive presence in the literature of the city, suffering a kind of anxiety of influence that leads them to write of anywhere save Dublin to avoid invidious comparisons with the master. In Magee, Lynott and Dunne MacAnna sees the beginnings of a literature that is resolutely 'anti-academic', that is outside, and owes nothing to, tradition, and hence is directly relevant to Dublin life. It is a writing of 'modern urban disillusionment', of alienation, poverty and violence, sex, drugs and rock music, as against Daniel Corkery's favoured themes of the land, nationalism and Roman Catholicism.

MacAnna's account culminates in the 'Renaissance' which completes his tripartite scheme, and which he sees as having been sponsored by the 1979 foundation of Raven Arts Press in Finglas by Dermot Bolger and Michael O'Loughlin.

> By the late 80s, Raven had become Ireland's leading underground and alternative press, publishing new work by many young Irish writers ... Bolger and O'Loughlin ... saw Dublin not as some ancient colonial backwater full of larger-than-life 'characters' boozing their heads off in stage-Irish pubs, but as a troubled modern entity, plagued by drugs,

---

3 Fintan O'Toole makes a better case for Leonard as a playwright of the new bourgeoisie. See O'Toole, 1988.

unemployment, high taxes, disillusionment and emigration. No city of 'The Rare Ould Times' here.

(MacAnna, 1991, p. 21)

Raven Arts Press published poetry, fiction, drama, journalism and pamphlets on literary, political, social, cultural and historical matters. MacAnna compares the literary work of O'Loughlin and Bolger to that of Swift; Bolger, introducing the *Letters from the New Island*, described that series of pamphlets, initiated in 1987, as an attempt to re-start the Dublin pamphleteering tradition of which the *Drapier's Letters* was the most famous example. MacAnna himself authored one of the first five pamphlets (Bolger, 1991b, pp. 7, 73–104).

In 1984, the Raven Arts publishing project was joined by the Passion Machine, a new Dublin theatre company. Founded by writer/director Paul Mercier, and John Sutton, this group established itself at the St Francis Xavier Centre on the North side of Dublin (the poorer side of the city containing such notoriously deprived areas as Finglas, Kilbarrack and Ballymun). Their opening production was *Drowning*, a rock musical by Mercier. This was followed by plays from Mercier – *Home*, *Wasters*, *Spacers* and *Studs* – and from Roddy Doyle – *Brownbread* and *War*. The Passion Machine has been very successful, transferring productions to larger mainstream Dublin theatres and abroad. It has also successfully built up its own audience base, from its own locality.

In 1986, Doyle published *The Commitments*, the first novel of what has been retrospectively entitled *The Barrytown Trilogy* (Doyle, 1993). *The Snapper* (published 1990) and *The Van* (published 1991) followed, the latter being shortlisted for the Booker McConnell Prize. Doyle's next novel, *Paddy Clarke Ha Ha Ha* (published 1993) won the Booker, and this, combined with very successful films of *The Commitments* and *The Snapper* and *The Van*, has made Doyle an international figure, and the most popular and best-known writer of MacAnna's 'Renaissance'.

Doyle's work is comical, but also partakes of the quality of the comic-strip: it is riotously vulgar, light-hearted, heavily larded with obscene and scatological vocabulary. It is relentlessly dialogue-centered, especially in the early novels, and the lack of narration gives the novels a sense that context is wholly cultural, never physical. Religion hardly figures at all, violence is deployed to comic effect, drastic circumstances (unemployment, crisis pregnancy) are shrugged off cheerfully with few emotional or psychic consequences. The cultural world evoked is that of television, British newspapers, English soccer, fast-food, rock music and unemployment. In 1994, the BBC and RTE produced a four-part television series, *Family*, which seemed to take Doyle into the territory of Dermot Bolger. *Family* was an appallingly bleak picture of working-class estate life, raddled with violence, adultery, abuse, pornography, not to mention crime, drugs, poverty and unemployment. It is difficult to avoid concluding that Doyle felt the need to produce a ferociously Manichaean corrective to the cheerfully vulgar suburban vision of the earlier work, but this also calls into question the accuracy of either version of Dublin working-class life that he has produced.

MacAnna rightly identifies the Passion Machine's work as the comic analogue of the bleak world of the Raven Arts writers. Taken together, they amount to an impressive surge of activity. But the 'creative writers' have been paralleled by a group of journalist-intellectuals, who could be described in Gramscian terms as the 'Renaissance's' organic intellectuals. These writers have all been published by Raven Arts also, and include Fintan O'Toole, Colm Tóibín, Katie Donovan, John Waters, as well as MacAnna and Bolger themselves. Some of these writers – Tóibín, O'Toole, Waters – emerged out of the 1970s and 1980s alternative press in the Republic. By this, I mean magazines such as *Hot Press* (a rock magazine), *In Dublin* (a listings magazine), *Magill* (a current affairs magazine) and *Hibernia* (a fortnightly newspaper). O'Toole is the most important of these intellectuals, as a columnist with the *Irish Times*, contributor to the international liberal press, presenter of *The Late Show* on BBC 2 television, member of the editorial board of *Fortnight*, a cross-Border political and cultural magazine. He has published three volumes of journalism, a study of the playwright Tom Murphy, a study of corruption in the Irish beef industry and a biography of the playwright Richard Brinsley Sheridan. O'Toole writes as a polymath intellectual, as happy emulating the semiology of Umberto Eco or Roland Barthes as discussing education policy or party politics. He is familiar with intellectual trends such as poststructuralism or second-wave feminism or Frankfurt School Marxism, though the dominant ideological position for these intellectuals consists in their sense of having left Irish nationalism behind. This is the conclusive mark of their modernity, as of the entire 'Renaissance'.

But this modernity has not produced a literary modernism. MacAnna'a strictures on Joyce for producing 'academic' work, or on the Co-Op writers for their experimentalism and tendency not to write about the city suggest that he holds a limited and rather prescriptive notion of the representative Dublin writer. For him at least, the stress is chiefly on a limited idea of mimetic realism, that of simply representing what has not previously been represented, and on the matter of whether the writer comes from the city. The status of *representation* as such does not trouble him, and hence, with his stress on Dublin, he seems to be led to a kind of identitarian literary politics. The paradox must then be that in his rejection of experimental Dublin writing, he echoes the quarrels between early twentieth-century Irish propagandists such as D.P. Moran, editor of the *Leader*, on the one hand, and the Literary Revivalists on the other (Cairns and Richards, 1988, pp. 69–71). Just as Catholic Nationalists, such as Moran and Arthur Griffith objected to the poetic and dramatic innovations of Yeats, Synge and Lady Gregory on the grounds of the inadequacy of their representation of the realities of Irish life, so MacAnna dismisses contemporary literary experiment. Yet MacAnna would see himself as opposed to a cultural dispensation which he would trace to the legacy of Moran. This is not to suggest that Doyle, or, as we shall see, Bolger, simply employ a bland realism or naturalism. On the contrary, their writing seems to betray a sense that such ontologically and epistemologically authoritative modes are unavailable to them.

Raymond Williams sets out a broad typology of cultural movements and organisations, ranging from mediaeval craft guilds to the Modernist avant-gardes of the earlier part of this century (Williams, 1981, pp. 57–74). Broadly speaking, the earlier the movement, the more likely its organisation is to be explicitly codified or rule-bound, and the more likely it is to be concerned with matters of internal coherence, authority, tradition, training and relations with patrons or the market. When Williams describes the twentieth-century movements as most likely to be characterised by 'a particular style or more general cultural position', we begin to recognise the group centred on Bolger and Doyle. Such an association is not necessarily defined by membership of anything. It may be manifest in group productions or exhibitions – in this case, the *Letters from the New Island* pamphlet series (Bolger, 1991b), or the volume of essays, poetry and photographs, *Invisible Cities: The New Dubliners* (Bolger, 1988). Chiefly it is a loose association, defined in this case primarily by shared practice, the social relations of its members being often nothing more than the ties of a group of friends who share common interests.

Williams suggests analysing such groups by looking firstly at their modes of internal organisation, and then at their proposed and actual relations to other organisations in the same field and in wider society. He lists three modes of internal organisation: those based on formal membership; those organised around some collective public manifestation (such as an exhibition, a journal or a manifesto); and those in which, while not arranged around formal membership or a collective public manifestation, there is evidence of 'conscious association or group identification' (Williams, 1981, p. 68). It is clear, then, that the 'Dublin Renaissance' can be understood as a movement of this third kind. It is a movement, but sufficiently flexible and spacious as to allow the incorporation of writers on grounds less of class than generation (such as the poet Sara Berkeley, or the journalists Tóibín and Waters, who come from Wexford and Roscommon respectively). We see that the Raven

Arts Press/Passion Machine grouping is constructed around sets of friends and colleagues. O'Toole, Waters and Tóibín, for example, are all sometime editors of *Magill*; O'Toole, Waters and Vincent Browne (proprietor of *Magill*) are *Irish Times* columnists; in his 'Acknowledgements' to his volumes of journalism, O'Toole pays tribute to Browne, Waters, Tóibín and Bolger as supports and influences (see O'Toole, 1990, 1994). Doyle and Mercier were friends prior to Mercier's commissioning of *Brownbread* and *War*. The group is thus marked by a shared practice, which is basically literary or journalistic; but not by a common theory. Indeed, many of these writers see themselves as transcending theory or ideology.

When it comes to external relations, between the movement and the rest of its field of activity, and then the wider social world, Williams again suggests three variants:

(a) *Specializing*, as in the case of sustaining or promoting work in a particular medium or branch of an art, and in some circumstances a particular style;

(b) *alternative*, as in the cases of the provision of alternative facilities for the production, exhibition or publication of certain kinds of work, where it is believed that existing institutions exclude or tend to exclude these;

(c) *oppositional*, in which the cases represented by (b) are raised to active opposition to the established institutions, or more generally to the conditions within which these exist.

(Williams, 1981, p. 70)

It seems very clear that the Raven Arts Press/Passion Machine formation is of type (b). It is concerned primarily with the representation of what Colm Tóibín has called 'crazy, unofficial lives', chiefly as they have been lived out in the suburbs of Dublin. In MacAnna's account, the mission has been to portray what had not been portrayed before, that is, the social conditions of that peculiar form of modernity that was unleashed in the Republic since the 1960s. Raven Arts Press and the Passion Machine have acted primarily as conduits for the production, exhibition and publication of work that had been excluded by existing institutions. Only in the essays by Anthony Cronin (significantly, one of the older writers published by Raven Arts) collected in *Letters from the New Island* under the title 'Art for the People?' are the existing conditions of production, exhibition and dissemination discussed, and then in terms of sketchy generalisation (Bolger, 1991b, pp. 148–87). There is little evidence of an attempt to articulate such a critique with actual writing or publication practice. In the work of Bolger and Doyle, there is no sign of any oppositional intent manifested in aesthetic strategy; the very rapidity with which these two writers have become 'mainstream' (exemplified by Doyle's Booker prize and the shortlisting of *The Journey Home* for the *Irish Times*/Aer Lingus Irish Literature Prize) seems only to confirm this. This applies to the other Raven Arts/Passion Machine writers already mentioned also. There is certainly nothing in this formation's project to match the thoroughness, grandeur and ferocity of opposition in the Modernist avant-gardes of early twentieth-century Europe, such as that of Surrealism, Dada or Constructivism. These movements were international, and were resolutely opposed, in their various ways, to the prevailing social, economic and political orthodoxies of bourgeois Europe. Their assaults were not merely a matter of representing communities or phenomena previously unrepresented, but amounted, in Dada, to denunciations of aesthetic ideology as such, and the dominant modes of production, presentation and dissemination of 'art'. These Modernist groups were in no doubt as to the political importance of their activities. Aesthetics and politics were linked intimately, though not always to progressive ends.

The ultimately apolitical character of the artistic productions of the Raven Arts/Passion Machine formation lies in the confusions about modernisation, modernity, postmodernity and ideology described in the Introduction. In a recent interview, Seamus Deane has suggested that in Ireland being labelled an 'ideologue' is a coded way of suggesting that someone is a Marxist (Callaghan, 1994, p. 45). I would suggest that 'ideology' also incorporates nationalism, and its absorption of oppositional energies, most especially since the start of the 'Troubles' in the late 1960s. The difficulty, as the Irish left has found for at least the last two decades, is that the crisis in the North has led to a drastic attenuation of the intellectual possibilities of the public sphere in the Republic. Therefore, any oppositional intellectual movement simply cannot afford to publicly name itself as Marxist (let alone to do so in such a way as to suggest an affinity or sympathy with the Northern minority). Closely related to this confusion and impoverishment is the fact that the image of heroic dissent that MacAnna claims for the 'Dublin Renaissance' writers is out of all proportion to their actual achievements, and its polemical stridency leads it into further contradiction. By this I mean that MacAnna overplays the moral and intellectual courage required of these writers to mount the critique they have of the national culture and the state. In his anxiety to prove their relevance, their organic relation to Dublin society, he overlooks too easily writers of earlier generations – Joyce, Beckett, O'Casey, Kavanagh, Flann O'Brien, O'Faolain, Clarke, O'Connor, McGahern, Edna O'Brien, Kate O'Brien – who worked in a much more censorious political and moral climate. These writers may often have come from outside Dublin, and may have dealt with social situations in rural settings, or in cities other than Dublin, but their critical impulse was in many ways similar to that now commandeered by MacAnna.

I drew attention earlier to Terence Brown's account of the difficulties attending the position of Irish writers in society from the 1970s onwards, noting that while the State had become much less censorious and repressive, and in fact was undertaking various measures in support of artists and writers, this had the confusing effect of removing from literary intellectuals the two main roles that had been available to them since Independence (Brown, 1985, pp. 312–25). These were, firstly, to buttress the authority of the national state by producing idealised images that conformed to the dominant ideology. Secondly, to act as honourable and lonely dissidents, producing writing, often 'realist' in mode and liberal humanist in philosophy, that showed the ideological orthodoxy to be sexually repressive, dehumanising, anti-intellectual, sectarian, and spiritually, morally, politically and economically impoverished and immiserating. Many of these earlier writers faced serious censorship or the banning of their work; some were publicly denounced in the press or from the pulpit (Brown, 1985a, pp. 67–78). Lives and careers were blighted in a way that seems almost unthinkable now. The following generation – figures active in the 1970s such as Banville and Friel, but also Tom Murphy, Thomas Kilroy, Aidan Higgins, Tom MacIntyre, John Montague, Thomas Kinsella – finding a more benign State and ideological climate, retreated into somewhat private worlds of formal experiment and personal, subjectivist exploration and meditation. (Other literary practices included the exploration of the dilemmas of the Southern Protestant minority, exemplified by William Trevor or Jennifer Johnston, or the farcical treatment of the vacillations of the new bourgeoisie, exemplified by the work of Hugh Leonard and Bernard Farrell.) The work of Banville and Friel discussed earlier was an example of this trend, a late efflorescence of Modernism. It was not, however, as I made clear, a particularly politicised or critical Modernism. This may explain why it has been invisible to a writer like MacAnna. This is the point made by Desmond Bell, when he reminds us that modernism arrived late in post-1945 Ireland, and then not as a symptom or critique of social ferment, as it had been in Europe and the United States in the early twentieth century. Rather it was already an exhausted political movement, and one which had been absorbed by the forces it had once opposed. So, in '1960s Ireland "modernism" as pseudo-international style and sensibility was championed not by a radical avant-garde but by the purveyors of consumer capitalism' (Bell, 1988, p. 229). It seems, crudely, that there was nothing left to oppose. The fear now must be co-option by the State or by the corporate sector that dominates the economy, cultural production now having been so thoroughly and obviously capitalised. The problem lies too in the way that a coercive dominant ideology apparently naturally called forth an answering ideological project of resistance – secular, humanist, liberal, rationalist, 'pluralist'. This we might now call 'revisionist'. What has been disappointing about this 'turn' has been its uninterestedness in feminism and the women's movement, and its downright intolerance of socialist, nationalist or anti-imperial critiques, all of these being seen as in cahoots with Northern republicanism. The lack, in an Irish historical context of conflict and colonisation, of agreed critical meta-languages produces a kind of performative contradiction in Irish 'liberalism', when it does appear in the form of 'revisionism'. This causes it to seek to sat-urate the entirety of intellectual debate and not to tolerate its discursive rivals, in rank contradiction of its own founding principles. As I argue in my chap-ter on Banville and historical 'revisionism', this tendency suggests an ideo-logical relationship with and dependence on the state. Indeed, the writer's dilemma may be formulated in the shift from a cultural policy based on repression to one based on support (via agencies such as the Arts Council and Aosdána, and the setting-up of tax breaks and grant aid for writers and artists) which can be conducive, in more subtle ways, to conformism and acquies-cence. This confusion of oppositional alternatives for aesthetic activity is made manifest in the work of the 'Dublin Renaissance', even as it tries to sketch out the contours of a new oppositional discursive space. In this light, it is perhaps significant that the one serious engagement with women's issues in the *Letters from the New Island* pamphlet series, Katie Donovan's *Irish Women Writers: Marginalised by Whom?* (published in 1988), is, as its title sug-gests, concerned chiefly with the ways that it reckons that women's writing has been marginalised by the aesthetic and thematic strategies adopted by women writers. Here we see the cost of putatively 'post-ideological' intellec-tual positions. Donovan writes as a 'post-feminist', and approvingly cites fig-ures such as Nuala Ní Dhomhnaill to make her point (Bolger, 1991b, pp. 146–7). The paradox, of course, is that she issues her call for confident Irish women writers to enter the mainstream from the pages of a pamphlet pub-lished by a putatively 'fringe' press. Much of the authority of her position is derived from its supposedly marginal enunciative location.

The choice of Swift as an exemplar is perhaps significant in this situation. An Irish Protestant of English descent, ill at ease in Ireland (resentful of his loss of influence in London) but critical of its treatment by the English gov-ernment, Swift seems to stand outside of ideological positions. This means for the Raven Arts writers those positions relating to Anglo-Irish relations: Swift was neither an Irish nationalist nor an uncritical *colon*, but was never-theless fiercely worldly, engaged, an endless fount of indignation (something the Raven Arts project aspired to). He therefore has an iconic status as an intellectual with a powerful but ambivalent sense of critical geography, in his personal sense of exile and distance from both England and Ireland. This makes him attractive to the Raven Arts writers with their fundamentally ruptured sense of place and of identity, both within Ireland and on the margins of Europe. MacAnna's invocation of the rhetoric of class and of realism is contradictory. He is keen to describe the new writing as a realistic description of (working-class) everyday or contemporary life. To accommodate Bolger, he extends this to a 'poetic realism', and the Passion Machine's drama constitutes a 'comic-strip realism' (MacAnna, 1991, p. 24). The new work is, he says, more a product of environment than of tradition. Despite this 'realism', or 'heightened social realism' or 'Dirty Dublin Poetic Realism', he sees himself and the new writing as opposed to any realism that serves an overt ideological purpose – socialist realism (so the new drama takes no cue from O'Casey, though O'Casey's most famous plays, the 'Dublin Trilogy', are, in fact, a testament to liberal humanism, and and yet produced urban images of precisely the kind that MacAnna objects to); or the nationalist realism of Corkery, concerned with the land, Roman Catholicism and nationalism. Indeed, he sees the Passion Machine's work as (healthily) non-ideological. Their plays are 'comic fantasies' (shortly after they constituted 'comic-strip realism') whose 'purpose is to entertain', not to offer 'a tidy moral message' (MacAnna, 1991, p. 25). MacAnna's remarks here, and his attacks elsewhere in this essay on academics, coupled with his assertion that the new Dublin writing depicts areas and experiences that 'many people – politicians, media, the complacent middle-classes, older writers – had tried to ignore or sweep under the carpet', seek to elaborate the oppositional position of the new writing. Even the Co-Op writers are castigated for their experimentalism (though this does not prevent MacAnna from including avowedly middle-class cosmopolitan experimentalists such as Ann Enright, Sebastian Barry (formerly of the Co-Op but acceptable because published by Raven Arts Press), and Aidan Matthews. The point is that MacAnna is interested for polemical purposes in constructing a homogeneous group – contemporary literary (especially critical) intellectuals in the Republic – whom he can accuse of propagating a monolithic culture, which the new Dublin writing lies outside of. The new writing is therefore non-ideological, post-nationalist, post-socialist, post-postmodernist (it is 'a deconstructionist's nightmare' (MacAnna, 1991, p. 29)). MacAnna is interested here to construct an identitarian politics of writing – only Dubliners (preferably of his generation) can write about Dublin with validity. This link between place, identity and representation is most explicit in the premise of *Invisible Cities*, where Bolger writes in the Introduction that 'This anthology is ... an attempt to chronicle the lives of the new Dubliners in the new Dublin as it has been lived by them' (Bolger, 1988, p. 10). Bolger goes on to suggest that certain areas are excluded because no-one has yet emerged to 'speak of them'. Later, I will demonstrate the working-out of this thinking – a grossly empiricist form of realism – in

Bolger's own writing. In this context, it is worth remembering the critique offered by David Lloyd, and cited earlier in the context of Friel's theories of the national writer, of the idea of the 'representative writer', with its link, in the Irish context, to Corkery's literary-critical nationalism, representation, and normative aesthetic criteria (Lloyd, 1993, pp. 42–7). The paradox is, of course, that Corkery is the kind of figure that MacAnna sets himself up to oppose, on grounds of generation, culture and politics.

The critics MacAnna does cite are not insignificant: Fintan O'Toole and Edna Longley. These two hold positions on the editorial board of *Fortnight*. O'Toole, as I suggested earlier, is the primary intellectual presence among the Raven Arts writers; he provided an Introduction to a collection of Bolger's plays, *A Dublin Quartet* (Bolger, 1992). Longley I will discuss at some length later, but of relevance here is her trenchant critique of Field Day, the group of writers and critics founded in Derry in 1980 by Friel and the actor Stephen Rea. Field Day, in its pamphlet and anthological work, has provided much of the academic background (with its interest in literary theory ('deconstruction') and politics) that MacAnna inveighs against. Bolger has specifically attacked the term 'post-colonial' as used to describe Ireland, to this extent aligning himself with Longley (Bolger, 1993, pp. xii–xiii). This critique is inspired, in both Bolger and Longley, by the wish to move beyond the conflict in the North, though they have somewhat different reasons for wishing to do so. Longley believes that the 'intersection' of literature and politics is 'unhealthy', especially in the Northern context, because she reckons it inflames an already culturally tense situation. Bolger and the Raven Arts writers reject the label 'post-colonial' because they reckon it elides contemporary issues, and sends the writer and critic back to the glorious literary past of the Revival. To this extent, one can say that the Raven Arts movement, as it is characterised by MacAnna, is 'revisionist'.

The invocation of Longley brings with it certain problems, however. If literary prescription of a Corkerian kind is what is feared, and 'deconstruction' (though MacAnna never indicates what he imagines this might be) is to be thwarted, then Longley's definition of the literary may not turn out to be wholly safe either. Ironically, MacAnna cites Longley's description of the poetry of Paul Durcan as 'extra-literary' with approval (Longley, 1982, p. xi). More recently, Longley has suggested that Friel's 1988 Field Day play about Hugh O'Neill, *Making History* (Friel, 1989), concerned as it is with the making of historical myth and the political exigencies of the narrativisation of lived experience, is a tame exercise in revisionism compared to Durcan's poetry (Longley, 1992d, p. 12). She might well have been thinking of the Durcan poem quoted by MacAnna, 'Making Love outside Áras an Uachtaráin', with its images of young lovers being stalked down by de Valera, and being ordered to 'Stop/Making love outside Áras an Uachtaráin'. Leaving issues of aesthetic judgement aside (a very un-Longleyan strategy) this is an example of what Shaun Richards, characterising the Raven Arts project, has called 'pissing on the hearthstone of ancient pieties' (Richards, 1992, p. 7). But the crucial term is 'extra-literary'. It is significant because it allows Longley to admit a resolutely worldly and political (in the widest sense) poet to her discourse, without altering its terms significantly, and to valorise him. Durcan is not, in this discourse, 'ideologically' motivated – he is a liberal humanist. Friel, on the other hand, is ideologically motivated – he is a nationalist – and hence can never match Durcan. This is despite the fact that many of Friel's plays deal with abstract issues such as language, politics, narrative, memory, and political, social and institutional discourses, from a profoundly humanist perspective. Of course, to open the debate a little wider, it is partly in reaction to cultural and intellectual formations such as the *Crane Bag* and Field Day that groups or journals as various as the Raven Arts Press, *Fortnight* and the Cultural Traditions Group have arisen. Certainly the *Letters from the New Island* pamphlets can be seen as a direct answer to the Field Day pamphlets; furthermore, recent anthologies of Irish fiction edited by Bolger (1993b) and Tóibín (1993b) position themselves self-consciously in opposition to the *Field Day Anthology of Irish Writing* (Deane, 1991). So the invocation of Longley marks an affiliation that locates the Raven Arts project as part of a broader Irish 'culture war' of the 1980s and early 1990s. These discursive struggles, in turn, can be understood in relation to yet wider contexts, such as the debate over historiographic 'revisionism', and the realisation in Irish intellectual circles that the project of 'modernisation' initiated in the 1960s was deeply flawed. All of this suggests a greater degree of continuity between the 'Dublin Renaissance' and earlier literary/cultural movements than an account such as that provided by MacAnna allows.

The term 'extra-literary' is one fraught with dangers and ambiguities for MacAnna. The 'non-literary' background that he claims for the new literature is precisely what makes it powerful 'literature' for MacAnna, hence his confusion. He suggests that it may be 'too early for literary critics to explain or come-to-terms with or even understand a new movement that seems non-literary in origin and avowedly anti-academic in its preoccupations and intentions' (MacAnna, 1991, p. 29). But MacAnna is obviously mistaken in his view of a cosy consensus having historically existed between 'writers' and 'critics'. The history of modern literature is marked by various antagonisms, collusions and confusions between critics and writers. The Raven Arts and Passion Machine writers are hardly the first to have a hostile attitude to the critics (except certain critics). Yet if one looks at the most recent act of, if not canonbuilding then 'definition', in Irish writing, the *Field Day Anthology*, Bolger,

O'Loughlin, Barry, Jordan, Matthews, O'Toole and Durcan all appear. The inclusion of some of Doyle's work on the Republic's secondary school English curriculum has already been seriously debated.

MacAnna's difficulty is that he wishes at once to excoriate the concept of the 'literary' as he believes it stands in Ireland at present (especially in the academy), and to assert the 'Dublin Renaissance' as a new literary movement. He stands on the borders of the discourse, looking both ways at once. To enter it is to deny, or at least to distance himself from, the milieu and the mass culture from which he believes the new writing draws its power, its materials and (implicitly) its audience. But to refuse to enter is permanently to consign the new writing to marginality, or at least to mark an unbridgeable distance between it and conventionally defined high or mandarin literary culture. This position might be an interesting one if it were held with an attitude of self-consciousness and irony. But this is not the case with MacAnna. Longley has suggested that Seamus Deane's critical writing is marked by a 'powerful sense of Palestinian dispossession' (Longley, 1994, p. 183). Leaving aside the matter of whether this is an accurate portrayal, and the ideological implications of such an analogy, it is worth noting that the motif of internal exile is equally applicable to the Raven Arts project, both in its novelistic manifestation (as we shall see with Bolger) and in its criticism (migrancy, exile, diaspora, emigration are all recurrent themes of O'Toole's work).

When he sets out what he sees as the main tenets of the new Dublin writing, MacAnna is perhaps at his weakest. It is, he says, a literature of social disenchantment. As I noted earlier, he seems incapable of recognising or acknowledging the social critique inherent in the work of many of the greatest pre- and post-Independence Irish writers. The sources of the new writing 'are essentially non-traditional, even anti-literary (social issues, local environment, urban disillusionment, political corruption, rock music)' (MacAnna, 1991, p. 29). All these matters have received copious literary treatment previously, even rock music, albeit in the different but roughly socially analogous form of the street-ballad, in *Ulysses* (see Lloyd, 1993, pp. 88–124).

MacAnna's criterion of 'extra-literariness' is important. It enables him to escape categorising the 'Dublin Renaissance' as a purely working-class writing, while enabling him to retain the portrayal of urban life as a touchstone of 'authenticity'. For MacAnna, this authenticity is a matter of geography rather than of class. This permits him to include middle-class writers in his survey. As I suggested earlier, a stress on working-class writing would lead MacAnna in the direction of 'ideology', something he wishes to avoid, being redolent of a kind of literary Zhdanovism. It also denies him the possibility of aspiring to that gratifying literary space of liberal humanism, the 'universal', that seems to be implied by the invocation of Longley and Durcan. But such universality might politically emasculate the 'Dublin Renaissance', and obscure its specificity, its main value in MacAnna's eyes.

If MacAnna and Bolger locate the power of the new writing in its authentic rendering of Dublin and its environs, however, they also run the risk of providing only the obverse of the literary tendency they set out to criticise. That is, they run the risk of once again perpetrating the kind of geographic essentialism that they, but also counter-Revivalists long before them such as Flann O'Brien, Beckett, O'Faolain and O'Connor, found in the Literary and Gaelic Revivals. If Yeats posited the existence of a certain racial or social ideal in a poem such as 'The Fisherman' (Yeats, 1962, pp. 67–8), then MacAnna, Bolger and Doyle risk a deeply negative 'style-as-cynicism' in their overwhelming will to expose and flaunt the 'realities' of modern Dublin (Richards, 1992, p. 6). The image that results is just as partial as anything purveyed by Yeats or Synge.

Somewhat schematically, the continuities that lurk behind the writing of 'modern Dublin' can be understood as follows. At the end of the nineteenth century, the Revival writers, such as Yeats, Lady Gregory and Synge valorised the landscape, culture, language and people of the Irish West. This latter represented a Gaelic, pastoral ideal place, where a people confident and self-sufficient in their cultural identity lived out lives ontologically at one with the land. Said argues that the landscape poetically imagined by Yeats at this time was part of the anti-colonial project of cultural nationalism, the forging of a coherent unifying national identity to be pitted against the coloniser (Said, 1993, pp. 265–88). The new national imagination required a national landscape to inhabit. As such, it was a necessary geographical, cartographic and cultural reaction against the *morte main* of the imperial imagination, an act of symbolic re-possession and re-investment in the national landscape. Said demonstrates the intermeshing techniques, both material and ideological, used by the coloniser to control the landscape. Thus resistance to this colonising project had to imagine a new kind of space. In Yeats and others, this new space drew much of its inspiration from the West, which seemed the part of the island least tainted by colonial influence, or by modernity, often seen in nationalism as a corruption brought in by the coloniser. So, in Said's account, Yeats' West of Ireland was the invention, by a nationalist organic intellectual, of a new national landscape, in the service of the project of creating a new national-popular consciousness.

Said is building here on Seamus Deane's reading of Yeats, by establishing a continuity between Yeats' early Celtic mysticism, and the later occult and fascist writings (Deane, 1985, pp. 38–50). In an effort (not without problems) to locate Yeats in the history of worldwide decolonisation, Said suggests that this late rebarbative work be understood as an example of *nativism*, comparable to the *negritude* of Leopold Senghor. The problem with such an essential-

ist construction or discovery is that, as Said points out, such an 'identity politics' remains part of the ideological dialectic of empire. Empire and colonialism, as part of their cultural strategies of self-legitimation, posit a Manichaean
model of civilisation versus barbarism, rationality versus irrationality, mascu-
line versus feminine, cultivation of the land versus its neglect, culture versus
nature. The coloniser appropriates the first term of these binaries in his self-
justifying rhetoric, arrogating to himself the mantle of civilisation, culture and
rationality. The native is projected as a barbaric creature of nature who cannot
or will not maintain the land in a rational manner, and who is feminine or
childlike, thus requiring civilising, assistance, or, if recalcitrant, punishment.
Deane detects these tropes in their benign form in Matthew Arnold's writings
about the Irish. In *The Study of Celtic Literature* (Arnold, 1912), Arnold reckoned that the philistine culture of bourgeois utilitarian England could be
redeemed by an infusion of Celtic spontaneity, imagination, proximity to
nature, poetry, emotion. As Deane puts it, Arnold's Celt

> is already encroaching upon the territory of Yeats and Synge – where
> folk-tales are preferred to the 'English diet of parliamentary speeches
> and the gutter press', where speech is highly flavoured, where peasants,
> be they Christy Mahons or figures from a Jack Yeats painting, have the
> vigour and vitality the anaemic city dweller has lost.
>
> (Deane, 1985, p. 25)

However, Deane also notes that for Arnold the colonial link is still necessary,
for while 'everything the philistine middle classes of England needed, the Celt
could supply' (Deane, 1985, p. 25), the opposite was also the case. Thus the
concomitant of Arnold's benevolent view of the Irish is their continuing need
for British government.

Thus we see that the Revival promoted a kind of essentialism, one that
took its discursive boundaries from the structures put in place by the colonial
relationship. To resist meant to establish a firm identity, and a firm identity
was held to be one that was pre-colonial, prior to the sectarian divisions that
were all too evident in Ireland in the late nineteenth century, prior to modernity. Such an identity was reckoned to be re-discoverable in the rural West,
as I have already suggested. But this discovery also rested on a corresponding
negative aesthetic of the city. This is clear in Yeats' distaste for materialism
and the sense that modernity brought with it a levelling tendency, expressed
most famously in poems such as 'September 1913' and 'The Second Coming'
(Yeats, 1962, pp. 46–7, 97–8).

We should not be surprised, then, to find an urbanist counter-current, and
this was expressed in much of the work of Joyce and O'Casey. Later, the

hegemony of ruralist ideology was disputed and parodied by Flann O'Brien. So the 'Dublin Renaissance' is the latest expression of a cultural current that has been running from the time of the Revival itself. What is new is the iconoclastic vulgarity of its expression, at times (in Doyle) to comic but also to ambiguous effect:

> – The Irish are the niggers of Europe, lads.
>   They nearly gasped: it was so true.
>   – An' Dubliners are the niggers of Ireland. The culchies have fuckin' everythin'. An' the northside Dubliners are the niggers o' Dublin. – Say it loud, I'm black an' I'm proud.
>
> (Doyle, 1993, p. 13)

The contradiction is that such an assertion is taken to be a break with the past, even where, as here, this break is asserted in a metaphor so obviously related to the experience of empire and of racialisation. This is not to suggest that this racialisation is itself lacking in paradox. Much of the humour of *The Commitments* lies in the distance between the characters and their community of Barrytown, and black culture in the United States. But this central conceit of the novel also inhabits difficult and debatable ground, since the distance between rhetoric and reality is one that confers safety and strength. So it is amusing for the Commitments to invoke the rhetoric of James Brown and his musical negritude, over against a kind of Irish nationalist nativism, at least partly since they are so obviously (and therefore safely) not black. Doyle is aware that soul was the music of a black working-class; what he may not realise is that this black proletariat had been faced with a similar abrupt change, within one generation, from rural to urban poverty.

I would like to turn now to Bolger's *The Journey Home* (Bolger, 1991a), on MacAnna's account the 'consummation' of the 'declaration of artistic intent' implied by Bolger's earlier work as a playwright and poet, and, I would add, as a publisher, commentator and intellectual (MacAnna, 1991, p. 26). I am passing over Bolger's plays (Bolger, 1992) – *The Lament for Arthur Cleary*, *The Tramway End* (two one-act plays, intended to be produced together, *In High Germany* and *The Holy Ground*), *One Last White Horse* – and his first two novels – *Night Shift* (Bolger, 1993a) and *The Woman's Daughter* (Bolger, 1987) – because *The Journey Home* encompasses and sums these works up.[4] Its themes of emigration, poverty, drug addiction, of the return of the exile from Europe, of the deterritorialisation of identity, of political corruption, of the

---

4 *The Lament for Arthur Cleary* was first performed in 1989, *The Tramway End* in 1990, and *One Last White Horse* in 1991.

repressiveness of the social order of the 1960s and earlier – these can all be found in relatively discrete forms in the plays and novels that preceded it.

In 1985, O'Toole delivered a paper to the Yeats Summer School in which he suggested that

> For the last hundred years, ... Irish writing has been marked by [a] dominance of the rural over the urban, a dominance based on a false opposition of the country to the city which has been vital to the main-tenance of a conservative political culture in the country.
>
> (O'Toole, 1985, p. 111)

For O'Toole, the key markers of the precedence of the rural over the urban in Irish writing have been:

> (a) The pull of the past, the movement in the direction of the world of a previous generation, (b) the impulse towards a knowable community in which the individual has an identifiable place.
>
> (O'Toole, 1985, p. 114)

Citing Bolger and Michael O'Loughlin as hopeful examples, O'Toole suggested that what had been missing in Irish writing had been a Utopian writing of the city, which sees the urban as the space for a transformative future. In 1988, O'Toole again welcomed the same writers, and suggested that their work could 'contribute to a critique of the received values' (O'Toole, 1988, p. 35). I will be suggesting here, in line with my earlier comments on the 'Dublin Renaissance' generally, that *The Journey Home* represents not an escape from what O'Toole, quoting Marx's *Eighteenth Brumaire of Louis Bonaparte*, calls 'the poetry of the past', but amounts in fact to an unhelpful re-elaboration of it.

The novel is set in the 1980s in the Republic, and takes great trouble to incorporate specific political and cultural references to locate it at that time – 'moving statues', the political instability of minority Fianna Fáil administrations, and their re-adoption of traditional nationalist rhetoric (Bolger, 1991a, pp. 187, 231).[5] The novel is made up of three narratives. An omniscient realist narrative depicts the flight of Francis Hanrahan (Hano) and Katie, to the wilds of Leitrim from the edge of Dublin where they have murdered Pascal

5 In the village of Ballinspittle, in Co. Cork, the statue of the Virgin in the local Marian shrine was seen to 'move' by many thousands of people in the late 1980s. Sean Doherty, Junior Minister for Justice in the Fianna Fáil government of 1982, was compelled to resign after allegations that he illegally arranged phone-taps on the telephones of two prominent journalists.

Plunkett, a sadistic and corrupt gombeen entrepreneur who has dogged Hano's life (and that of his parents) and sexually assaulted him. A second narrative, addressed by Hano to the sleeping Katie in the basement of the ruined 'Big House' where they finally hide, tells Hano's autobiography up to the point at which their flight began. A third narrative, elliptical in form, reveals itself to be the voice of the dead Shay, Hano's great friend and Katie's lover. Speaking from the grave, addressing Katie, Shay recounts details of her history – her move, after her parents' deaths, from Leitrim to Dublin, her alienation and drug addiction – and also his death, murdered by the Plunkett dynasty. These three patterns are played out simultaneously, cutting across each other, together reducing the overall scheme of the novel to a series of relatively discrete episodes. The effect is one of circularity, as Hano's and Shay's narratives are extended flashbacks, and Hano's is recounted from the endpoint of the omniscient narrative. The result is a sense of stasis in a novel centrally concerned with movement and migration, and, hence, futility. This is the first indication, on a formal level, of Bolger's retreat from any semblance of the Utopian aspirations O'Toole projects for him.

Georg Lukács suggested that the novel was the epic of the bourgeois age and that it was characterised by 'transcendental homelessness' (Lukács, 1971, p. 88). Here, in an attempt to narrate the experiences of a new Irish urban proletariat, struggling to adapt to conditions of 'peripheral postindustrialisation' (Jacobsen, 1994, pp. 10–17), homelessness is no longer merely a metaphysical condition. Every character in *The Journey Home* is displaced, an exile: Hano's parents from Kerry; Shay from the inner city; Katie from Leitrim; the 'old Protestant woman', whom Hano befriended on teenage hitching trips from Dublin, and with whom he and Katie take refuge, has been driven from her house. Even the Plunketts, the visible face of power in the novel, are exiles from Mayo. The great desire, and nostalgia, enunciated here therefore is for 'home', and for the sense of wholeness, authenticity and self-presence founded in a stable geographical location. Hano puts the problem thus:

> I didn't understand it then, but I grew up in perpetual exile: from my parents when on the streets, from my own world when at home … How can you learn self-respect if you're taught that where you live is not your real home?
>
> (Bolger, 1991a, p. 8)

However, Hano found that when he travelled, at the age of fourteen, into what he calls 'my father's uncharted countryside', he discovered there a reality beyond his father's comprehension: 'long-haired Germans in battered vans picking up hikers; skinheads battling outside chip shops in Athlone' (Bolger,

1991a, p. 8). Hano's father was of a generation that came to maturity around 1960, when the ruralist national culture promulgated by de Valera and carica-tured by MacAnna had yet to actually confront the Lemass/Whitaker 'mod-ernisation' initiated in 1958. On his deathbed, he told Hano that he had only ever liked the suburban house he raised his family in because in its garden he had, by planting potatoes and raising chickens, tried to re-establish a sense of home, a memory of the farm he had come from (Bolger, 1991a, pp. 126–7). But to no avail. For he had also breathed in the confidence of the Lemass era, hoping that with the new economic dispensation, his children might be able to stay in Ireland and not be forced to emigrate, as he and his siblings had been. Hano's father, in other words, had hoped that, as Terence Brown has put it, modernisation could be nationalised (Brown, 1985a, pp. 246–7). With hind-sight, we might consider Lemass' success in this ideological project as a matter of some cynicism, since the main vehicle for this modernisation was to be transnational capital, a shifting force that would eventually lead the Republic, in the 1980s in which the novel is set, back to conditions of severe economic slump, unemployment and emigration, though the terms of cultural and migrant geography had changed. *The Journey Home* is marked by an uneasy sense of solidarity and difference with the Lemass generation: fury and disgust at what Bolger sees as the corruption, hypocrisy and self-aggrandisement of the powerful of that generation; sympathy for those disenfranchised by it.

The novel is about journeys, as its title suggests: journeys physical, cul-tural and metaphysical. Said has noted the spatial characteristics of the real-ist novel as a major bourgeois cultural institution of the nineteenth century, how it is crucially concerned with the way the 'novelistic hero and heroine exhibit the restlessness and energy of the enterprising bourgeoisie' and how 'they are permitted adventures in which their experiences reveal to them the limits of what they can aspire to, where they can go, what they can become' (Said, 1993, p. 84). Bolger's social world may not be that of the bourgeoisie, but his characters travel constantly in search of home and of themselves. Hano travels into the country, as a boy; Shay travels to Europe in search of liberation, as one of the 'young Europeans' so beloved of IDA promotions; Katie and Hano flee to the country, in order to escape the forces of the coun-try that have taken over the city; Hano travels from boyhood to manhood, working for the state bureaucracy and then becoming embroiled in the cor-rupt and criminal world of Pascal Plunkett.[6] In Bolger's world, however, even

---

6 The IDA is the Industrial Development Authority, the state agency responsible for the pro-motion abroad of the Republic as an industrial location. In the 1980s, its campaigns stressed the youth of the Irish workforce, in conjunction with the state's membership of the European Economic Community.

the Irish representatives of the 'enterprising bourgeoisie' turn out to be 'the niggers of Europe'. They are peripheral small players on the European stage. Their explorations of European social space end in failure. Patrick Plunkett, Pascal's corrupt politician brother and the father of Justin, may be a Junior Minister, his future may be as a European Commissioner, but Shay meets him trawling sleazy gay bars and clubs in the Hague, a lonely outsider in the heart of the continent. This only mirrors Shay's own experience of Europe as that of the *gastarbeiter* suffering exploitative labour conditions, living in shacks. When he returns to Europe, later in the novel, it is having betrayed himself and, it turns out, Katie, by working for Justin Plunkett as a drugs courier.

Hano's narrative, then, is in some ways a conventional Irish *Bildungsroman*, except that rather than describing a conventional bourgeois history of growing social confidence, stature and definition, achieved if necessary by migration, here, all possibilities are thwarted (Brown, 1985a, pp. 318–19). This blockage takes place in the city, because, as O'Toole suggested, of its provinciality and domination by country people. Hano is dogged by his feelings of alienation from his country parents, and his feelings of guilt and betrayal in relation to what he perceives as the dominant ethos and culture (in line with MacAnna's thesis), which is characterised as being obsessed with the rural past, nationalism and Anglophobia. It is hypocritical, corrupt, pious, money-grabbing. The world of work, exemplified by the Plunkett empire and the Voters' Register's Office, where Hano and Shay work, is similarly corrupt or bureaucratic, semi-criminal or a matter of unproductive paper-shifting. It suits both Bolger's characters' existential quandaries and his ideological purposes, to plunge them into the alternative subterranean world of flatland, dope, rock music and general cynicism since it offers them (and the readership the novel is seeking to construct for itself) some temporary relief, and the pleasure of debunking the dominant cultural myths.

Bolger's vision, therefore, is an ambivalent one, contained within a Manichaean framework. Ireland is divided between the country and the city. Dublin is split between rural colonisers and the 'crazy, unofficial lives' of denizens like Hano and Shay. Europe is split between bureaucrats like the Irish Embassy official in the Hague who refuses to help Shay when he is destitute, and the Turkish migrant workers with whom he makes common cause in Germany (Bolger, 1991a, pp. 192, 205). But this split is not a wholly negative phenomenon, for what really offends Bolger is the close co-existence of country and city, the idea of a rural bourgeoisie, or the possibility of alienated rural labour. This is illustrated in Hano's description of a pub Shay takes him to, in 'a warren of cobbled laneways off Thomas Street':

The downstairs bar was thick with smoke, countrymen nursing pints, a figure with a black beard gesturing drunkenly in the centre of the floor. Two old women sang in a corner, one lifting her hand with perfect timing at regular intervals to straighten the man beside her who was tilting on his bar stool. Nobody there was under fifty, no one born in the city that was kept out by the steel door.

'Gas, isn't it' Shay said. 'Knocknagow on a Friday evening'. He gazed in amusement, then headed downstairs to the cellar. Here the owner's son reigned, the father never coming closer than shouting down from the top step at closing time. Four women with sharp, hardened faces sat in one corner drinking shorts ... I began to suss how the locked door kept more than the industrial revolution out. The girl across from me was rolling a joint; the bloke beside Shay passing one in his hands ... Two of the women in the corner rose and ascended the stairs ...

'The massaging hand never stops,' Shay said. 'Pauline there left her bag behind one night so I brought it over to her across the road in the Clean World Health Studio. She was clad in a leather outfit after skelping the arse off some businessman ...'

(Bolger, 1991a, pp. 32–3)

The reference to the industrial revolution is crucial. Industrial modernity is fatally compromised for Bolger. Hano may enjoy the liberation he experiences in Shay's company: 'Home', he says, 'like an old ocean liner, broke loose from its moorings and sailed in my mind ... I could see it retreating into the distance ... as I took each euphoric step ... towards ... the adventures of crossing the city through its reeling night-time streets' (Bolger, 1991a, p. 36). The horror arises at the blurring of boundaries that is a concomitant of modernity, or, more accurately, at the peculiar cohabitation of tradition and modernity that characterises contemporary Ireland. In the upstairs/downstairs relationship described above, it is rural traditionalism that is upstairs and implicitly dominant, keeping both the liberatory potential of modernity (figured by young people and marijuana) and the perverse reification characteristic of modernity (prostitution and masochism) downstairs and hidden. It is even more of an affront that this is taking place in the city. Modernity in Bolger is both exhilarating and alienating, but the alienation derives from the persistence of the rural, its ability to co-exist with modernity. Consequently, the ideological polemic of the novel is directed at the idea of a bourgeoisie that has rural origins. Bolger would not fully recognise Marshall Berman's description of modernity, which stresses both the joy and anguish of modernity, as well as its capacity to transgress *all boundaries*, geographical, political, cultural (Berman, 1982, p. 15). That is, Bolger attributes the 'anguish' of modernity to its domination by a rural culture that is, finally, monolithic. He can see that rural Ireland has experienced deracination and trauma *in the past* – this is what brought Hano and his family to Dublin – but not in the present. In the present, Irish rural culture and ideology, as exemplified by the Plunketts, is consolidated. The anguish and trauma of modernity may be experienced by the Plunketts in psychic terms – this is expressed in their perverse homosexuality – but it does not affect their power, which is expressed in the totalising vision enunciated in the words of Hano's boss at the Voters' Register's Office. Mooney (from Monaghan) tells Hano ominously: *'I see everything in this office'* (Bolger, 1991a, p. 28). This power is present in spatial terms also. It is expressed in Shay finding that he cannot escape the 'bog Irish', even in Europe (Bolger, 1991a, p. 206). They are the invisible co-workers who beat him up when he supports equality for Turkish and European labourers, and they are present in Patrick Plunkett's horrific sexual assault on him. Ireland has become a totally administered society, where there is no escape from the circle of corrupt power.

The 'bog Irish' and their scandalous presence on the continent become the most striking aspects of Shay's discovery of the contradictions and ambiguities of modernity. If Leitrim or Kerry are the 'country' to Dublin's 'city', then, in this novel, Europe is the 'city' to Dublin's 'country'. Unlike Dublin, however, Europe is represented as exclusively urban. It is a place of factories, railways, shacks, restaurants, bars, clubs, cafes and brothels. Dublin, paradoxically, contains pastoral spaces, like the Botanical Gardens, where Shay and Hano enjoy strolling, or the Fifteen Acres in the Phoenix Park, where they play soccer on Sunday afternoons.

The novel, and O'Toole's article, are based, then, on a belief in the incompatibility of an ideology based on tradition and an economic practice based on modernisation. What both fail to account for is the fact that the construction of a cohesive nation-state was often a precondition for the development of industrial capitalism in European history. This is not to deny that it is a contradiction, in an era of multinational capital and international institutions such as the European Union. The Republic's problem has been precisely that it has engaged in national modernisation in the era of multinational late capitalism. But Bolger and O'Toole take 'traditional Ireland' at face value when they attribute such power to it as we see in *The Journey Home*. Furthermore, the *Bildungsroman* form is one which dramatises on the level of the individual subject the universalising narrative of modernity that nationalism proposes at the level of the ethnic group. Luke Gibbons points out that the ideology of valorising rural Ireland was, as I suggested earlier, one produced by the Revival, that is, urban middle-class intellectuals for the most part, and he goes on to demonstrate that this image of rural Ireland was not a matter of *continuity* with the past but rather a *break* with the past (Gibbons, 1988, pp. 208–10). The Arcadian imagery conformed to the real experiences of country people no more than to those of city-dwellers. In fact, the imagery of a national pastoral idyll served the 'modernisers' of the 1960s very well, by masking the discontinuities that were to disadvantage country people further, and by inhibiting their potential resentment and resistance. The fact is that Bolger and O'Toole are closer to their Revival antagonists than they think. Both Yeats and Dermot Bolger proceed from an assumption that nationalism and modernity are incompatible. To Yeats, modernity represented a levelling tendency in society, a social degeneracy and corrupt materialism that was incompatible with the noble new people-nation he imagined. To Bolger, modernity should wash away the atavisms of sectarian nationalism. But nationalism is an aspect of modernity (Anderson, 1991; Gellner, 1983) and capitalist development has for much of its history been driven by the nation-state. Bolger and O'Toole forget that capitalism has served to differentiate and fragment space as much as to homogenise it. Bolger takes this vilification of nationalism to the extreme of comparing the victims of the Plunketts, especially Katie and her junkie companions, to the Jewish victims of the Holocaust (Bolger, 1991a, p. 246), thus conflating state nationalism and totalitarianism. The polemical point is to suggest that modernity in the Republic has been betrayed by nationalism; this forecloses any discussion of the nature of modernisation itself, or of the kind of modernising development initiated by Lemass. This approach, however, is typical of the novel, and of Bolger's work more generally, which tends to depict the condition of Irish modernity, but not to offer a sustained analysis of it.

On the formal level, the rural is the locus of Bolger's omniscient realist narrative (the account of Hano's and Katie's escape to Leitrim), whereas the urban, in its chaos, exhilaration and terror, can only be rendered subjectively, in Hano's and Shay's narratives. However, this formal split undermines the novel's polemical drive. Bolger is forced in two contradictory directions. The first is to produce a subjective narrative – Hano's autobiography, spoken to the sleeping Katie – marked by an overmastering will to name, enumerate, tabulate, in almost obsessive empirical detail. This produces an account that is at once subjective and yet yearns for authority. But, if we accept that realism is a narrative mode of stability and totality, dependent on the availability of an accepted and hence authoritative metalanguage, then for Bolger to produce an omniscient realist narrative of the city would be to collude or identify with the totalising ruralist discourse of Mooney. Bolger's problem is how to discuss the 'state of the nation' in such a way as to evade the incorporating stabilities of the state, which he believes is corrupt, and of the nation, which he believes no longer exists except in the degenerate rhetoric of Plunkett's party. Yet representational realism is precisely the narrative mode that Bolger adopts to describe the flight through the countryside. The irony is then that Bolger produces a narrative that while apparently critical of rural ideology, manages to collude with the elisions made by precisely that ideology in its idealised representations of the country.

By this I mean that Bolger's description of the countryside, as compared to Dublin, is one which almost entirely suppresses *work* as an element of rural life. Hano and Katie steal vegetables from a 'tiny field', worked by an 'old man ... his felt cap pulled down, oblivious to the weather' (Bolger, 1991a, p. 185). They even rest by a dolmen, at which point Bolger informs us that 'The only sign of man was the high-frequency wires strung out between humming pylons that bisected the sky. Otherwise the landscape looked the same as had greeted druids who tramped here to lay down their dead thousands of years ago' (Bolger, 1991a, p. 146). Opposed to this primeval image are only the crude depredations of short-term, irresponsible, cynically commercial, ruthless exploitation, or the colonising presence of the German woman who now inhabits Katie's parents' cottage (Bolger, 1991a, pp. 95–107). From this one concludes that for Bolger the country would be acceptable if only it was devoid of its actual denizens. The rhetoric that is associated with the country is that of the Plunketts, one of power and of material interests. Poverty, underemployment, emigration, disillusionment and also labour – or its repression in the form of the dole queue – become prerogatives of the city. Raymond Williams made the point admirably:

> This teeming life, of flattery and bribery, of organised seduction, of noise and traffic, with the streets unsafe because of robbers, with the crowded rickety houses and the constant dangers of fire, is the city as itself: going its own way. A retreat to country or coast, from this kind of hell, is then a different vision from the mere contrast of rural and urban ways of life. It is, of course, a rentier's vision: the cool country that is sought is not that of the working farmer but of the fortunate resident. The rural virtues are there but as a memory ... What is idealised is not the rural economy, past or present, but a purchased freehold house in the country, or 'a charming coastal retreat', or even 'a barren offshore island'. This is not then a rural but a suburban or dormitory dream. And it is in direct reaction to the internal corruption of the city: the rise of the lawyer, merchant, general, pimp and procurer; the stink of place and of profit; the noise and danger of being crowded together.
>
> (Williams, 1993, pp. 46–7)

Bolger's characters may not be 'fortunate residents', but the description holds nevertheless. Other than the link of the Plunketts and their political party (which is transparently the Fianna Fáil of the early 1980s Haughey administrations, with their atmosphere of corruption and invocation of the stalest traditional nationalism), *The Journey Home* fails to suggest the connections between rural and urban economies. Bolger is open to the idea that the European core may exploit peripheral Ireland: this is what is so offensive about the Germans, who accumulate wealth at the expense of the continent's margins (Ireland, Turkey) and, on that basis, are able to buy out the landscape of the margins there to fulfil their variously post-apocalyptic and primitivist fantasies. But in Bolger's Ireland, the capacity of the core to exploit the periphery is only to be measured by the extent that the country has succeeded in conquering the city. Thus, Bolger ends up producing a discourse of the countryside that is not, in fact, so far from the Revivalists that he so resolutely seems to be turning away from.

Appropriately, then, in the Irish countryside that Hano and Katie traverse in the course of their escape from Dublin, it is visions of a modernising rural economy, of man's domination of nature, that draw negative associations. Just before Katie and Hano reach the woods in Sligo owned by the 'old Protestant woman', Hano's secret friend from his boyhood travels, with whom they aim to shelter, they happen upon a political rally in a nearby village. It is a gathering to celebrate the victory of the local candidate of Plunkett's party which has just won another general election. The exultation of the villagers, an apparently monolithic, undifferentiated mass, is expressed in 'animal roars' and screams that are 'wild' and 'inhuman' (Bolger, 1991a, pp. 231–2). A platform speaker reminds the villagers that 'we have always looked after you and you have always looked after us', and promises a new parish hall and sports complex (Bolger, 1991a, p. 233). He bullies the local Gardaí into not endorsing pub licences in the event of all-night drinking: 'There are no guards here tonight, only Irishmen'. This is a negative caricature of clientelist Irish rural politics; it is also based on a widely-rumoured incident involving Brian Lenihan in the early 1980s. But Bolger's point is not only to lodge his narrative in the immediate past, but to give a portrait of the political face of modernisation in rural Ireland. Any opposition to it is dismissed as the irrelevant opinion of a 'fucking jackeen' (Bolger, 1991a, p. 183). Thus Bolger castigates the rural bourgeoisie and petit-bourgeoisie in terms which paradoxically recall J.M. Synge's revulsion at their 'rampant double-chinned vulgarity' (Synge, 1983, p. 117). This is the element in rural society that is responsible for the ostracisation and victimisation of the 'old Protestant woman', who refuses to sell her remaining land to permit her neighbours to expand their holdings. It is also responsible for the crass and irresponsible despoiling of nature that the old woman tells Hano about.

It is in the company of the Protestant woman that the couple finally take refuge. It is at this point that we have circled back to almost Yeatsian ground. The former mistress of the local 'Big House', the old woman now lives in a caravan, a refugee on her own land (as Hano and Katie are internal exiles) while her home runs to ruin. However, unlike Hano, Katie and Shay, she has succeeded in making a relative virtue of her homelessness. She is the lode-stone of the novel's moral geography, as well as its narrative endpoint. Formerly a landowner and therefore an agent of power in the countryside, she is now as outcast as the couple she takes in. It is with this woman that Hano and Katie, or, as they have become at the end of the novel, Francis and Cait (Bolger, 1991a, p. 189), find a redemptive space; in Bolger's terms, 'home'. The old woman is a metaphor for many things. She stands for liberal enlightenment, for internationalism as against nationalism, for a non-sectarian spirituality. She is an updated and subversive version of Cathleen Ni Houlihan, except that she shelters her son rather than sending him out to fight for her 'fourth green field'. Of course, she has lost most of her fields, and they are no longer green, because of local industrial pollution (Bolger, 1991a, p. 180); this explains her advocacy of green politics. It is worth remembering at this point that ecology frequently manifests itself in the discourse of Romantic anti-modernity, which was also an element of the Celtic Twilight. As Gibbons suggested, this was an ideology produced overwhelmingly by *urban* intellectuals, cut off by capitalist reification from the real material links between the city and its rural hinterland. Compared to Hano's parents, who actively worked their garden plot in the city, the old woman keeps her woods for spiritual reasons only. In her 'green' consciousness and somewhat 'New Age' spirituality (she is given to hugging trees in moments of stress), she figures an authentic, because un-modern and un-capitalised, non-instrumental relationship to nature. At the novel's conclusion, she, with Hano and Katie, are held to have transcended the system, where they are simply marginal to it. Politically and existentially, the old woman is summed up thus:

> One wall of the caravan held rows of pictures from her past: the house before the war; her family who were all dead; friends from around the world; everyone from street traders in Morocco to political prisoners in Turkey. She fought a hundred causes from the caravan. The post-man brought mail from The Kremlin, Chile, South Africa, and places Hano had never even heard of. The only government she had no correspondence with was her own ... it was as if she had withdrawn from

her own land, knowing it was impossible to change the Plunketts who carved it up, and had concentrated on creating her own country within her caravan instead.

(Bolger, 1991a, p. 178)

Clearly, Anderson's 'imagined community' is here no longer limited or sovereign (Anderson, 1991, pp. 6–7). But the old woman's transcendence of the system is also her abandonment of hope in it, and part of Bolger's rather hysterical polemical linkage of Irish state nationalism and totalitarianism (change is possible in the Soviet Union and South Africa, but not in Ireland).

When the young couple take shelter in the basement of the 'Big House', this act is preceded by a ritual laying-to-rest of the ghost of a former servant of the house who, wrongly accused of theft, had committed suicide. Leading Hano down the stairs reading from the Bible, Katie frees the ghost. Then she turns to Hano and says 'It's time you came home, Francis' (Bolger, 1991a, p. 280). Home, Hano announces in the last sentence of the novel, is the arms of Katie, redemption comes in the love of a woman and the continuity implied in the son he is certain he has fathered upon her. It has also come in the reconciliation of the two social groups that Brown suggests were marginalised at the foundation of the Free State: the Protestant minority and the working-class (Brown, 1985a, Ch. 4). This is implied in the exorcising of the servant's ghost, and his replacement by Hano and Katie. We are back to an upstairs/downstairs arrangement again, in a decayed Ascendancy home. O'Toole suggested that the malign literary influence of the country over the city was to be found figured in the 'pull of the past' and in the attraction of the 'knowable community' where the individual knows his/her place. As examples he cited the tenement dramas of O'Casey and Behan (O'Toole, 1985, pp. 114–15). That, however, is precisely what we find here in Bolger. After brutalising encounters with urban modernity, Hano and Katie flee to the country. There they make common cause with and shelter in the home of a member of the former Ascendancy. Cut off from their immediate past by crime, internal exile and disillusionment, Hano and Katie retreat to a deeper past, with the 'old Protestant woman', who, displaced from her home, is similarly cut off. The entire negative inventory of the old woman's Ascendancy patrimony is cancelled out by her poverty and exile. In the old woman's spiritual reconciliation with the ghost of the wrongly-accused servant, and her alliance with Hano and Katie, who, after all, are but peasants at one remove, we see an reinvention of what E.P. Thompson called the 'moral economy', whereby the rural social system is ideologically understood in terms of paternalism and a reciprocal dependency, as against economic exploitation (Thompson, 1971; Lloyd, 1993, pp. 140–7). The irony in this is that, as F.S.L.

Lyons and David Cairns and Shaun Richards with their differing emphases make clear, the Ascendancy antiquarianism of the early nineteenth century and the Celtic Twilight of the turn of the century both projected idealised relationships between Ascendancy and peasantry, that strategically bypassed the burgeoning Roman Catholic middle-classes that threatened the Ascendancy the most, and constituted the primary motive force of Irish nationalism (Lyons, 1979, p. 28; Cairns and Richards, 1988, pp. 25–8). At this point one realises the appropriateness of the Raven Arts invocation of Swift. Michael McKeon has pointed out Swift's alignement with a strain of Tory radicalism, that produced an alliance, in early eighteenth-century England, of a 'backwoods gentry' and the urban poor, in the name of a conservative anti-capitalism (McKeon, 1987, pp. 170–1). This appears to be precisely the partnership that is being resurrected here. Hano and Katie may not be the idealised peasantry envisaged by Yeats, but they are the true dispossessed, the detritus of nationalised modernity. In their condition of stripped-down, almost negative identity ('Just be your fucking self', Katie tells Hano early in the novel), the young couple have passed beyond class and beyond national identity. So also has the old woman, and thus their sense of community is predicated on an individualist, humanist subjectivity. Yet, as I said before, this community is distinctly reminiscent of an earlier Yeatsian 'organic' society. The future is positively envisaged only in the conservative dynastic or filiative sense implied by the son Katie will bear Hano:

> Woods like this have sheltered us for centuries. After each plantation this is where we came, watched the invader renaming our lands, made raids in the night on what had once been our home. Ribbonmen, Michael Dwyer's men, Croppies, Irregulars. Each century gave its name to those young men. What will they call us in the future, the tramps, the Gypsies, the enemies of the community that stays put?
>
> I do not expect you to wait for me, Cait. Just don't leave, stand your ground. Tell him about me sometime; teach him the first lesson early on: there is no home, nowhere certain any more. And tell him of Shay, like our parents told us the legends of old; tell him of the one who tried to return to what can never be reclaimed. Describe his face, Cait, the raven black hair, that smile before the car bore down and our new enslavement began.
>
> ... Sleep on, my love. Tomorrow or the next day they will come. I will keep on running till they kill or catch me. Then it will be your turn and the child inside you. Out there ... commentators [are] discussing the reaction of the nation [to the election results]. It doesn't matter to internal exiles like us. No, we're not exiles, because you are

> the only nation I give allegiance to now ... When you hold me, Cait, I
> have reached home.
>
> (Bolger, 1991a, pp. 293–4)

Here we find an implied narrative of victimhood as simplistic as any
Whiggish story of eight centuries of national struggle. Here we find a retreat
from *Gesellschaft* to *Gemeinschaft*; in the place of the nation, the patriarchal
nuclear family as the ideal locus of identity-formation; the fathering of children as the centre of social reproduction; a woman as the redemption of a
fallen man. The irony is that these tropes have all been mobilised before in
the service of precisely the project of nation-building that Bolger purports to
reject, even transcend, so decisively. Here we find a dismal shrinkage of the
geography of hope, resistance and the imagined future community. *The
Journey Home*, it seems to me, narrates a return to putative origins that in its
sentimentality, reconstructed traditionalism and attenuated historical vision
is in fact a sorry shadow of the ideology and social system that Bolger set
himself, and O'Toole had wished for him, to oppose. It would seem, therefore, that neither Bolger nor Doyle, at least partly because of their reaction
against an aesthetically radical but apparently institutionalised Modernism,
have found a way of avoiding the nets of Romantic Revivalism. Therefore,
one is forced to conclude, without wishing to dismiss the movement *tout
court*, that the most prominent figures the 'Dublin Renaissance' has yet produced have thus far failed to create a true alternative to the tradition from
which they are in flight.

CHAPTER 4

Film and politics: Neil Jordan, Bob Quinn and Pat Murphy

Here I hope to demonstrate that the political and cultural ambiguities of the post-Lemass modernisation and its discontents in terms of which I believe the work of Friel, Banville and Bolger can be understood, also are traceable in major Irish films of the period. But I wish to start with some remarks that will link my discussion very directly with the Lemass period. Firstly, film, along with television, is the cultural product most obviously *of* the 'age of mechanical reproduction' of the forms that I have considered (Benjamin, 1992, pp. 211–44). Since it is a capital-intensive activity, it unsurprisingly displays a relationship to economic and political vicissitudes that one could reasonably call 'mechanical causality' (Jameson, 1981, p. 25): film, as an industrialised art, reflects the processes by which the Free State/Republic has 'peripherally postindustrialised' (Jacobsen, 1994, pp. 10–17), often in relatively crude, direct and unmediated ways. Secondly, as a collaborative and expensive art-form, the production of a 'national' cinema is difficult in a small marginal economy, and therefore, by its very nature, film goes far in exploding any comforting narrative of economic nationalism or autarky that the nation may tell itself.

These issues are set out conveniently for us in the two main strands of Southern state policy towards film, the cultural and the industrial. Kevin Rockett points out that, since Independence, the state has overwhelmingly regarded film production as an industry, the main interest of which is its capacity to attract foreign capital and provide employment (Rockett, Gibbons and Hill, 1988, pp. 95–122). This attitude has been evident from a time that long predates the opening of the economy to multinational investment in the late 1950s, though Sean Lemass was the central exponent. As early as 1946 and 1947, as Minister of Industry and Commerce, Lemass made two submissions to Cabinet, which expanded on the report of an Inter-Departmental committee set up in 1938, *The Film in National Life* (completed in 1943, but never published). Lemass proposed investment of £500,000 on a National Film Studio, and guarantees on capital investment in film. He was opposed by Frank Aiken, Minister of Finance, who espoused a version of the 'cultural' argument, suggesting that state money should be spent 'on the production of Irish films by Irish organisations', and not on facilities that while attractive to foreign producers would not suit low-budget indigenous production. A decade later, the house and estate of Ardmore, outside Bray, Co. Wicklow, was purchased by Emmet Dalton and Louis Elliman for their production company, Dublin Film Productions Management. They were encouraged by their success with two play adaptations, *Professor Tim*, originally written by George Shiels, and *Boyd's Shop*, by St John Ervine, in 1957. Lemass aided the studio with a grant from the Industrial Development Authority, and a loan from the State Development Bank, the Industrial Credit Company. Rockett writes:

> In his opening address on 12 May 1958 Lemass emphasised the employment and export, rather than cultural, value of the studios. He said that it was marking an important development in the economic history of Ireland and as such the occasion was one of great national importance.
>
> (Rockett, Gibbons and Hill, 1988, p. 99)

In the priority given to the 'economic' as against the 'cultural' imperative, and the concomitant and somewhat paradoxical conflation of the 'economy' and the 'nation', one recognises Terence Brown's observation of Lemass' ability to cast economic development, in the absence of an accompanying intellectual project, as nevertheless a national project to rival or displace the 'National Question' (Brown, 1985a, pp. 246–7).

The history of Ardmore, as Rockett goes on to chart it, is characterised by the same pattern of economic pragmatism or 'modernisation' as described earlier, in the hope of some kind of notional 'trickledown' effect taking place in the economy of the Republic from the presence of foreign capital or international film productions. Most of the time, this proved to be a pious hope. Even at the level Lemass projected for it, that of facilitating international productions, the Ardmore studio was an abject failure, changing hands repeatedly through the 1960s, and going into receivership three times by 1973. In 1980, Louis Marcus estimated that, since 1958, £10 million (at 1980 prices) had been lost by the state through Ardmore (Rockett, Gibbons and Hill, 1988, p. 103). It failed utterly in providing opportunities for Irish film-making, or the development of a skilled Irish film workforce. For example, in 1960, Dalton persuaded the Industrial Credit Corporation to set up the Irish Film Finance Corporation. Marcus has called this 'an inducement to foreign film producers to use Ardmore', and, according to Rockett, it

> ... almost inevitably led to a restrictive agreement between Ardmore management and the English film technicians union, ACTT, whereby Ardmore would be regarded as a UK studio for purposes of Eady

finance, if only ACTT members were employed on these productions. Any lingering hope of Irish people gaining experience on visiting productions vanished.[1]

(Rockett, Gibbons and Hill, 1988, p. 100)

This situation was of no more benefit to Irish film producers than to technicians. Securing backing from the IFFC meant providing a guarantee of distribution, and this was almost impossible for small, unknown Irish film producers operating in the British exhibition market which was dominated by Rank and ABC. The result was that British producers, already benefitting from Eady finance, could also avail of IFFC funding. So the ironic situation obtained that British film production in Ireland, which because of the ACTT agreement excluded Irish labour, was being assisted by Irish state finance. A better example of dependent development could hardly be wished for.

Films made at Ardmore have, overwhelmingly, been international productions. In the early years, under the aegis of Dalton, a series of adaptations of Abbey plays were made. International productions with Irish settings and themes included *Shake Hands With the Devil* (1959), *A Terrible Beauty* (1960), *The Quare Fellow* (1962), *Girl with Green Eyes* (1963), *Ulysses* (1967), *Paddy* (1969), *Philadelphia Here I Come!* (1970) and *The Mackintosh Man* (1973). The cultural irrelevance of the Irish location of the studio was demonstrated by the fact that films having nothing to do with Ireland were made there, such as *The Spy Who Came in from the Cold* (1966) and *The Vengeance of Fu Manchu* (1967).

Rockett suggests that the experience of Ardmore led governments to espouse a policy of direct aid to film production in the 1980s, where the stress before had been on the provision of fixed plant. Nevertheless, the state remained interested chiefly in the idea of developing a commercial, non-subsidised industry, even though it was the 1980s that saw the life of Bord Scannán (The Film Board), a state aiding agency, with only £500,000 annually at its disposal, and which, according to Rockett, 'made the most significant contribution to the development of an Irish cinema' (Rockett, 1994, p. 128). Bord Scannán was founded in 1981; it was shut down in 1987. In that time, it part-funded ten feature films, twenty short fictions and documentaries for television, as well as fifteen experimental shorts. It also grant-aided script development and pre-production work on sixty projects (Rockett, 1994, p. 129). The Finance Act of 1987 included two tax schemes, Section 35 and the Business Expansion Scheme, which provided new tax breaks to encourage film production. '$9.4 million' (*sic*) was invested in eleven projects under the

---

1 'Eady finance' was a funding pool for British film production set up by the post-1945 Labour government, based on a levy of cinema ticket sales.

auspices of Section 35 in the period 1987–92; '$1.18 million' (*sic*) was raised by ten projects under the BES in the period 1987–91.

The period from September 1992 to March 1993 saw a flurry of positive developments in Irish film culture. In September 1992, the then Taoiseach, Albert Reynolds, opened the Irish Film Centre in Dublin, a facility which houses theatres, a library and the National Film Archive. Mr. Reynolds also announced the establishment of a Working Group on the Film Industry with a brief to report in three months. Before that report was completed, there was a change of government (in January 1993) to a Fianna Fáil/Labour coalition, which resulted in Michael D. Higgins being appointed to the position of Minister for the Arts, Culture and the Gaeltacht, the first time an arts minister had been given full Cabinet status. In March 1993, on the morning that Neil Jordan's Oscar for *The Crying Game* was announced, the Government revealed that the Film Board (Bord Scannan) was being resurrected, with an annual budget of £2.5 million. New tax schemes, related to Section 35 and the BES, were also announced, and the 'cap' on RTE's advertising revenue (its main excuse for the curtailment of the commissioning of independent productions) was lifted (Rockett, 1994, pp. 130–1). The beneficiaries of this grant-aid in the 1990s have been predominantly international productions.

From the mid-1960s onwards, State cultural policy relevant to film changed. Censorship laws pertaining to literature and film were relaxed. (According to Rockett, the first forty years of Independence saw the banning of approximately 3000 films and the cutting of approximately 8000 more: Rockett, 1994, p. 128.) The 1973 Arts Act increased the Arts Council's budget and permitted it, for the first time since its inception in 1951, to make funds available for film. One significant expression of this was the institution in 1977 of the Arts Council Film Script Award. Other, less defined (and not necessarily mutually supporting) developments included the growth of a cadre of Irish art school graduates, from both the Republic and the UK, who began to experiment in cinema; film-makers and technicians who had gained their experience in State-sponsored documentaries or in television work in RTE, or in commercial advertisments began to experiment with fictions; lastly, film societies such as the Project Arts Centre and the Irish Film Theatre contributed to the production of a cine-literate audience.

These developments helped to produce a generation of independent film-makers in the Republic in the 1970s who had a powerfully self-conscious relationship both to Irish cultural traditions and to the mainstream of international film production (represented in Ireland most concretely, but not solely, by Ardmore). Such activists included Bob Quinn, Joe Comerford, Thaddeus O'Sullivan, Pat Murphy, Cathal Black, Kieran Hickey, Neville Presho, Tommy McArdle, Robert Wynne-Simons and Neil Jordan.

It will be immediately clear that the developments here outlined parallel significantly the development of 'revisionism' discussed earlier, and that the rise of the group named parallels the resurgence of violence in Northern Ireland. If one also acknowledges the censoriousness of the atmosphere surrounding the exhibition of film in the Republic, the wave of attempts by the independent film-makers, to engage with social and political change in Ireland, with the recrudescence of violence and with the 'tradition' of filmic representations of Ireland (mostly international in origin), that characterised the 1970s and 1980s becomes understandable. My intention is to look most closely at two independent productions of this period, as it has been in the independent sector that the most sustained critical engagement has taken place. This engagement, with society and politics, with history, with stereotypical representations of Ireland in film, and with film language, can all be understood as being related to the 'revisionism' debate, often in the more self-conscious sense I have discussed in Friel and Banville. The issue is neatly set out by Luke Gibbons, who writes that

> From its beginnings in the early decades of the present century, Irish cinema has been dominated by a number of pervasive and inter-connected themes: the idealization of the landscape, the legacy of the past, the lure of violence and its ominous association with female sexuality, and the primacy of family and community.
>
> (Gibbons, 1983, p. 149)

It follows, then, that films that engage with this traditional imagery, which has been formidably buttressed by a host of productions ranging from *Man of Aran* (1934) to *Far and Away* (1992), are those that should interest us most. The danger remains, even then, of a film being appropriated back into the tradition to which it has opposed itself. However, before I move on to such a discussion, I should make some interlinked comments about the films of the two most commercially successful Irish directors to date, Neil Jordan and Jim Sheridan, the commercial sector as such, and the ideology of geography that may suggest links between the political aesthetic of commercial films and their independent counterparts. For the fact is that such commercial films can often be seen as 'revisionist' in the more conservative sense, and to fall back into the repository of traditional images that Gibbons sets out for us, as well as other regressive tendencies in film.

In distinguishing between the independent and commercial sectors, I am drawing attention to the constraints that film-makers working in the latter may be subject to. Commercial directors are, generally, more likely to be restricted when it comes to self-conscious experiment, to the exploration and challenging of genre, mostly because of the perceived audience or constituency that the film is being pitched to by its producers. Even when a film is not Irish-produced, marked differences may arise between films that are funded or sponsored by the British Film Institute or Channel 4, and those with more explicictly commercial backers. In many ways paralleling the literary or paraliterary activity of Dermot Bolger and the Raven Arts writers were a series of films made in the 1980s, both independently and commercially. Small-budget films made by first-time young film-makers concentrated on Dublin as a locus of urban decay, crime, unemployment, drug culture, violence, powerlessness and alienation. Films such as *The Courier* (1987) and *Joyriders* (1988) in the commercial sector, and *Pigs* (1984) and *Boom Babies* (1987) in the independent sector produced images of 1980s Irish modernity that were almost uniformly bleak and hostile. These films were the home-produced pessimistic analogues of the international productions of the 1980s and early 1990s, such as *The Commitments* (1991), *The Snapper* (1993) and *My Left Foot* (1989). In *The Commitments* and *The Snapper*, we see the adaptation of Roddy Doyle's almost narrationless novels into the filmscripts they so resemble. Novels almost totally lacking social texture or context are translated into a world of urban-decay-turned-post-industrial-*chic* (*The Commitments*), and working-class-estate hermetic detachment (*The Snapper*). Of necessity, the medium of film must provide these narratives with a greater sense of physical location than was the case in their novelistic manifestations, where place was cultural or linguistic rather than physical (or risk a commercially unacceptable theatricality). So, the abundance of references to mass culture – television programmes, music, newspapers, fast food – found in the novels gives way in the films to more traditional international stereotypes of 'Irishness', such as loquacity, bucolic jollity, vulgarity, 'soul'. We also see increasingly familiar signs of Dublin urban geography, such as the Ballymun apartment towers (which also featured prominently in Doyle's television series for the BBC and RTE, *Family*, 1994), the Dublin Area Rapid Transit (DART) railway system and industrial or postindustrial wastelands.

In the films of the major new commercial director to emerge in the late 1980s, Jim Sheridan, we see a landscape, whether rural or urban, of nostalgia. In *My Left Foot*, a vision is presented of 1950s and 1960s Dublin that is almost Victorian in its sentimentality. The film depicts a working-class culture of honest hardworking men, and stoic suffering wives. The humanity of a tortured and imprisoned soul (Christy Brown's) is given expression through the heroism of his mother, and his surrogate mother (the doctor who gives Christy therapy and who realises that he has literary and artistic 'talent' and ambitions). The narrative that results is a gratifying 'portrait of the artist as a young handicapped man'. It portrays the progress of this man from his mother's kitchen floor, where he reveals his ability to write, to the street outside, where the 'lads' incorporate him into their football games, to his hospital therapy, and eventually to the launch of his autobiography in the home of a member of the Ascendancy, where in the company of the philanthropic 'great and good', he gains pleasing bourgeois acceptance. This progress is mirrored by his increasing spatial freedom and mobility, as he moves from the claustrophobic confines of his parents' terraced house to, at the end of the film, the announcement of his engagement atop Killiney Hill in south Dublin, with its panoramic views of the sea and the city suggesting the final delightful freedom from the ghetto and his social class that the hero has attained. This has been achieved through an aesthetic, 'transcendent' conception of artistic activity and, paradoxically, his disability, which has served to bring his innate humanity into greater relief.

In Sheridan's *The Field*, we see a similarly humanist and nostalgic re-working of John B. Keane's play. The play was written in 1965 and set in North Kerry in the late 1950s, but Sheridan relocated it in 1930s Connemara. Sheridan focussed the film more resolutely on the central character, 'The Bull' McCabe, who was played by Richard Harris, a recognisable international 'star'. This downplays the social context of the narrative (a conflict over possession of the field of the title between McCabe, the long-time tenant, and a returned emigrant with modernising ambitions), because the magnetic presence of a star marginalises lesser characters and shifts emphasis onto a humanistic notion of individual acting 'performance'. Sheridan's screenplay also excised an array of references to the accoutrements of modern life and to modern technology from the play, which made explicit the play's context in a modernising society. The play, with its emphasis on social conflict and change, is thus transformed, in the film, into a contest of human will and conscience. Keane's setting, on the eve of the Lemass modernisation, and the fact that his returned emigrant was coming back from England, gave his play a much sharper socio-political edge than Sheridan's film. In the latter, the returnee was an American (played by another recognisable star, Tom Berenger), and the period being the 1930s allows the film to set a much more comfortable distance between its primitive, almost elemental characters, and its audience in 'modern' Ireland, which is thus saved the trauma of recognising its own recent past. Sheridan's moving the physical location of the film to the beautiful and rugged terrain around Killary Harbour, on the mountainous border of Mayo and Galway, as against the pastoral country of North Kerry, also permits him to frame the action in such a way as to make McCabe's drama one of epic human struggle with the wilderness. Thus, his motivation shifts from being one of simple economic investment in the field, to some much more romantic love of the land itself. In conclusion, it is worth mentioning that in *Into the West* (1992), a film directed by Mike Newell, an Englishman, from a script by Sheridan, the narrative is predicated on the flight 'into the West' of Ireland of the two children at the centre of the story. The fact that this journey is effected on back of a magical white horse named Tír-na-nÓg (recalling that used by Niamh to lure Oisín away from the Fianna) lifts the film onto the level of fantasy, but not before it has sketched in the now-typical portrait of Dublin as a city of crumbling modernist tower blocks and urban deprivation. It also relates the film to the Western, and reminds the viewer that a persistent trope of Irish films of this time (both independent and commercial) was 'the road', where alienated (mostly urban) characters take a kind of refuge in mobility (mostly in the countryside). This motif of deracination and quest appears in such films as *Hard Shoulder* (1990), *Joyriders*, *Traveller* (1982), *Angel* (1982) and *Reefer and the Model* (1988). In *Into the West*, certainly, we find that, as in the case of Dermot Bolger, the project of critical modernism is thrown out in a blind critique of the results of uneven modernisation, a kind of replay of Yeatsian geopolitics, with its nostalgia for 'Romantic Ireland' in the face of the 'greasy till'.

It may seem perverse that I do not intend to deal at great length with the career of the Irish film-maker of the highest profile to have emerged over this period, Neil Jordan. He produced a very substantial body of work beginning in the early 1980s, mostly British or American-financed, overwhelmingly in the commercial sector: *Angel* (1982), *The Company of Wolves* (1984), *Mona Lisa* (1986), *High Spirits* (1988), *We're No Angels* (1989), *The Miracle* (1990), *The Crying Game* (1992) and *Interview with the Vampire* (1994). Jordan wrote the script for Joe Comerford's *Traveller*, and has had a successful career as a short-story writer and novelist. Of these films, *Angel, High Spirits, The Miracle* and *The Crying* Game could be considered as 'Irish', in that they treat of Irish subjects, Irish characters or Irish locations. However, I have felt that, for reasons I will outline below, these films do not step usefully beyond the confines of traditional representations outlined by Luke Gibbons.

Most obviously, in *High Spirits*, Jordan tried to produce a kind of 'Big House' film, and fell foul of the market-driven expectations and requirements of his Hollywood backers. The story of the owner of a dilapidated Anglo-Irish country house who in an effort to raise money turns his home into a 'haunted castle' hotel for (American) tourists, and is then perturbed to find that his machinations awaken real ghosts, the film might have been a cinematic examination of the Irish Gothic in a contemporary setting, and ought to have been, according to Jordan, 'the Marx Brothers meets A Midsummer Night's Dream'. It became instead a crude star vehicle for Darryl Hannah and Steve Guttenberg, and a demonstration of special effects. Jordan was very unhappy with the result, and effectively disowned it, calling the production 'a dreadful heartbreaking experience' (Maher, 1995, p. 17). *The Miracle* was conceived by Jordan as a way of returning to his roots and to the kind of smaller, non-Hollywood project with which he had originally made his name. Set in Jordan's home town of Bray, Co. Wicklow, it is an Oedipal story of an adolescent boy who falls in love with a mysterious older woman who turns out to be his mother. This theme of awakening and ambivalent or potentially transgressive sexuality is a recurrent theme in *The Company of Wolves, Mona Lisa, The Crying Game* and *Interview with the Vampire*. The concern with sexual identity and ambiguity is reprised in *The Crying Game*, a much more ambitious film where conflict that finds its origins in the 'national question' is displaced into the realm of sexual politics and the private sphere. This is not necessarily a criticism of *The Crying Game*, which boldly mixes issues of national, racial and sexual identity in a manner rare in a mainstream film. It replays the theme of the 'reluctant gunman' familiar from earlier British films about Ireland such as *The Informer, Odd Man Out*, and *A Prayer for the Dying*, and it also interestingly presses the kind of relationships between enemies, prisoners and their captors portrayed in Frank O'Connor's famous short story 'Guests of the Nation' to new limits. Nevertheless, it is noticeable that the representation of, arguably, progressive sexual politics in the film does not preclude the indulgence of negative stereotypes in relation to nationalism and 'terrorism'. This relates the film to the anomalous condition of Irish postmodernity. By this I mean that peculiar conjuncture that has led to a situation where, as Desmond Bell suggests, aesthetic postmodernism is espoused in the *absence* of a powerful indigenous modernism. Bell, it will be remembered, noticed how Irish postmodernity is characterised by a variety of 'post' discourses, that are predicated on historical movements or narratives that have not, in fact, taken place or been completed in Ireland:

> We are experiencing for example – in the sphere of economic ideology, 'monetarism' without a prior social democracy; in politics a 'new right' without an old left, 'post-nationalism' with the national question materially unresolved; at the social level, a return to family values without the advances of feminism; at the cultural level, the nostalgia and historicist pastiche of 'post-modernism' without the astringent cultural purgative of modernism.
>
> (Bell, 1988, p. 229)

So, in this case, we find a film engaging in a typically postmodern displacement of *national* identity by *sexual* identity.

John Hill delineates two broad approaches to Irish subjects taken by British films and those of Hollywood respectively (Rockett, Gibbons and

Hill, 1988, pp. 147–93). While American cinema, because of the Irish presence in the United States as both activists (most famously John Ford) and as audience, is able to take a pastoral or nostalgic view of Ireland (again, most famously, and commercially successfully, in Ford's *The Quiet Man*, 1952), British cinema, being closer to the governance of Ireland, is more likely to take a dark view of the country. Of these two views, Hill argues that

> both sets of images imply a contrast between the characteristics of Irish society and those of an apparently advanced and modern civilisation. In the former case, this usually assumes the form of a lament for the simple virtues of rural life which the advances of urban-industrial society have destroyed. In the latter, it is more usually a lament for the Irish themselves and their failure to accomodate to the standards of reason and order characteristic of a modern and 'civilised' society.
>
> (Rockett, Gibbons and Hill, 1988, p. 147)

Hill relates the inclination of British cinema to work within the second of these imagologies to the long history of imperial discursive constructions of the Irish dating back to Giraldus Cambrensis and Barnaby Rich. He points out that the persistent attribution to the Irish of the stereotypical characteristics of 'indolence, superstition, dishonesty and a propensity for violence' helps to shift the colonising project into the terms of a civilising mission, but also begs the question as to *why* the Irish so doggedly resort to violence and refuse the benefits of that civilisation (Lebow, 1976, p. 78). According to Hill,

> The answer, of course, was implicit in the designation of the Irish as violent. Violence, in this respect, was not to be accounted for in terms of a response to political and economic conditions but simply as a manifestation of the Irish 'national character'. By this token, the proclivity for violence was simply an inherent characteristic in the 'nature', if not the blood, of Irish natives ... For what British films about Ireland maintain is not simply the traditional inclination to portray the Irish as violent but also the inability to provide a rational explanation for the occurrence of violence. Two main attitudes to violence predominate. In the first case, violence is attributed to fate or destiny; in the second, to the deficiencies of the Irish character. Both attitudes share an avoidance of social and political questions. It is only metaphysics or race, not history and politics, which offer an explanation of Irish violence.
>
> (Rockett, Gibbons and Hill, 1988, p. 149)

Hill goes on to explain that differences in British and American cinematic narrative traditions account for differences in attitudes to violence as a theme. In the American tradition, violence is containable in the narrative; indeed, it is often, in such genres as the Western or the gangster film, a necessary dynamic force that is used to resolve problems and overcome difficulties. So, it is a major component of what Hill calls 'the positivism and dynamism of American cinema' and supports a teleological ideology of film narrative (Rockett, Gibbons and Hill, 1988, p. 151). In British film, however, violence is problematic, a troubling force that upsets generic conventions such as the 'light comedy or domestic drama', where narrative tends to the circular rather than the linear, and where the status quo is re-affirmed rather than change being instituted. So, in British film, violence is the problem, which must be resolved by the narrative. Hill writes that

> be it comedy or problem drama, violence in the British cinema characteristically thwarts drives and ambitions, indicates character flaw or lack of self-identity, exacerbates problems and tensions and signifies either regression or fatalism.
>
> (Rockett, Gibbons and Hill, p. 152)

Hill concedes, of course, that British cinematic representations of Irish violence are not simply monolithic and unchanging. Films rework old images to meet current political and social contingencies, and also to match generic requirements. Nevertheless, a definite continuity is traceable between such films about IRA violence as *Odd Man Out* (1947) and *Shake Hands with the Devil* (1959), and *The Long Good Friday* (1979) and *Cal* (1984). That *Cal* was directed by an Irishman (Pat O'Connor) and adapted from his own novel by a Northern Irishman (Bernard MacLaverty) ought to alert us to the degree to which Irish cultural production can be interpellated by traditions or ideologies from outside the island. As is evident in the case of Jim Sheridan, Irish writers and film-makers are no less capable of producing ahistorical stereotypes than their international colleagues. This is Hill's persuasive case against Jordan's *Angel*. So, he takes issue with the unhistorical critique provided by Richard Kearney, who suggests that

> *Angel* debunks the orthodox portrayal of Irish political violence and deromanticises several of its stock motifs – most notably that of the national hero at arms. Rather than conforming to any specific ideology, this film exposes the hidden unconscious forces which animate ideological violence, irrespective of its Republican, Loyalist or British Imperialist hue. Jordan's cinematic exploration of the psychic roots of

violence permits him to cut through ideological conventions and discloses that fantasy world of inner obsessions which, he believes, is the source of both our political and poetic myths.

(Kearney, 1988a, p. 175)

Hill rightly points out the similarity between this film and *Odd Man Out* and demonstrates the degree to which it portrays Northern violence as incomprehensible and destructive. By adopting highly self-conscious aesthetic and formal strategies (a script dense with literary allusion, non-naturalistic dialogue, settings and lighting, traces of *homage* to *Point Blank*, the director of which, John Boorman, was a mentor of Jordan's and who was Angel's executive producer) the film produces a putatively 'universalistic' or 'pure' portrayal of violence, stripped of all context. The film's revenge narrative is entirely negative and futile. (But if, as Luke Gibbons suggests, masculinity, violence and sublimated sexuality are the values on which the *affirmative* role of the hero of classical narrative film are based, it is difficult, *contra* Kearney, for the film to wholly escape the lure of the violence of which it purports to offer a critique.) But the production of an image of violence that is explanatory only at the metaphysical level simply renders all social or political explanation irrelevant. All violence is placed on the same level. It is disingenuous to suggest that the film lacks all context, in spite of its aesthetic techniques. It is recognisably set in Northern Ireland. One must then consider the implications of such a 'universalising' discourse on violence in terms of media and other images of the Northern conflict. If the violence of the 'lone gunman', Danny, who, is the anti-hero of the film, is decontextualised and 'purified', then so is that of agents of the state. Indeed, the final killing in the film, by a policeman, of another man holding Danny at gunpoint, is not portrayed in any detail or from the point of view of the killer. Thus, murder, or 'ad hoc execution', by the state is not shown to have any of the unpleasant or troubling psychic consequences that Danny's revenge killings have had. This is what would be required for Kearney's essentialistic analysis of the film to hold true. So the film turns out to be true to the form that Hill establishes for British films, that is, affirmative of the status quo. Notably, Hill compares the film's portrayal of Northern violence to comments made by Philip Schlesinger about the media portrayal of the North generally:

> Philip Schlesinger, for example, suggests how British television's coverage of Northern Ireland has relied on 'a series of de-contextualised reports of violence' which have failed 'to analyze and re-analyze the historical roots of the conflict'. And this, he continues, cannot but help

to reinforce a dominant view of the 'troubles' as 'largely incomprehensible and irrational'.

(Rockett, Gibbons and Hill, 1988, pp. 177–8;
Schlesinger, 1978, p. 243)

To Schlesinger one can add remarks made by Edward Said, who has written cogently on the rise to public prominence of the discourse on 'terrorism' in the 1980s. Said alludes to the fact that the 'very indiscriminateness of terrorism, actual and described, its tautological and circular character, is antinarrative.' Furthermore, '[S]equence, the logic of cause and effect as between oppressors and victims, opposing pressures – all these vanish inside an enveloping cloud called "terrorism"' (Said, 1994a, p. 257). Said has also pointed out that

> In the contemporary contest between stable identity as it is rendered by such affirmative agencies as nationality, education, tradition, language, and religion, on the one hand, and all sorts of marginal, alienated, or, in Immanuel Wallerstein's phrase, antisystemic forces on the other, there remains an incipient and unresolved tension. One side gathers more dominance and centrality, the other is pushed further from the center, toward either violence or new forms of 'authenticity' like fundamentalist religion. In any event, the tension produces a frightening consolidation of patriotism, assertions of cultural superiority, mechanisms of control, whose power and ineluctability reinforce what I have been describing as the logic of identity.
>
> (Said, 1994a, p. 353)

Said and Schlesinger together remind us of the wider discursive context of films such as *Angel*, and of the relationship between the production of such films and the political and military struggle in Northern Ireland, at a time when the political-discursive struggle to name the 'Troubles' as either 'political' or merely 'criminal' was extremely intense. *Angel* was made at the time that the IRA hunger-strikes in the Maze prison were underway. These hunger-strikes, and the consequent deaths of ten 'volunteers', firstly and most famously Bobby Sands, led to a surge in support for Provisional Sinn Féin. They originated in protests by republican prisoners for their 'political' status to be acknowledged, something to which the Thatcher government in the UK seemed resolutely opposed. To this we can also add the evidence of the British Army manual *Land Operations*, in which is to be found the accumulated knowledge of dozens of counter-insurgency operations: it speaks of dealing with 'a technique of revolutionary warfare that relies mainly on popular support for its success', and consequently defines a primary military objective as being to isolate the enemy 'physically and psychologically from their civilian support' (Curtis, 1984, p. 229). In this light, representations of the insurgent that portray him removed from his social, economic and political context, that dehistoricise him and deprive him of a narrative to place him and explain him, so that he appears to burst on the scene in the manner of one of his own 'outrages', take on a kind of 'worldliness' and discursive power that overrides Kearney's analysis and lets us see that, in this case at least, the aesthetic project and the project of state security are coterminous. The only narrative permitted Danny is that of revenge (the 'terrorists' he pursues murder a beautiful young mute woman with whom he makes love early in the film), and he finds that violence has a logic of its own. Thus the need to contextualise violence is obviated – it is all a matter of the irrationality of a lonely and pathological individual. Of course, this also has the useful effect of reducing state violence to the level of error, or the action of a 'maverick', who falls outside the rationalities of the system.

Unfortunately, there is little evidence in *The Crying Game* to suggest a change of approach. Here we find a reluctant gunman, Fergus, who (as in 'Guests of the Nation') befriends his hostage, Jody, makes the mistake of revealing his identity to the hostage, and undertakes to visit his girlfriend and break the news of his death to her. The IRA hideout is raided and destroyed by the British Army, the hostage is accidentally killed by an Army vehicle in the process, the other members of the IRA cell are apparently killed. Fergus disappears to London, disguises himself as a building labourer, and tracks down Jody's girlfriend, Dil. Before he can bring himself to tell Dil what has happened, he finds himself becoming emotionally and sexually attracted to her. At this point, he discovers that Dil is in fact a cross-dressing man. Fergus initially recoils from Dil at this discovery, but before he can resolve the relationship, his old IRA colleagues re-appear and entrap him in a fresh plan to assassinate a senior British judge, as a test of his commitment which had been deemed lacking in the previous operation. The new plan goes awry because of Fergus' involvement with Dil, one of the terrorists is killed and the other tries to kill Fergus, only to be shot by Dil. Fergus sets himself up as the killer and serves his sentence, visited, supported and loved by Dil.

The Crying Game purports to be a radical and unsettling exploration of identity. However, it halts that exploration at certain crucial points, which mostly concern Ireland, nationalism and insurgency. It is true that the film gives a sympathetic portrayal of a 'terrorist'. Fergus, it is true, is not a conventionally masculinist national hero, and chooses at the end of the film to declare his love for another man. But the difficulties arise when we look at the boundaries that cut across the narrative. Kevin Maher has suggested that the film was ... deconstructing political and sexual differences in front of more people than it could have possibly imagined.

In its most basic state the film is about border crossing, about breaking boundaries, and removing parameters/perimeters. It is an act of clarification, carrying a formal element that permeates the entire film.

(Maher, 1995, p. 17)

The problem with this formulation is that while it correctly draws attention to the play on gender distinctions that the film sets up, it pays insufficient attention to the resultant displacement of these distinctions into the realm of the political. In other words, an examination of the narrative and semiotic grounds of possibility of the union of Fergus and Dil reveals a structure as ahistorical, depoliticising and even reactionary as anything in *Angel*.

Maher, and the film, seem to set up a facile homology between sexual and political identities. Maher suggests that the film is concerned with 'border crossing', a metaphor at variance with 'deconstruction', which properly ought to have more to do with the *dissolution* of borders. But the film actually leaves a surprising number of boundaries in place. Fergus and Jody may exchange personal information while the latter is held hostage, but it is Jody's social background and community that is explored, when Fergus moves to London. Ireland is left behind, as the place of violence and of public politics. Fergus moves to England, and must adapt, if not to civilised society then to 'pluralism' in terms of sexual choice. But this pluralism also extends to race: Jody is represented as a successfully assimilated black Englishman, who remarks that Northern Ireland is the only place where he is called 'nigger' to his face, and who would have no difficulty in passing Norman Tebbit's infamous test of allegiance in terms of cricket. Jody is from Tottenham, and so has been comfortably 'civilised', an implicit example to Fergus, the Irish *kern*. The film is not interested to develop the issue of the politics of race in the British armed forces; even though Jody tells Fergus that soldiering is for him 'only a job', his very professionalism and therefore putative objectivity is a figure for the standard British assertion of neutrality in the Northern conflict, a claim that is not beyond contest. It is difficult, then, to avoid comparison between the representation of the Antiguan British soldier Jody, and the *Paris-Match* cover image of an African soldier saluting the French tricolour made famous by Roland Barthes in his essay 'Myth Today': both stand as figures of the successful assimilation to the metropolitan culture of the formerly colonial oppressed (Barthes, 1973, p. 116). Here, in *The Crying Game*, it is Fergus, named for the great mythic Ulster hero who defected to the army of Queen Maeve, who changes. In Ireland, we see a sexual seduction that is deceptive (that of Jody by Jude, Fergus' female colleague, named for the patron saint of lost causes), because it is prostituted (and indeed, Jude's appearance in this scene is that of the 'tart', in dated miniskirt, big earrings and blond hair) to the interests of war and of violence. In England, we see a seduction that is a deception in the interests of love (that of Fergus by Dil). If Ireland is the space of 'public' politics, then England is the place of the 'private' politics of the private and sexual sphere. This formulation thus constructs England as an apolitical public space, which is of course an obviously ideological notion. The film utilises the geographical divide between Ireland and England, it pre-supposes their political and economic interconnection, but evacuates this interconnection of any historical or political content. The film is profoundly uninterested in *why* Jody is serving in Northern Ireland, in why Fergus is fighting him, in *why* it is in fact entirely plausible for Fergus to take refuge in the heartland of his 'enemy'. Behind each of these narrative moves or geographic inscriptions lies a massive complex history of conquest, resistance, territorial acquisition, economic interpenetration and dependence, decolonisation, unemployment and impoverishment, migration and ghettoisation. All of this is stripped away, leaving us with a gratifying image of the 'good terrorist', who finds the space for love and the expression of his true humanity in England.

As if to confirm this, we have, in the sudden re-irruption of Fergus' violent former comrades (who it transpired survived the Army attack on the hideout) into the narrative (negating its movement in much the way described by Hill and suggested by Said), the appearance of the 'bad terrorists'. Most interestingly, and negatively, the worst of these terrorists is Jude, the aggressively heterosexual woman. Sarah Edge has recently provided a powerful critique of the film's representation of women and Jude especially (Edge, 1995). Jude, Edge argues, is the transgressive character in the film, in that she aggressively steps outside of the subject-position allotted her under the patriarchal symbolic order – she is sexually aggressive, and also militantly so. She has 'de-natured' herself by virtue of her assertive sexuality, and her aggression. So she, unlike Dil, whom Fergus courts in the most conventional manner, is not a 'real' woman (although she is the only female character in the film). In the film's first scene, Jude demonstrates her 'de-natured' sexuality by luring Jody into an IRA ambush. During his captivity, Jody, who has been educated to believe that the Irish are all 'tough … motherfuckers', who will not release him because it is not in their nature, tells Fergus a fable about the scorpion who is given a ride across a river by the kindly frog, but who cannot resist stinging the frog 'because it is in his [the scorpion's] nature'. This is followed by a scene where Jody accuses Jude of having no compassion; she pistol-whips him, revealing herself to be a 'scorpion'. As Fergus says, 'she can't help it'. Fergus, in contrast, takes the hood off Jody's head, and treats him gently, revealing his froggish amenability to interpellation by the ideological narrative of humanity and civility. So, interestingly, as Fergus and Jody bond, become more 'feminine' and thus display the ability to transcend their 'nature', Jude is shown to be stuck in her 'unnatural' (because republican and feminist) 'nature'.

In London, Jude's re-appearance makes explicit the film's weaving together of the most regressive images of assertive, feminist women (characteristic of films such as *Fatal Attraction* (1987), *Basic Instinct* (1992) and *Disclosure* (1994)) and the woman terrorist. Jude returns as a femme fatale, appearing initially surrounded by shadows, with a black sharply defined bob wig and bright red lipstick. But while Jude may alter her physical appearance, her 'nature', scorpion-like, cannot change. To emphasise the point, Jude is given a haircut by the shape-shifting Dil, as is Fergus. But Fergus' alteration is more than skin-deep. The film's underlying misogyny is suggested by the image of a woman being educated in the ways of feminine beauty by a man who has colonised femininity. Jude's kinetic unstoppability recalls Alex Forrest, the psychotic, sexually predatory, careerist woman who troubles the all-American, middle-class family in *Fatal Attraction*. She is 'hard', a 'bitch': on meeting Fergus again, she grabs him by the genitals and orders him to 'fuck' her. But she is also a 'terrorist', and hence doubly bad and doubly transgressive. Jude is now the 'phallic woman', complete with lethal firearms, returned, having been repressed, from the space of deceitful and failed relationships (Ireland), to split and terrorise the dyad that has been possible in England. As Edge puts it,

> Within this film it may be possible to see an analogy between Jude as a member of the IRA who threatens boundaries in relation to 'colonial' power, and national/cultural identity and Jude as a transgressive woman who also threatens the imaginary border between what Kristeva describes as 'the paternal law' of the father and the place of 'maternal authority'. In this sense, it is possible to read the character of Jude as threatening two borders that separate order from disorder – where the stable and dominant definitions operate to legitimize the existing orders of society.
>
> (Edge, 1995, p. 180)

As a transgressive woman, Jude's fate is to be either recovered for the patriarchal order (married off), or punished. The latter, of course, is her fate: she is shot dead. Again, her violence is given no social depth or context. Like the 'good' (because self-doubting, and hence 'human' and reformable) 'terrorist', the 'bad terrorist' does not emerge from any kind of social or political narrative, formation or history. Moved only by personal revenge, the obverse of the sexual lust that is her 'unnatural nature', Jude explodes tautologically into the narrative. Her offensiveness lies precisely in her status as narratively uncontainable.

This, then, is the space of possibility of Fergus' and Dil's union. Their mobility, their humanity, their 'femininity' (or 'New Man' sensitivity) is made possible because the space of the feminine has been evacuated by the unwomanly Jude. On the same basis, one can say that Fergus' assimilation into civility is made possible by the destruction of Jude, the feminist republican terrorist. Fergus' mobile human masculinity is set over against Jude's static, inhuman, voracious, excessive femininity.

If Jordan's films have exhibited a tendency to ahistorical reproduction of certain stereotypes, a powerful rejoinder exists in the work of Bob Quinn, one of the most important and certainly the most prolific major independent filmmaker in Ireland in the 1970s and 1980s. From *Caoineadh Airt Uí Laoire* (Lament for Art O'Leary, 1975) to *The Bishop's Story* (1993), Quinn's work has been marked by an uncompromising will to confront and debunk stereotypes, to challenge the Irish film industry and its imbrication with the international industry, and to generally offer itself as an *oppositional* cinema (Said, 1985b, pp. 157–8). In this sense, he has challenged not only traditional stereotypes but the ersatz 'modernity' and cosmopolitanism that was ushered into the Republic with the Lemass/Whitaker programmes after 1959. Quinn worked in RTE in the 1960s, until he left in 1969, when he set up Cinegael, a film production company, in Galway, which has produced all his independent work since. He has also written a novel, *Smokey Hollow* (1991).

Caoineadh Airt Uí Laoire was made in 1975, a commission by Official Sinn Féin. This in itself is enough to make the film of interest, since that party was undergoing a period of intense strain and change at the time. The failure of the IRA Border campaign of 1956–62 to produce any serious shift in Southern policies with regard to the North or to any significant change in the style of governance of Northern Ireland (indeed it led to internment on both sides of the Border) had led to a shift to the Left in Sinn Féin, and the development of a grouping less interested in the 'national question' as it had been traditionally conceived, and more interested in an all-island class politics. This group was also prepared to compromise on the question of abstentionism (the traditional Sinn Féin policy of refusing to take up seats won in either Leinster House or Westminster). This trend culminated in the split between the 'Provisional' IRA and the 'Official' IRA, and a concomitant split in Sinn Féin. It was encouraged cynically by elements of the Fianna Fáil government in the Republic (who were nervous about the emergence of a potent fusion of republicanism and socialism) and exacerbated by the resurgence of violence in the North. This schism might also be understood in North/South terms, although the 'Official' IRA was involved in early military activity in the 'Troubles', and 'Provisional' Sinn Féin was initially known as 'Sinn Féin, Kevin Street' after the location of its Dublin headquarters. This quarrel and trend manifested itself in 'Official' Sinn Féin's changing its name to 'Sinn Féin – The Workers' Party'. Since the 1970s, the party has undergone further changes of political hue and of name, dropping 'Sinn Féin' in the early 1980s, and then splitting again in the early 1990s, to become 'Democratic Left'. These changes are as much related to developments in 'actually-existing socialism' and the collapse of the state socialist regimes of Eastern Europe, as to Irish politics. But *Caoineadh Airt Uí Laoire* is about revisionism of a specifically Irish nationalist kind, much as its sponsors may have passed through Marxist revisionisms later. It is worth mentioning here that the Gaelic poem on which the film is based has also been re-appropriated and re-worked by more recent literary-historical revisionism, specifically that of Dermot Bolger, whose play *The Lament for Arthur Cleary* is an adaptation of the poem to his concerns in 1980s Dublin. This point reinforces the point made earlier that Bolger's writing, for all its disavowal of the discourse of the nation, remains as imbricated with that discourse as the literary modes that it sees itself as replacing.

The *Caoineadh* is a Gaelic poem, a lover's lament, spoken for Art by his wife Eibhlín Dhubh Ní Chonaill, in the wake of his murder by the bodyguard of the High Sheriff of Macroom, Co. Cork, Abraham Morris. Ó Laoire was one of the 'Wild Geese', the Gaelic Roman Catholic gentry dispossessed after the Williamite victory in 1690, and socially, economically and politically disempowered by the Penal Laws of the early eighteenth century. After many years' mercenary service in the Hungarian Hussars, Ó Laoire returned to Ireland in 1767, only to run foul of the new dispensation. The actual incident took place in 1773. The poet was a member of the O'Connell family of Derrynane, Co. Kerry, and an aunt of Daniel O'Connell.

Quinn's film is both a re-telling of the story of Art, and a Brechtian reflection on that re-telling, its circumstances and on the contemporary resonances of the poem and its story. The film gains further significance in that it was the first independently-produced film in the Irish language and, in fact, 'the first independent fiction film produced in Ireland since Tom Cooper's non-professional feature, *The Dawn*, made in 1936' (McLoone, 1994, p. 158). It was a collaborative effort, with the English playwright John Arden, and the Corrandulla Arts and Entertainment Club. It is worth adding that the film was made at a time when a retreat by the state from the commitment to Irish language restoration was counterpointed by an expansion in the mass youth market for Irish traditional music.

The film's dramatic scenario is that of a theatre group in contemporary Connemara rehearsing a 'mixed media' performance based on the *Caoineadh*. The director (John Arden) is an Englishman, by turns arrogant, patronising, exasperated and despairing of his cast of bilingual locals. The 'performance' involves filmed sequences which shift between realism (for example, Art rides, in eighteenth-century costume, through Macroom) to Brechtian self-consciousness (the camera pulls back from Art, to reveal that he is riding through a modern Irish town). A further level of reflexiveness is added when the actor playing Art (who is himself called Art) interrupts the showing of the film, objecting that 'Macroom' is in fact Galway. So we have a film within a play within a film. Roughly, the film's narrative follows the final years of Art's life from his return from Europe, through his marriage to Eibhlín, to his fatal confrontation with Morris. The narrative is, however, continually broken, and verisimilitude is constantly affronted by various alienating effects, most obviously, direct address to camera, by both characters in the costume drama film, and by contemporary characters or 'actors'. This makes explicit the passive complicity of the viewer in the filmic construction of the putatively authoritative illusion of reality. In addition, the viewer is confronted with another set of 'viewers' watching a film and reacting to it. Further, the scenes in the film-within-a-film of the 'past' are deliberately non-naturalistic – actors are in costume, but the impression is theatrical or pageant-like. The film sets up a series of polarities (audience vs. film, past vs. present, illusion vs. reality, history vs. myth, Irish vs. English (both linguistically and ethnically)) and sets out to shatter them. Authority (of narrative, of history, of the national hero, of the director of the 'performance') is inscribed, only to be unsettled.

The film is exceedingly rich, but not without its problems. It attacks the myth of the national hero, by portraying Art as arrogant, selfish, and loutish. It at the same time attacks the English, both in the form of the New English planter and the English theatre director. Both are shown to be smug, patronising and dismissive of history. The film opens with a quotation from James Connolly: 'Fortunately, the Irish character has proven too difficult to press into respectable foreign moulds' (Connolly, 1987, p. 21). The film's portrayal of the mutually antagonistic relationship between director and Art (the actor), and Morris and Art Ó Laoire, demonstrates in fact that the 'Irish character' has been quite susceptible to 'foreign moulds', but that these 'moulds' have been created partly in the effort to rationally govern (or direct) the Irish. Stereotypical behaviour (the director's alternately patronising and hectoring treatment of his actors) is shown to be in a mutually reinforcing relationship with other stereotypical behaviour (Art, in both past and present, is rude, disruptive, given to drink, self-occupied and hence an irritant to his Irish brethren). To this extent, authority is seen to be justified in its treatment of him.

This represents a considerable act of courageous demystification in the context of the heroic tradition of Irish nationalism, and coming in a film sponsored by the political inheritors of the national revolution. Given the relationship between those inheritors and the embattled Northern minority, it could also be understood as an act of revisionist betrayal. Tomás MacGiolla, leader of Sinn Féin – The Workers' Party, wrote of the film at the time as follows:

> [It] is not another exercise in futile probing of myths, but essentially a comment upon reality in the present Ireland of 1975 ... Defiance and resistance are not enough in themselves to liberate a people. Courageous campaigns of resistance, however noble their inspiration, will fail like the gesture of Art O'Leary if they try to ignore realities ... Romantic acts of heroism or defiance may inspire people but will never organise them.
>
> (Rockett, Gibbons and Hill, 1988, p. 138)

In other words, the vanguardist, 'blood-sacrifice' model of nationalist resistance, leadership and authority is being left behind, in favour of one that is *answerable* to a collectivity.

In the parallels the film draws between colonialist attitudes in the past, and the persistence of stereotypes and exploitation in the present, it is exemplary. Indeed, its willingness to confront politics generally, Anglo-Irish relations and the nationalist tradition head-on is rare and honourable in Irish film. However, this does not save it from eliding issues of class and gender in conservative ways, and also from betraying unease with its Brechtian formal techniques.

In regard to feminism, the film debunks nationalism's traditional masculinism, in showing that, while Art's murder leaves his wife and children bereft, his confrontation with Morris may have had as much to do with the macho posturing of a man with a tenuous grip on spousal and paternal responsibility, as with insurrection. The film's appropriation of a female narrative of grief, however, is not as critical or as reflexive as one might expect. The relationship between Art and Eibhlín played out in the film-within-the-film is ironically counterpointed with the fraught relationship that obtains between the actors who portray them, which emerges in the cracks forced self-consciously in the narrative. But ultimately, towards the film's conclusion especially, when past and present are blended increasingly seamlessly, the film reinforces a standard nationalist trope of femininity: that of Deirdre of the Sorrows. The primary role offered the female characters, past or present, is that of service to male authority. In the past, Eibhlín's choice is between father or lover. In the present, authority is vested in Art or the director. It is these male figures who provide narrative and semantic coherence. No space is opened for female agency, save in opposition to other women (Eibhlín's quarrels with her mother and sister over Art) or in collusion with the imperial English director (when the director complains about Art's use of Irish on the set, one of the actresses remonstrates with Art, saying that 'when in Rome, one does as the Romans do', to which he replies 'This is the bloody Gaeltacht!'). This lack of space for female agency is crucially linked to the lack of fully reflexive hermeneutical rigour in the film's use of the text of the poem as its structuring principle. This becomes clear early in the film immediately after a dramatised quarrel between Eibhlín and her mother over the use of Irish – Eibhlín regards any use of English as a sell-out, her mother is more pragmatic – when there is a sudden cut to Eibhlín, in costume, reciting the poem in a graveyard, with a ruin behind her. This amounts to a very traditional Revivalist image of Irish femininity. Consequently, the film depends on the poem as a literal, unmediated discourse of truth and humanity, and therefore can only allow Eibhlín to embody and enunciate grief. So the film disappointingly raises the issue of patriarchy (in actor-Art's chauvinist public remark that actor-Eibhlín is not fit to play a virgin, for instance) only to resolve it at the film's end with actress and actor dancing happily at the ceilidh held to celebrate the end of the rehearsal.

The issue of class is very important in the film. Again, it opens the issue up, only to eventually hide it in moving towards its conclusion. The narrative voice-over of the film-within-the-film tells us that Art 'straddled the lines between oppressor and oppressed'. This both alludes to Art's class position – that of a displaced aristocrat – and elides it with the categories of race and nation. The film highlights class division in various ways: its staging of the quarrels between Eibhlín and her mother and sister over Art; in its recounting, in voice-over, of complaints to the newly-formed Muskerry Constitutional Society in 1771 about Art's 'depredations on the poor people of this district'; in its description of Art's spurning of the Whiteboys and Ribbonmen, the rural secret societies that were the vehicles for land disputes in the eighteenth century; and lastly, in its enumerating of the Penal Laws, only to have Art intrude on the voice-over telling us that the historic Art was, as an aristocrat, mostly unaffected by them. However, this critical movement is negated by the return of an increasingly coherent narrative towards the film's conclusion. After we are informed by the voice-over of Art's final decision to confront Morris, the movement between past and present, between the conflict between Art and the director in the present, and Art and Morris in the past becomes increasingly seamless, broken only by shots of Eibhlín, in costume, reciting the poem. Thus past and present converge in an unproblematic narrative of insurrection. This illustrates the point that insurrectionary nationalism must finally fold the dissenting discourses with which it is initially in alliance (class and feminist politics) back into itself. The antics of the present actor-Art no longer undermine the heroics of the 'historic' Art. In fact, the 'rebellion' of the 'historical' Art is given a spurious communal legitimacy by the general insurrection against the director that takes place in the present, most explicitly in the cast's refusal to 'allow' Art to lose the horse race he enters, illegally, and in which he lost his mare. Inveighing against 'folk memory' and 'myth', the director instructs the cast to 'forget the tradition that Ó Laoire won the race'. But the cast is heard cheering on after the point when Art is meant to have 'lost'. The director is furious, dons the Morris costume, challenging the actor-Art to hand over the mare, which if it won the race must be worth more than £5 and hence beyond Art's legal entitlements. He attacks the actor in the rehearsal hall, who then pushes him over. So we see the director pouring scorn on 'folk memory' but partaking of the distortion of history in order to assault Art. The director's strictures on 'myth' and 'folk memory' inevitably resonate with statements made in the early 1970s by historians such as T.W. Moody and F.S.L. Lyons. This contemporary political resonance is even clearer in the depiction of the killing of Art, which is preceded by the director haranguing the cast about the necessity to be rational about such events, and telling them that with proper history-teaching, 'the North would never have happened'. This scene is intercut with apparent documentary interviews with liberal Southerners questioning Northern violence. The actual killing is performed with Eibhlín reciting the *Caoineadh* on the soundtrack. The director pompously reminds her that the poem is 'not ... Shakespeare', telling her she is being 'too emotional'. By now, the director has been constructed as the repository of inauthenticity, so his words serve in fact only to validate the poem.

The film ends with the cast attending the funeral of the historical Ó Laoire, which is broken by Art admonishing the viewer: 'If you think this playacting means my sort is finished, you're mistaken. Come, we'll drink to it.' The film then cuts to a contemporary traditional music session in a pub; Art enters, in part-costume, and dances with actress-Eibhlín. Thus, the film ends on a defiantly insurrectionary, but rather traditional note. It has succeeded in moving from an initial scepticism (in regard to history, authority, narrative, vanguardist revolutionism, the cinematic apparatus) to a position rather more comfortable with what Said has called 'the rhetoric of blame' (Said, 1993, p. 19).

The difficulty arises in the issue of historical interpretation. Firstly, the film, for all its cinematic Brechtianism, seems to have very little problem in integrating the discourse of the poem with that of documentary history, but in a way that takes little cognisance of the historical and ideological contexts out of which the poem emerged. The director enunciates such concerns, but at a point when whatever authority he once had has been thoroughly discredited. So, as suggested earlier, the poem emerges increasingly as a touchstone of authenticity in the film. This is not to say that the film suggests that the *cinematic* representation of the past is unproblematic – its techniques of theatricality, the use of hand-held cameras, the direct address to camera of costumed actors serve to deflect such thinking. But the poem itself is untouched, its interpretation is literal.

The opposition that arises between the old poetic narrative and the confused, broken and debatable modern one has, initially, at least two implications. Firstly, it denies the possibility of a Whiggish interpretation of the earlier 'events'. They are not now available for incorporation in a heroic and self-congratulatory narrative of legitimisation of the present. When the actor-Art yells 'Aha! History repeats itself!' when in confrontation with the director, he is correct, but what is unclear is the degree to which he is aware of the farcical nature of the repetition. So the viewer's attention is drawn to what separates the two sets of characters as much as to what unites them. Secondly, realisation of the shambolic nature of the contemporary forces the viewer to reassess his or her conception of precisely what the past 'events' may have been, and to recognise the degree to which their character and status as 'events' has been discursively constructed. The jarring contrast between the 'poetry' of the past, and the demotic 'prose' of the present distances the viewer from an aestheticised *cinematic* discourse of the past.

However, the parallels between past and present that emerge as the film develops have the effect of lending a spurious authority to that present, farcical though it may be. The clash between the English director and the actor-Art becomes one in which the viewer identifies with the actor. This illustrates effectively Desmond Bell's qualms about positing a move towards the legacy of the modernist avant-garde as a way out of the sterility of choices facing the Irish media – between the public service ethos, and the cynicism of the market and bland technocratic utopianism. These choices face film-makers as much as they do broadcasters, and they emerge in the stress, explained earlier, placed on industry, economic development and job creation in the legitimising discourse of Irish film-making. The result of this stress is the assumption that interest in film 'culture' is ideological and traditional. Ironically, among the figures Bell names among the avant-garde in Ireland is that of Quinn. He writes:

> This tack is not without certain difficulties. The sort of social and political engagement entailed in the media practice of the historic avant garde ... has gone out of fashion in the cynical eighties. Many of

the actual media practices of the constructivist avant garde have passed into the stylistic repertoire of today's advertising industry or are endlessly recycled in rock video products and have returned to mock us.

(Bell, 1988, p. 227)

So this film demonstrates the problem that the techniques of the avant-garde can be recuperated and used for conservative projects. In *Caoineadh Airt Uí Laoire*, the fault is that while the imperatives of the present are allowed to disrupt and, initially, to alienate the past, the 'present' itself is not subjected to the same sceptical scrutiny. So while the 'past' is revealed as a construct, the present is allowed to remain 'natural'. Ironically, documentary techniques that alienate and lay bare the reconstructions of the past (interviews delivered to camera, the hand-held camera) actually serve to naturalise and authorise what is a fictional scenario in the present. The point is made by Fredric Jameson when he suggests that pastiche is more characteristic of postmodern cultural production than parody. Pastiche, he argues, is an uncritical parody or 'blank irony' (Jameson, 1985, p. 114). That is the critical failure of Quinn's film – it forces us to re-examine the past, but it is not above allowing us to identify with the identification of the cast with that past. It is through the present that we are encouraged to re-appropriate the past in this film, but it fails to acknowledge, finally, the means it employs to manipulate our interest – principally, the construction of authority as foreign. Thus, the film slides into a crude anti-imperialism. It is as if the twenty-six county state had never been. In this, and in its consequent failure to draw attention to policies and trends that have been damaging to historiography, the Irish language, the West of Ireland, the position of women and the working class, the film is in an oddly collusive relationship with the revisionism it purports to condemn. The film ultimately loses its way while trying, very honourably, to elaborate a critique of both traditionalism, and bourgeois humanist cosmopolitanism, as they manifest themselves in Ireland. The difficulty is that a discourse that ironises its own authority leaves itself no space from which to speak the truth.

Pat Murphy's *Maeve* (1981) is perhaps more successful, in its self-conscious strategy of bringing nationalism, history and the Northern crisis into collision with feminism. Produced primarily with the support of the British Film Institute, but also RTE, it takes its cue from both second-wave feminism and republicanism. Like Quinn's *Caoineadh Airt Uí Laoire*, it is marked by an awareness of the European New Wave cinema, but in a less theatrical manner. *Maeve* confidently combines realistic narrative with reflexive techniques such as direct address to camera, non-naturalistic dialogue, unheralded flashbacks, and at least three temporal frames. Shot composition combines conventional realistic modes and self-consciously symbolic styles.

Barbara O'Connor has suggested that Pat Murphy is Ireland's only feminist film-maker, and while younger women have appeared, and critical independent feminist film-making has moved on since 1981 (most notably through the work of the Derry Film and Video Co-Op), it would be reasonable to assert that Murphy remains the most important female activist in the field.[2] Since *Maeve*, Murphy has made *Anne Devlin* (1984), a more formally conventional but nevertheless critical feminist excavation of the biography of Robert Emmet's female assistant and comrade during the 1803 Rising. O'Connor locates Murphy in the context of a 'feminist counter-cinema', which views the forms of dominant cinema as 'essentially patriarchal' (O'Connor, 1984, p. 79). For O'Connor, the Irish independent film-makers of the 1970s, including Murphy and Quinn, were deploying ideas drawn from the European New Wave to break up dominant representations of Ireland, Irish society, landscape, politics and history in film that had been accumulated during the post-Independence period, marked as it was by censorship and conformism. As she points out, this period produced images of Irish women that stressed their subservience to male authority when they were represented at all (O'Connor, 1984, p. 79). O'Connor's analysis is vitiated by the fact that she does not distinguish between independent and commercial, local and international productions, documentary and fictions, thus eliding many contributary factors to the representation of women, notably the fact that the bulk of fictions produced in this period were international in origin and in intended audience.

The narrative premise of the film is the return to her native Belfast of Maeve Sweeney, after a period living in London. Her various interactions and confrontations with her mother, younger sister, father and former boyfriend are interwoven with flashes back to her childhood, adolescence and young womanhood before she left Belfast, and to her time in London. The film, however, is framed by sequences featuring her father. That the film will consist in a confrontation with patriarchal ideology is clear from the start, as Sweeney, watching a war film on television, is disturbed by the war on the street outside. Soldiers order him out of the house because of a bomb scare, but allow him to stay inside provided he stays at the back, in the scullery. Thus local patriarchal authority has been domesticated, feminised and marginalised, by an external authority. Sweeney writes to his daughter, his letter

---

2   The Derry Film and Video Co-Op was one of a series of regional workshops in the United
    Kingdom funded by Channel Four. Its major work has been *Mother Ireland* (1988; dir. Anne
    Crilly), a video documentary on the subject of nationalism and the representation of women,
    and *Hush-A-Bye Baby* (1989; dir. Margo Harkin), a fiction concentrating on the effect of a
    crisis pregnancy on a Roman Catholic teenager in contemporary Derry.

spoken in voice-over. The final sequence of the film consists in a long monologue by Sweeney, with the camera trained on the side of his face. Most of
Sweeney's stories in the film, with which he tries to assert his narrative and
historical authority, are delivered direct to camera, thus preventing the 'nat-
uralisation' and hence authorisation of his discourse. Here, the camera angle
and the anonymous whitish-grey background suggest interrogation,
Sweeney's surrender to the imperious gaze of the camera. His tale bears this
out: it is one of incompetence and vulnerability on his part, as he tells how his
van was hijacked by the Provos, how he was arrested and questioned at
Castlereagh (a barracks of the Royal Ulster Constabulary), how the press mis-
interpreted the story, how he is always afraid now. His ceding of narrative
authority in the film has been preceded by struggles with other forms of
political and discursive authority – the Provisionals, the state, the media – all
of which he has lost.

A major concern of the film is the gendered character of traditional
nationalist history or myth. The film self-consciously stages political discussions, in non-naturalistic dialogue, between Maeve and her boyfriend Liam,
that turn on historical interpretation. But it also demonstrates this cinemati-
cally, and in terms of its deployment of the trope of landscape. Sweeney frequently takes his child-daughter on his delivery jobs in the countryside in his
van. They visit antiquarian sites, where he tells her the mythic histories that
he calls the 'stories in the stones'. Thus patriarchal history is naturalised in its
expression in landscape. In a flashback scene that Luke Gibbons has drawn
attention to, Sweeney stands in the middle of a ring fort (which suggests that
his view of history is circular and static) reciting one of his interminable tales,
as the child Maeve creeps around the perimeter wall. The camera tracks her
movement, over which his story is heard. At the endpoint of his story, he
appears in the frame, speaking directly to camera, with Maeve in the background. At the moment that he speaks his punchline, Maeve jumps off the
wall, symbolically turning her back on her father's patriarchal conception of
history (Gibbons, 1983, p. 151).

The antiquarian, or more accurately, Revivalist, link is made more explicit
in a flashback scene of Maeve and her then boyfriend, Liam, in his bedsit. His
landlady is a spiritualist, and while she and fellow-members of the 'Irish
Society of Spiritual Awareness' conduct a seance (reminding us of Yeats'
occultism), the young couple make love upstairs. The spiritualists are disturbed by these 'noises off', and thus sexuality is seen as disruptive of the politics of Revivalism. Later, as they lie naked in the afterglow of intercourse,
Maeve muses to Liam that something as 'contradictory' as sex or a seance
may be as valid an expression of identity as 'politics'. Maeve is content here,
replete with physical love, and yet aware that the private pleasures and free-

doms of sexual activity are inevitably compromised. 'Your fantasy is acted out in a shape that fits itself to your surroundings ... these are the basic romantic needs ... we know we've barricaded ourselves in'. These remarks are a critique of both her present situation and aspirations, and also of the more public, conventionally 'political' ideologies that might replace them. 'Barricaded' is the term that permits such articulation. Sex may be an evasion of certain realities, but public political narratives of liberation may be as 'romantic' or 'barricaded'. Ideology is inevitably a product of, and therefore limited by, its conditions of possibility.

The antiquarian link is present in the three self-conscious, jargon-laden debates staged between Maeve and Liam, that mark stages in the development of her feminist consciousness. The first takes place on the Cave Hill, associated with the United Irishmen, before Maeve leaves for London. Over a panoramic panning shot, we hear Maeve intone an elliptical, allusive, associative stream of words and phrases: '... a centre, a landmark, ... a space for things to happen, a technique, a way in, way out, a celebration, a guide, a release, a lie, a truth, a lie that tells the truth, a projection, a memory'. Maeve's discourse stands in deliberate and stark opposition to that of Liam, who is struggling with the traditional linear narrative of nationalist militancy. He envies the certainty this ideological world-view gave to his father, and feels that this is evidence of its expressing the desires of the oppressed. Even if it is inaccurate, it expresses what Brendan Bradshaw has approvingly called 'purposeful unhistoricity': myth can be positively appropriated (Bradshaw, 1994a, p. 213). But Maeve, standing outside such a tradition, simply sees it as invented, and accuses Liam of retrospectively arranging the historical record to suit his present political needs. She acknowledges the importance of the past, but only as it serves a project of opening the present. To Liam's need to remember, she complains that 'the way you remember excludes me'.

Later, Liam confronts Maeve in the midst of her new, comfortably bohemian life in London. He regards her move there as an avoidance of reality. When she suggests that London's size, anonymity and multiculturalism offer her a space in which she can find herself, in an individualist sense, he is outraged. London has acquired these attributes, he suggests, through its long and bloody history of imperialist accumulation, while places like Belfast suffer the 'colonial aftermath'. If London is to Maeve a 'centre of energy' which she can enjoy, to Liam Belfast, with its violent struggle, is the true site of intensity. Their different imaginative geographies render the movement between Belfast and London in polarised ways. To Maeve, London was a place the map of which she had memorised before she arrived, a place where everything was 'focused' and where she was pleased to find things where she expected them to be. Liam, conversely, describes his journey to London as unpleasantly *inevitable* yet unfamiliar, a passage where all roads lead to London, 'like there's no choice'. London for Liam is a 'leech' that sucks people in, where knowledge is difficult to come by. For Maeve, however, it is a place of geographical and epistemological openness. It is a place she knew before she came, where she determines her own cognitive possibilities in spatial terms. It is in Belfast, she argues, with its gapped, ruptured streets and bomb sites, that spatial knowledge is uncertain They are both living out the dialectic of identity conferred on them by the colonial relationship, by what Said calls 'overlapping territories, intertwined histories' (Said, 1993). Maeve's new-found individualist identity (where she has 'the right not to know what [she is] doing') has not fully or surgically separated her from the identity her Belfast provenance has conferred on her, while Liam cannot see beyond his communal identity conferred on him by traditional nationalism.

The third major debate between the two takes place after Maeve's return, significantly as they walk through Clifton Graveyard. The degree to which their discourses bypass or block each other is demonstrated visually: tracking shots frequently place the listening interlocutor behind a tree or headstone, out of the viewer's sight. She is now intellectually more than a match for Liam. She points out to him that while he may possess a project or narrative to give coherence to his life (militant nationalism), he is in fact still conforming to the dialectic of identity of Anglo-Irish relations, a logical part of the 'fictions' of 'Southern nationalism and of English late-imperial fantasies'. But for Liam, nationalism is still something he cannot bypass, and he sees himself as striving to break out of stereotypes. From his viewpoint, Maeve's feminism is a 'copping-out', a premature utopianism. Maeve has recognised the danger of fighting the enemy with his own discursive weapons, and also the danger for feminism of allowing its project to be subsumed within that of nationalism. This has resulted, she says, not in 'a recognition of our rights, but a moderation of our aims'. The feminist alternative is to fight on the terrain of the body, hence the crucial importance of sexuality for feminism. Liam responds that the hunger strikers and 'blanket' protestors in the Maze prison (IRA hunger strikes took place in Northern Ireland in 1980 and 1981, preceded by extensive 'blanket' and 'dirty' protests) are using their bodies as weapons.[3] Maeve suggests an alliance on that basis, but Liam rejects this, seeing feminism only as a diversion, a 'separatism' that he (with unconscious irony) denounces as 'reactionary'. When Maeve questions his idea of victory (will it

3 These protests were part of a campaign for the reinstatement of political status for paramilitary prisoners. 'Blanket' protests consisted in the refusal to wear prison clothing, using only a blanket instead. 'Dirty' protests consisted in prisoners daubing their cell walls with their own faeces.

be one that, for example, permits her free access to abortion should she need it?), he can only see such questions as a selfishly individualistic betrayal of community. Liam's arrogation to his traditional nationalism of the positive values of community extends to his telling Maeve that he in fact represents the women of Northern Ireland more than she does. Ironically, this comes shortly after Maeve has described the situation of women *vis-à-vis* men as that of colonised territory.

As an alternative to the troubled and failed political relationship with Liam, Maeve is depicted tentatively assembling new relationships with her sister, Roisin, and her mother. Yet, as Gibbons points out, the film's refusal of the conventions of narrative is echoed in Maeve's own decentering, and refusal to make anything happen:

> There is no question of Maeve adopting the kind of affirmative role normally accorded to the hero in a classical narrative, for this is based precisely on the values of masculinity, violence and sublimated sexuality from which she is seeking to distance herself.
>
> (Gibbons, 1983, p. 152)

Rather, we are presented with Maeve's conversations with Roisin and her mother, as discontinuous debates and interventions, much as Said suggests is the role of the critical intellectual (Said, 1994b, Chs. 1 and 3). There are barriers to this: Roisin's anti-social pub working hours, Mrs Sweeney's desire 'to be involved with marriages and children, and all of us living in the same neighbourhood', Roisin's inclination to read the anti-patriarchal character of Maeve's feminism as simply another version of her mother's Roman Catholic view that all men wish to take advantage of women. Maeve misunderstands her mother's desire for filiative bonds with her daughter (illustrated in Mrs Sweeney's desire to keep her drawing-room as a kind of sacral space for her daughters to entertain boyfriends in, as against Maeve's wish that she would use the room for her own [Mrs Sweeney's] comfort). Maeve is inclined to see in her mother's and Roisin's traditional version of female solidarity one that is finally collusive with patriarchy. In a heavily self-conscious and lingering shot, Maeve delivers a riposte to Roisin's view. Speaking to her in the room they are sharing, as they are both naked and preparing to go out for an evening, she tells Roisin, who is looking directly into camera (which is also the implicit position of the dressing-table mirror): 'The confusion is in this place. Women's sexuality is so abused that it's almost a liberation to turn yourself into a sex object. You take on a woman's role to get out of childhood. Then you've to find a way of getting out of that'. In psychoanalytic terms, the camera/mirror is the 'ideological apparatus' that interpellates the subject and gives her unitary identity and a sense of meaning. But this process is subverted by the film's deployment of Brechtian alienating tropes, here the overlong shot, the conflation of camera and mirror, the non-naturalistic jargon-ridden dialogue. In a brilliant move, the film has drawn its viewer's attention to the cinematic process by which that viewer is constituted, and to the way the subject is offered a position in the symbolic order, precisely by drawing that process out just long enough to break the illusion of reality.

Maeve is reminiscent of a *Bildungsroman*, a 'portrait of the intellectual as a young feminist'. Like Stephen Dedalus, Maeve leaves Ireland to forge a conscience, but for a woman, this necessitates the creation of a prior feminist critical consciousness. Unlike Stephen, she returns to Belfast, to reappropriate it as female space and not to do so in terms of the old filiative family bond. The new relationship is an affiliative, feminist one, with her mother and sister, who are now 'sisters' in the politicised feminist sense. The penultimate scene of the film is of a visit they pay together to the Giant's Causeway. There, they enjoy jokes and a drinking session. As Maeve watches the waves pounding the rocks, she is approached by a strange man, filmed from threatening low angles, who tells her a tale suggestive of Ulster Protestant exceptionalism: he claims to have counted the columns of the Causeway, finding only one out of a total of 38,000 that was not six or seven-sided. Asked which it is, he has forgotten. As Maeve climbs away from him, out of the frame and then back into it but now above him and hence implicitly reversing their roles, the man starts to recite parts of the Ulster Covenant of 1912, his voice rising to a yell. Turning their backs on him and the sea, the three women walk shoulder to shoulder inland, in a gesture reminiscent of Maeve's childhood rejection of her father's narratives in the ring fort. Gibbons has suggested that here female solidarity is asserted in the face of landscape, a visual trope usually romanticised in cinematic representations of Ireland (*Ryan's Daughter*, 1970, would be a famous example of this, though *The Field* repeats the trope). The rejection extends to traditionally conceived histories, as represented by the man speaking the Covenant, and the cultural nationalist narrative implied by the Causeway, with its association with the Ossian myth (Rockett, Gibbons and Hill, 1988, p. 247).

So we find, in *Maeve*, a critical cinema that can debunk traditional political ideologies (nationalism, unionism) without falling into an alternative authoritarianism, whether that is expressed in terms of history or in terms of narrative coherence. We also see a film that can be critical of the British presence in the North, or at least its military manifestation, without slipping into 'the rhetoric of blame'. This is illustrated, firstly in the scene where soldiers stop Maeve and Roisin in the street and order them to jump, so that they (the soldiers) can leer at the women's breasts. Secondly, it is demonstrated in

Roisin's tale of a soldier who appeared in the bedroom she was sharing with a friend, and made them choose which of them was to submit to him sexually. The soldier took fright and fled, but afterwards, Roisin found that her friend's republican brother and his comrades had been in the house the whole time. So the patriarchal practices of the state and of its putative opponents are shown up to be collusive when it comes to the subordination of women. To this extent, the film is a great advance on the subliminally anti-'terrorist' and misogynist work of Jordan, and manages to avoid the pull of some of the old verities that *Caoineadh Airt Uí Laoire* falls back into.

The confluence in *Maeve* of feminism, political and historical critique and formal self-consciousness make it a uniquely powerful and impressive text. It demonstrates the critical potential, at a formal, aesthetic level and on the level of manifest content, of feminism, the various strands of which constitute probably the most radical form of 'revisionism' in Irish cultural debate. *Maeve* is more successful than *Caoineadh Airt Uí Laoire*, because in it the Brechtian reflexive technique is articulated with another form of the critique of modernity, that of feminism, as against the Brechtianised insurgent nationalism of Quinn's film. *Maeve*'s renunciation of tradition is complete and uncompromising, whereas the dependence of *Caoineadh Airt Uí Laoire* on the lament-poem and its deployment of the politics of language lead it to a position of greater ambiguity.

CHAPTER 5

Intellectual politics: Edna Longley and Seamus Deane

Thus far, I have discussed a variety of aesthetic responses to the cultural, economic and political contradictions unleashed in Ireland, North and South, by 1960s modernisation. My efforts have been chiefly concerned with the drawing out of contradictions, failures, and compromises in the aesthetic strategies employed by the writers and film-makers discussed (with the odd more optimistic beacon, such as Banville's work, or *Maeve*). In this last chapter, I wish to turn to the work of the two critics whose positions could be seen to have dominated the period. It has been the salutary function of Seamus Deane and Edna Longley to have shaped decisively the ways that Irish literary culture has been understood in this time. In trying to analyse their stances, therefore, I am attempting to turn self-consciously back on the intellectual structures and discourses that have shaped my own thinking, whether positively or negatively. It is only in the open acknowledgement of such sources that the critic can ever begin successfully to elaborate his own position.

When Jean-François Lyotard describes the 'postmodern condition' as 'incredulity towards metanarratives' (Lyotard, 1984, p. xxiv), his point can be given an Irish inflection by realising that the end of the 1960s saw the failure of the legitimating narrative of modernising bourgeois or statist nationalism in the Republic. At the same time, the 'modernisation' and liberalism of Terence O'Neill in Northern Ireland proved itself incapable of resolving the contradictions it had unleashed by encroaching on sectarian privilege, as David Cairns and Shaun Richards have demonstrated (Cairns and Richards, 1988, pp. 141–2). Modernisation in Ireland, North and South, had proved itself incapable of dealing with what Raymond Williams called 'residual' and 'emergent' ideologies and social formations (Williams, 1981). In the North, O'Neill and his increasingly repressive successors, Chichester-Clarke and Faulkner, were ill-equipped to cope either with emergent radical leftist or Trotskyite movements (such as People's Democracy), or with more traditional residual movements of opposition (such as republican nationalism) or of reaction (Paisleyism or militant loyalism). In the South, similarly, mainstream political parties (Fianna Fáil, Fine Gael) were taken by surprise by both residual republican nationalism (as indicated by the Arms Trials) and by the demands of new urban working-class movements or the Women's Movement. Neither political mainstream had been able to understand its task in terms other than the economic-technocratic. Very little recognition was given to the fact that 'modernisation' requires self-conscious social and cultural intellectual elaboration as much as industrial policy initiatives. Modernisation forced wide the cracks that had always existed at the margins of the hegemonic cultures, North and South, and displayed the inability of these cultures any longer to convince their least dedicated members that, as Hayden White would put it, their fictions were truths. It revealed the implicit violence of the conventional communal narratives of the Republic and the North, and exposed the repressive aspects of the dominant systems of representation.

So the crisis could be said to be one of narrative. If the late 1960s and early 1970s witnessed an explosion of interest and identity groups, based on religion, sex and class, each such group sought to legitimate itself in narrative terms. Narratives help to locate communities historically, spatially, politically, metaphysically, mythically, ethically. Narratives permit communities to plot their futures. They can be understood as assertions of the will, of power. Narratives can be normalising or liberating. Every human being produces narratives, be they banal personal narratives or the official histories of whole communities. If one links this idea to Gramsci's observation that all men are intellectuals, but not all men have in society the function of intellectuals, one arrives at the realisation that official or dominant narratives are elaborated by socially authorised intellectuals (Gramsci, 1971, p. 9). So it is in these terms that we can understand John Wilson Foster's suggestion in 1985 that

> The critical condition of Ireland at the present time seems undivorceable from the condition of criticism in Ireland. The failure of Irish society is the failure of criticism.
>
> (Foster, 1991, p. 215)

Returning to Chomsky, and drawing on the review of intellectual culture in the Introduction and in my discussion of historiographic revisionism, we can say that the intellectual 'modernising' technocracy of the 1960s was primarily responsible for the failure that Foster refers to. The irony of the situation is that the reaction of the Southern state to the Northern violence was to shut out critical discourses – Marxist and neo-Marxist theories of economics, dependency and culture – that would have helped to explain the crisis *in the Republic*. The failure was one of the absence of universalising or 'value-oriented' public intellectuals and of the consequent lack of new, enabling ideologies. Into the space left by professional intellectuals, encompassed as they were by the state and corporate capital, sequestered in universities, into the gap left by an attenuated and media-dominated public sphere, stepped the discourses of extremism and, ultimately, violence. The failure of the intellectuals to elaborate an oppositional discourse, a critical counter-narrative to the hegemonic ones, must be seen as contributory to the violence of Northern Ireland after 1969. Thus, the political arena was open to the paramilitaries and the British State after 1972 in Northern Ireland, and the intellectual arena was vulnerable to the 'invention of tradition', or the old oppositional ideological narrative of Ireland, nationalism.

To a considerable extent, the careers of Edna Longley and Seamus Deane can be seen as opposing responses to this crisis, though both of these critics have been formed by it also. Longley's work, in this formulation, is related to the empiricist technocracy described above, concerned as it is chiefly with 'close reading' of (overwhelmingly) poetry, in the style of the New Criticism. Deane's work shows the influence of more recent critical modes, such as American poststructuralism, and colonial discourse theory, as well as the older but recently revived Frankfurt School Marxism. All of these are inflected in Deane with Northern nationalism. Both critics have found different ways of coping with the Northern crisis, and its relationship to intellectual perfor-mance and the crisis of the public sphere, North and South. I should make it clear here that I am not seeking to dispute specific readings of either, but rather I am offering a critique of their intellectual positions.

Longley was born in the Free State in 1940, and educated at Trinity College, Dublin. She met her husband, the poet Michael Longley, at TCD, and later moved to Belfast in the early 1960s. There, they became part of a literary/poetic circle, including Seamus Heaney, presided over by the English poet and critic Philip Hobsbaum. Longley's argument for Hobsbaum's influ-ence over Northern Irish poetry explains in historico-biographical terms, her detailed and minute concern with poetry in her work (Longley, 1994, pp. 17–22). This comes as a part of a larger discussion of the fate of the Protestant minority in the Free State/Republic since Independence, Longley's overall point being that a non-sectarian institution (TCD) and a non-sectar-ian discourse (poetry) provide the ground of what she sees as the 'revisionist' strain in her work. The weakness of this argument is that it still accepts the sectarian framework that Longley is rightly concerned to criticise. The prob-lem then arises as to how to move beyond that framework, without moving into an absurd series of intellectual and analytical Chinese boxes, each smaller and more isolated, but more morally powerful, than the last.

Earlier in the same essay, Longley makes a comparison between the lib-eral Catholic nationalism of Sean O'Faolain and the liberal Protestant nation-alism of Hubert Butler (Longley, 1994, pp. 12–14). Butler, she suggests, deliberately exploited the tension between being a Southern Protestant and a Nationalist, in such a way as to offer a critique of both post-1920 statelets, North and South. This seems indisputable, and the kind of liberal criticism offered by Butler in the 1940s and 1950s remains relevant today, when the Northern crisis is perhaps beginning to achieve resolution. However, Longley also seems to be implying that Southern *Protestant* dissent has somehow been more significant, or courageous, or 'dissenting' than other forms. Longley concludes a fascinating essay about Louis McNeice, John Hewitt and Hubert Butler later in the same book, *The Living Stream*, by quoting William Drennan, the United Irishman and Belfast Presbyterian who believed that 'The Catholics may save themselves, but it is the Protestants must save the nation' (Longley, 1994, p. 149). But she does this without any irony or apparent sense of the arrogance contained in such sentiments. It seems invidious to produce such moral hierarchies, while one can also envisage other social, economic or political categories that might provide even more powerful critical positions. The most obvious of these would be class; another might be gender. Both might operate to complicate the tradition of dissent that Longley is intent on constructing as her own habitation, with its foundations in TCD and Northern poetry, but neither is mobilised in the context of the intellectual historical-biography she is building here – it never seems to occur to her to question the makeup of the student body of Trinity in class or gender terms (though she is keen to invoke the fact of gender elsewhere, to trouble nationalism, as in her essay 'From Cathleen to Anorexia' (Longley, 1994, pp. 173–95)). Furthermore, her concentration on the question of religion (not in itself an analytical category to be ignored, of course) has the effect of producing a body of critical work as interested in, if not actually reinforcing then drawing attention to, sectarian divisions, as in healing them. Her remarks about the difficulties of being a dissenting Southern Protestant make fascinating comparison with those of W.J. McCormack, who stresses a much more class-based analysis. McCormack's intellectual background is that of 'literary history', strongly influenced by Hegelian Marxism (Georg Lukács and the Frankfurt School), and this accounts for his critique of Longley's 'sectarian sociology of art' (McCormack, 1986, pp. 51, 65).

It may also be that the category of minority religion offers Longley an intellectual home that, unlike the categories of class or gender, does not involve her in explicitly affiliating herself to a political or social movement. Thus she apparently avoids what Julien Benda called 'la trahison des clercs' (the betrayal of the intellectuals) (at least in the context of her critique of the Republic), and can maintain a Platonic self-image of the intellectual (Benda, 1955). In her autobiographical references, Longley recalls proudly her father's courageous decision formally to break with the Roman Catholic Church when ordered to end his association with TCD (T.S. Broderick was Professor of Pure Mathematics there from 1944 until 1962), and in the face of the divisive *Ne Temere* papal decree (which stipulates that the children born of a

Catholic–non-Catholic marriage should be raised as Roman Catholics). In Longley's account, her father's move is cast as the dissenting stand of a secular Roman Catholic intellectual, who affiliates himself with the liberal humanist values of the university rather than those of the Church, and this, combined with his decision to raise his daughters in what Longley calls the 'Anglican compromise' (her mother was a Scottish Presbyterian) is implicitly held up as both a paradigm example of liberal intellectual principle, and also as a legitimating narrative for Longley's own position (Longley, 1994, p. 12). Longley's frankness and willingness to attempt some examination of the historical grounds of her critical position is admirable, but her account of her father's position is limited. She admits that TCD's history began in sectarian circumstances, but locates this in the very deep past (1592). Against this she sets the Roman Catholic Church's ban on Roman Catholics attending TCD, concentrating on the authoritarianism of Cardinal Cullen (in the nineteenth century) and of John McQuaid, Archbishop of Dublin (1940–72). She makes no allusion to class or economic factors influencing university attendance patterns. For Longley, the problem is one of Roman Catholic authoritarianism (in the hierarchy) and subservience and conformism (among the laity), as compared to TCD's values of secularism, independence, individualism. There is an implication that her father's ability and decision to align himself with TCD means that any Roman Catholic could do so. Professor Broderick was affiliating himself to an institution Terence Brown has described as bearing, in the 1930s, 'a striking resemblance in social terms to the Big Houses of the countryside – each symbolizing a ruling caste in the aftermath of its power', though, of course, he is unlikely to have seen it in this way (Brown, 1985a, p. 116). My point here is that the intellectual may be examined not merely in terms of her or his pronouncements, but also in terms of affiliations and filiative relationships, to institutions such as religion, class, professional guild or position, or overt political position. So, the array of choices the intellectual makes bearing on his or her location in civil society, the trajectory of his or her career – these are legitimate objects of critical examination. If such critique seems *ad hominem* in tone, then it must be remembered that, as in the example of Edna Longley, intellectuals may choose freely to expose their personal histories publically.

Seamus Deane's background is almost diametrically opposed to Edna Longley's (Deane, 1992, p. 28). Born also in 1940, he comes from Derry's Roman Catholic Bogside. He was a beneficiary of the 1947 extension to Northern Ireland of Britain's 1944 Butler Education Act. He studied at Queen's University, Belfast, and at Cambridge. From the late 1960s, he taught at University College, Dublin. From 1980 until 1993, he was Professor of English and American Literature at UCD. In 1993, he was appointed Keogh Professor of Irish Studies at Notre Dame University in Indiana. Thus, as Longley has moved North, Deane has moved South. Each might be tempted to make the *ad hominem* criticism of the other that their exile has in fact been a matter of political adjustment, Deane's nationalism being better suited to the Republic, Longley's 'regionalism' to the North. Deane's movement to the United States, however, also signifies another factor. His work is more explicitly 'theoretical' than that of Longley (accepting that there is no criticism without a theory), who is capable of using the generalised term 'theory' as a smear – in her 'Belfast Diary' essay published in the *London Review of Books* in the wake of the appearance of the *Field Day Anthology*, she compares Deane's intellectual politics to those of Paul de Man (Longley, 1992b). Deane's move to the United States is entirely logical, for he has thus placed himself physically at the heart of Anglophone literary debate. Indeed, it may be argued that the centre of gravity of *Irish* literary-critical debate is now located in the United States. Major Irish writers, such as Thomas Kinsella and Seamus Heaney, Eavan Boland and Paul Muldoon have residencies at American universities. Major Irish critics (Denis Donoghue, John Wilson Foster, David Lloyd, and now Deane) teach at North American universities. American-based critics bulk large among the contributors to such journals as the *Irish Review*, *Bullán*, or the *Irish Literary Supplement* (which is actually published in New York). The American Conference for Irish Studies and the Canadian Association for Irish Studies hold large annual conventions/conferences on both sides of the Atlantic. With regard to Field Day, the non-university enterprise Deane has been most associated with, major American critics such as Fredric Jameson and Edward Said have contributed pamphlets (which have since been reissued, introduced by Deane, by the University of Minnesota Press). More than half of the first print run of the *Field Day Anthology of Irish Writing*, of which Deane was the General Editor, went to the United States. The point of this recital of crude facts is to show that Deane, in moving to the US, is acting on the knowledge that 'discourse is the power which is to be seized' (Foucault, 1981, p. 53). Deane recognises that a very powerful influence can be exerted over Irish literary and cultural debate via the last superpower. The irony, of course, is that the United States is also the source of much that Deane is critical of in Ireland. This is an irony that his criticism has yet to fully address. He recognises that the Irish cultural sphere is deeply penetrated by American influences, whether this is at the level of high culture and intellectual trends, or at that of popular culture. But his work only rarely self-consciously locates itself. Yet when it does, as in his General Introduction to the *Field Day Anthology*, where he acknowledges the vulnerability of the *Anthology* to the present moment, or at the end of the essay 'Wherever Green Is Read', Deane does so in a manner that is characteristically intertextual: 'history also reads and writes us' (Deane, 1994, p. 244). This makes an interesting and entirely typical contrast with Longley's empirical personal history.

Longley's posture is that of the New Critic, with her concentration on subtle, formalist 'close readings' of a rather narrow group of poets, especially contemporary ones from Northern Ireland. She has edited the work of Edward Thomas, published a study of Louis MacNeice, co-edited a collection of essays on the 'Protestant Imagination in Modern Ireland' (Dawe and Longley, 1985), and published two collections of essays, *Poetry in the Wars* (Longley, 1986) and *The Living Stream* (Longley, 1994). She sits on the editorial board of the *Irish Review*, and on the Advisory Board of *Fortnight*, a cross-border cultural/political magazine. She has also been involved with the Cultures of Ireland Group, and edited the 1991 Conference proceedings. In her essays, we find a concentration on such writers as Yeats, Louis MacNeice, Derek Mahon, Seamus Heaney, Paul Muldoon, Tom Paulin, Medbh McGuckian, Hubert Butler, John Hewitt, Paul Durcan. The emphasis is very heavily on the contemporary, on poetry (by men, mostly) and on the North. As well as helping to run the Hewitt Summer School, Longley has formulated a 'regionalist' position based on Hewitt's suggestions for a non-sectarian Ulster identity, in the belief that culture provides a realm beyond politics where the divided community of the North may be reconciled with itself.

For Longley, in Derek Mahon's words, 'a good poem is a paradigm of good politics'. Her polemical essay 'Poetry and Politics in Northern Ireland' remains her best-known statement of this position. 'Poetry and politics, like church and state, should be separated', she writes,

> And for the same reasons: mysteries distort the rational processes which ideally prevail in social relations; while ideologies confiscate the poet's special passport to *terra incognita*. Its literary streak, indeed, helps to make Irish Nationalism more a theology than an ideology. Conor Cruise O'Brien calls 'the area where literature and politics overlap' an 'unhealthy intersection'; because 'suffused with romanticism', it breeds bad politics – Fascism and Nationalism. But it also breeds bad literature, particularly, bad poetry, which in a vicious circle breeds – or inbreeds – bad politics. As Yeats says: 'We call certain minds creative because they are among the moulders of their nation and are not made upon its mould, and they resemble one another in this only – they have never been foreknown or fulfilled an expectation'. Ulster poets today are sometimes the victims of improper expectations. Whatever causes they may support as citizens, their imaginations cannot be asked to settle for less than full human truth. And no cause

in Ireland (unlike, say, opposition to Adolf Hitler) carries such an *imprimatur*. This does not let the poet off the hook of general or particular 'responsibility' towards political events. The price of imaginative liberty is eternal vigilance.

(Longley, 1986, p. 185)

From this paragraph, we can, I think, infer much about Longley's criticism, and her intellectual stance. We are given a set of carefully demarcated fields – poetry, politics, church, state, criticism. Intersections of these fields are to be negotiated carefully, often avoided altogether. 'Poetry' is conceived of as a Platonic ideal, which it is the mission of criticism to rescue and protect, most especially from 'politics' and 'ideology'. Criticism is subservient to poetry. Where 'poetry' and 'politics' *do* intersect, the result is bad politics, and bad poetry. 'Poetry' is reserved a privileged position, in the Yeatsian formulation provided, where it is able to reflect on the world, but the world does not impinge on it. The poet moulds the nation, but the nation does not mould the poet. This implies that the poetic consciousness lies outside of language while using it, and outside of history while participating in it. However, alongside this poetic consciousness exists the rationalistic consciousness of the 'citizen', which is held to be 'responsible' to events. Longley assumes the easy separation and rejoining of these components. The true poet is the one who, in fact, can manage this mental shuffle distinctly. This presupposes a particular view of the subject as fully self-aware and autonomous, and as capable of poetically grasping 'full human truth'. So we are given a set of oppositions, whereby 'poetry' is associated with 'mysteries' and '*terra incognita*', while 'politics' is linked with 'ideologies'. One is therefore led to ask, is 'poetry' a secular religion? Is 'politics' transparent? Do the concepts of 'politics' and 'ideologies' exhaust each other?

A major difficulty of Longley's formulation is that poetry and politics are separable only to the degree that church and state are. But in Northern Ireland they are not, as yet. Much of the strenuousness of Longley's critical prose derives from her efforts to lift poetry out of its political context. She seeks to separate poetry and politics in advance of, perhaps as an avant-gardist example to, church and state. I would argue, however, that the effort to carve out a non-ideological 'poetic' discursive space is itself a political act. The New Critical focus on the text only, as an internally resolved balance of paradoxes and complexity, allows it to combine an apparently rigorous concentration on the 'literary' while also not exposing the text to the risk of historical, political or economic reductionism. In other words, New Criticism is itself a kind of critical functionalism, an ultimately 'conflict-free' model of literary analysis, that seeks to explain the text exclusively on its own terms but also raises the text above the encroachments of other discourses. The poem can be examined with brilliant subtlety, but the value of 'Poetry' is put beyond question, and in fact poetry becomes a framework through which we can reflect back upon the quotidian world, a unique and privileged form of knowledge that can offer insights on the grubby terrain of politics and history without itself being tainted by them.

Therefore, Longley's position as a putatively non-theoretical critic leads her into contradiction in making public statements (publishing, lecturing, debating). So criticism itself must be political, and therefore ideological. But all critical ideas, even those advanced by a modest empiricism such as Longley's, aspire to the hegemonic, discursive capture of the public sphere. Any self-respecting criticism also aspires to represent its object to an audience. But this constitutes a capture of that object, which does not hang well with Longley's view of criticism as subservient to poetry. The result of the collision of poetry and criticism – that is, any kind of intersubjective existence for the text – must be a politicisation of poetry. The ironic corollary of this is that it is the poetry or literature that is most criticised, interpreted and hence publicly recognised (i.e. canonical literature) that is rendered most political. The articulation of these ideas in conjunction with a critique of nationalism as 'romantic' and 'theological', due to its 'literary streak', calls up Terry Eagleton's point about Irish Arnoldianism, directed almost certainly at Longley:

> There are Irish critics and commentators who deploy the term [the 'aesthetic'] today as a privileged mark of that decency, civility and cultivation of which an uncouth nationalism is fatally bereft. In the stalest of Arnoldian clichés, the poetic is still being counterposed to the political – which is only to say that the 'poetic' as we have it today was, among other things, historically constructed to carry out just that business of suppressing political conflict.
>
> (Eagleton, 1988, p. 13)

The problem with Longley's subsequent objection to Eagleton's 'colonisation' of Irish criticism is that his intervention gains much of its force and relevance from the Arnoldification of the disciplinary field by critics such as herself (Longley, 1994, p. 29).

Longley's literary demarcations are paralleled by and closely related to political and geographic ones. In a manner comparable to her setting-up of a privileged poetic consciousness that offers to 'revise' literary and political categories, 'Ulster' appears as a similarly privileged region:

Both Irish Nationalism and Ulster Unionism must accept the reality of the North as a frontier-region, a cultural corridor, a zone where Ireland and Britain permeate one another. The Republic should cease to talk so glibly about 'accommodating diversity' and face up to difference and division. This would actually help the North to relax into a genuinely diverse sense of its own identity: to function, under whatever administrative format, as a shared region of these islands. At which point there will definitely be no such person as Cathleen Ni Houlihan.

(Longley, 1994, p. 195)

This is characteristic of a position which McCormack noted in his commentary on *Across a Roaring Hill*. This is that the New Critical stress on the autonomy of the text in Longley's criticism assumes an outmoded notion of the autonomy of the human subject and an arguably exclusivist politics; hence, Longley's use of Hewitt's concept of regionalism and her wish to defend the integrity of Ulster. Noting the overwhelmingly textual nature of the 'imagination' explored in *Across a Roaring Hill*, McCormack suggests that

Abjuring the abstraction inherent in painting and music, avoiding the dialogism and action of theatre, *Across a Roaring Hill* longs for an embodiment of the imagination in the self ... The defence of the Self, of the integral text, is inevitably a political apology for the present.

(McCormack, 1986, p. 66)

John Barrell has teased out the politics of New Critical 'close reading' of the kind Longley advocates. He points out that the stress on the 'integrity' of the text and on 'full humanity' amount to a refusal of history, and therefore of the political. To seek to evaluate the text (most characteristically the poem) in terms only of its relationship to the 'tradition' and to itself, is to deny the historically-determined nature of literary judgement, and to posit a transcendent notion of literary value, and of 'human nature'. Along with the refusal of history goes a stress on literary 'balance', which implicitly refuses the expression or embodiment of political values in the text, because they are held to be too urgent, emotional or partisan. It is this that leads Longley to castigate Deane and Paulin for their vision of differences where unities exist (Longley, 1986, pp. 197–9). As Barrell puts it,

The notion of balance, as something which proceeds from a position beyond the political, is in fact a thoroughly political notion. That position, a middle point between and above all merely partial and particular situations, bears a close resemblance to a certain ideal construction of the situation of the middle-class – neither aristocratic nor vulgar, neither reactionary nor progressive. And similarly, the balance and resolution which literary texts seek to achieve bear a close resemblance to the political balance which, in England especially, was both cause and effect of the increasing power of the middle class, and which has made the notion of 'balance' itself a term of value with a crucial function in middle-class ideology, underwriting the political authority of 'consensus', or the 'middle ground', by representing as irrational extremism whatever cannot, or whatever refuses to be, gathered into the middle ground.

(Barrell, 1988, pp. 5–6)

The linkage of the integrity of Ulster poetry and the 'province' is made by Longley herself, when she suggests that '"Ulster poetry" complicates conventional poetics and canons (in the Republic, Britain, the United States) as Ulster complicates politics' (Longley, 1992a, p. 63). Further, 'Northern Irish poetry ... owes some of its recent variety and intensity to an interaction between literary traditions which also has social roots. It is perhaps the most complex cultural map we have' (Longley, 1992b, p. 21). Longley's idea of the North as a 'cultural corridor' is an interesting one, but it is viable only in a situation where culture is depoliticised. The parallels between this cultural and geographical model, and the practices of the New Criticism are only too clear. As that critical method seeks the resolution of the text's ambiguities within itself and raises up a Platonic ideal of the 'poem' as a source of knowledge, so Longley's cultural geography stresses the uniqueness of Ulster, Ulster poetry and the need for internal solutions to both. It also seems to imply that while the Republic may permeate the North *culturally*, only the existing status quo (that is, the UK) can permeate it culturally and *politically*. She is led into contradiction when she suggests that the Republic should desist speaking of 'accommodating diversity' and face 'difference and division'. The British equivalent in Northern Ireland is the Cultural Traditions project, sponsored by the Northern Ireland Office. But Longley has actively affiliated herself to this project. Yet Northern nationalists have interpreted its underlying intention in the same manner as Longley does the Republic's official discourse of accommodating diversity (Murphy, 1993, pp. 24–5). So, if the UK were to face difference and diversity, what would the implications be for the Union? Conversely, one can argue also that Northern Ireland's divisions and diversities that require facing obtain in the political as well as the cultural realm, and that the latter may not be exhausted by religious differences alone – class, gender, locality, the rural – urban divide will come into play also. If 'pluralism' implies a serious decentering of the Southern state, how will this apply to the North, or to Britain? Northern Ireland is to be allowed (by the Republic) to 'relax into a genuinely diverse sense of its own identity'. It is notable that the North can contain 'diversity' within its 'identity', but the Republic is faced with 'difference and division'. The hard choices face the South, not the North. When Longley attacks Seamus Deane for his 'hospitable' metanarrative of Irish writing in the *Field Day Anthology*, she is assuming at the same time the legitimating presence in the North of the Union and the British state. This ought to be hidden by the transcendence of politics by literature, but this is unsustainable in Northern Ireland. The idea of a transcendent cultural realm is only sustainable in a stable and legitimate state. Northern Ireland has not been either in a full sense.

Longley accuses Tom Paulin, in his Field Day pamphlet, *A New Look at the Language Question* (Paulin, 1986) of paying too much attention to linguistic differences. Likewise, she detects a Manichaean tendency in Deane's 'Civilians and Barbarians', in his portrayal of the discourse of the oppressors *vis-à-vis* the oppressed in Irish history (Deane, 1986a). This may be correct, but it is nevertheless vital to retain the kind of systematic overview that Deane provides, lest we lose that sense through albeit necessary attention to detail and complexity. As Deane himself says, to suggest that the closer one gets to an issue, the less one is able to make judgements about it, is a 'scandalously unintelligent' position (Deane, 1992, p. 32). Deane's critique of modernity and liberal humanism in Ireland – in his Field Day pamphlets and also in his critique of historical revisionism – is clearly influenced by poststructuralism and the Frankfurt School's critique of Enlightenment rationality (Deane, 1986a, 1986b, 1994). This leads him to posit the existence of a 'system' where none apparently exists, as befits the condition of late capitalism. To do this is to recognise with Said that the very 'quixotic' character of such an enterprise, the sheer difficulty of such generalisation is itself part of the contemporary cultural situation, and, therefore, all the more necessary (Said, 1985b, pp. 135–6). This is perhaps the greatest difference between Longley and Deane. There is at times in Longley's criticism an implicit assumption (cultural corridors notwithstanding) that Northern Ireland is as normal as Finchley; that its experience of modernity and humanism has necessarily been the same as that of the rest of the United Kingdom. This is to fail to take account of the fact that in a sectarianised society, where the legitimacy of political structures is *not* beyond question, where religious identity *has* been related to access to power, liberal modernity and humanism take on a different aspect.

The problem is exacerbated when Longley appears to actively promote a 'sectarian sociology of art', as in her interest in the 'Protestant imagination' (McCormack, 1986, p. 65; Dawe and Longley, 1985; Longley, 1994). In properly humanist terms, this category is surely oxymoronic. But Longley's case is, I feel, contradictory. She argues for the separation of poetry and politics in her critiques of Northern nationalist writers (Deane, Heaney, Paulin, Friel) but not in her championing of an anarchic Southern humanist (Paul Durcan). She accuses the Field Day team of opening up differences through their nationalist readings of literature, but she is confident in her explorations of religious sentiment in poetry. Along with R.F. Foster, she is keen to posit varieties of 'Irishness', but seems less tolerant of varieties of Ulsterness, be they Unionist or Nationalist. She is quick to question the stability of Irish national identity, but is still capable of viewing critics such as Eagleton, Said, Fredric Jameson and David Lloyd as 'foreign'. (Interestingly this does not apply to a figure such as John Wilson Foster, an Ulsterman resident in Canada.) These critics are Marxist, or at least engage with various Marxisms. This makes them 'imperial' in Longley's rhetoric (Longley, 1992a, p. 68). Borrowing from John Hewitt, she deploys the term 'archipelago', in the effort to find a non-coercive, apolitical description of the British Isles (Longley, 1992b, p. 21). Yet she mocks Said's comparison of Ireland to other formerly colonised countries, mostly in the Third World: '… the land of saints and scholars, missionaries and imperial civil servants seems to have gone float about – perhaps to the Caribbean' (Longley, 1994, p. 30). This is an example of geographical empiricism on Longley's part. What her critical geography does not admit is what is of necessity obvious in Said's: that geography is an interpretative discourse, that it to a degree constructs its object in the process of describing it. Said's geography is no more imaginative or inauthentic than Longley's. The term and concept of an 'archipelago' is polemically useful to Longley, in that it 'grounds' and legitimises her cultural descriptions in the 'facts' of the physical adjacency of England, Ireland, Scotland and Wales. But the relationships between these units, and others that subdivide or cut across these, and the means we have at our disposal to understand these relationships, are necessarily linguistic, cultural and historical. Said, when comparing the relationships between, say, Britain and India, France and Algeria or the United States and Vietnam, has only the cultural and historical links suggested above to work with. Further, because the use of the 'archipelago' model is an attempt to give the authority of empirical fact, and hence, objectivity, to Longley's cultural discourse, it overlooks relations of power, which is something that Said's model, in spite of its oversights, does not do. Thus, Longley's 'archipelago' is not unrelated to her critical model, or to her ideal of the separation of politics and culture, or humanistic disciplinary fields. It is something of a 'well-wrought' artefact, that internally resolves its differences or safely stages different voices in an enclosed rhetorical space. Of course, the political geographer Jim MacLaughlin has been arguing that Ireland has been experiencing deterritorialisation, on economic grounds, for at least two centuries anyway (MacLaughlin, 1994, p. 3). This makes Longley's attack on Said seem somewhat disingenuous, since it implies that Ireland has been 'floating about', as an economy peripheral to the world-system, for rather longer than simply since Said intervened in Irish debates. For Longley, 'il n'y a pas de hors-texte', to a much greater extent than for Deane, in spite of her castigating him for 'deconstruction'. In this light, it is ironic that she should use the metaphor of a map to describe Northern Irish poetry, while criticising the *Field Day Anthology of Irish Writing* as 'a hegemonic attempt, a heavy-gun emplacement' (Longley, 1992b, p. 21). Longley dislikes the militant, even military rhetoric employed at times by Field Day, but it must be remembered that a map is itself another form of text. A map is the textual representation of the results of a survey, itself a kind of anthology. The historical, legal and political origins of cartography need not detain us here – suffice it to say that the map is a textual form as totalising, selective, proprietorial, *territorial* (for Longley, the aesthetic should transcend the territorial) even military, as any anthology. But one of Longley's main criticisms of Field Day generally, and the *Anthology* particularly, is that it claims for a certain brand of Derry-based, 'Jacobite', anti-Partitionism the authority to speak for the entire country, or at least to speak for all of Irish nationalism (Longley, 1994, pp. 23, 39–40). Longley's charge is vitiated by the fact that she frequently claims for Northern poetry the power quoted above to 'complicate' ideas or canons of poetry, as Northern politics 'complicates' the politics of both the Republic and the UK, and has the potential to 'complicate' European politics as well. It is not that this is entirely false, but rather that such a suggestion attributes a coherent and self-present subjectivity to Northern poetry or the North, and, at least rhetorically, puts it beyond question. This cultural-political unit is able to shake the literary foundations of the Atlantic Anglophone world. 'Ulster' and 'Ulster poetry' complicate politics and poetry, but not *vice versa*. Ulster may trouble the outside world, but the outside world shall not trouble Ulster.

Longley's empiricism leads her into interesting debate over historiography and literary-critical method. At the end of an essay on MacNeice, she suggests that his

> empirical aesthetic matches his empirical philosophy: 'An "empiricist" may be someone who lives from hand to mouth. Or he may be someone who follows an ideal that is always developing, implicit rather than explicit.'
>
> (Longley, 1986, p. 93)

Here we find an explicit match of aesthetic and philosophy (or ideology), in the context of an essay on a writer whose work and positions have been central for

Longley. Taken with Longley's other statements on 'poetry' and 'politics', we find that it is a version of the aesthetic that, in Longley's work, fits neatly with the tendency of other fields of humanistic endeavour identified earlier: the stress on (New Critical) technocracy, on the separation of fields, the refusal of a narrative projection of intellectual activity, the refusal of utopian thought, the resistance to totalising thought or theory. In the American context, the relationship of the New Critics and practical criticism in the 1950s to a contemporaneous functionalist social science has been noted by John Fekete and Paul Bové (Fekete, 1977; Bové, 1986). In Ireland, the analagous relationship is between Longley's empiricist New Critical practice and the dominant tendency in historiography. Stanley Aronowitz has argued that 'the new criticism was the literary expression of empiricism, the dominant philosophical position of the mid-twentieth century ... the New Criticism's rigid formalism may have proved compatible with the general desire of critics to find ways to perform their task in the discourse of science' (Aronowitz, 1994, p. 45). Aronowitz points to the appeal of the New Criticism in the 1930s, when the choice had seemed to be between either a vulgar but powerful and putatively scientific Marxism, and a weakly subjectivist liberal criticism dependent on the category of 'taste'. This reminds us of the opposite but nearly contemporary choices made by British Marxist historians such as Hobsbawm and Kiernan and Thompson, on the one hand; and Irish revisionists Moody and Edwards on the other. Unsurprisingly, then, for Longley, 'Literary-critical revisionism has not kept pace with the historians' (Longley, 1992a, p. 63). I have argued earlier that in fact it is the historians who have not kept pace with textual criticism, exemplified in historiography by the work of Hayden White, a matter alluded to by historians such as Tom Dunne, Ciaran Brady and M.A.G. Ó Tuathaigh (Dunne, 1992; Brady, 1994b; Ó Tuathaigh, 1994). But for Longley,

> Whereas Irish historiography has long been led by scholars bound up with Ireland's changing condition, homegrown literary criticism, though now increasing in influence, has been overwhelmed by the international fixation on Joyce and Yeats. This chronic deficit underlies the current stand-off between historians and theorists.
>
> (Longley, 1994, p. 44)

This passage contains a curious logical back-flip. For Longley, Irish historiography has been progressive and up-to-date for a long time, because concerned with 'Ireland's changing condition'. Irish criticism has, however, been retarded by outside influences and their obsessions. This goes some way to explaining Longley's hostility to 'foreign' critics and methodologies (though her intellectual debts are to British empiricism, Arnold and the New Critics), even when these are domesticated by groups such as Field Day. But the accounts cited earlier, by Brady (1994a) and Bradshaw (1994a), of the origins of the 'new history' suggested that that movement was powerfully motivated by a concern to update Irish historiography to international standards, and to respond to German historicism. Further, while Irish criticism, including that of Field Day, has remained fixated on the Revival and writers contemporaneous with it, it has also been writers such as those vilified by Longley, such as Deane, David Lloyd and Eagleton, and others such as McCormack, Richard Kearney and Cairns and Richards, who have employed outside influences such as Critical Theory, phenomenology, poststructuralism and psychoanalysis to elevate Irish criticism onto the same plane as critical debate elsewhere in the Anglophone world. Therefore, the 'stand-off' is due less to Field Day's anti-Revivalism, than to the stagnation of the theorisation of history in Ireland. The 'stand-off' is also related to the lack (noted by McCormack) of a classical or Marxist sociology of culture in Ireland, which has resulted in a 'revisionism' chiefly concerned with producing a critique of the Catholic, ruralist character of the dominant post-Independence Roman Catholic rural bourgeoisie, as against of its bourgeois character. One thus concludes that the kind of literary-critical revisionism Longley would like to see would be the New Criticism, and it is this notion of critical 'progress' that enables her to see the 'theorists' as out of date.

What Longley does not seem to recognise is that her criticism, in its relationship to empiricism, is closely related to the intellectual and developmental imperative evident in 'modernisation theory' and the 'new history', that has done more (in the form of multinational-led 'modernisation') to erode the autonomous realm of the aesthetic than any of the politicisation of criticism sponsored by Deane or his allies. One concludes that it is this that also leads John Wilson Foster to accuse sociologists of a 'crypto-Marxist tendency' that hides a disappointed nationalism which rejects Northern Ireland and 'the promiscuous multinational desires of the Republic' (Foster, 1991, p. 240). This results in Foster's petulant claim that

> ... the autonomous individual may be a bourgeois humanist fantasy, but many of us in Ireland would like to enjoy that fantasy, thank you very much ... it would be foolish for us to embrace the psychological socialism of poststructuralism before reaping the rewards of psychological *embourgeoisement*.
>
> (Foster, 1991, p. 231)

Where Deane's work *has* been important and salutary is in its recognition of the bankruptcy of this brand of Arnoldian humanism. Longley accuses Deane of writing with a Derry-nationalist angle, and this indeed may be true. It is nevertheless necessary to not simply dismiss his work on that basis, but to ask *why* this is the case, and to realise that its power derives from its tendency to stand outside the cosiness of Foster's 'embourgeoisement', and Deane's own history, which locates him beyond the confines set by the uncritical phrases 'many of us' and 'promiscuous multinational desires'.

Deane's biography, as a Roman Catholic nationalist born in the Unionist statelet of Northern Ireland, who manages to haul himself up to the peak of Irish academia, is in many ways the opposite of Longley's, and he has characterised it in this manner himself (Deane, 1992, p. 28). Coinciding as his career did, via study at Cambridge and then later in the United States, with the radicalisation of cultural studies, the rise of the New Left, student activism and the Civil Rights movement, whether in its Irish or American manifestations, it is inevitable that he should have acquired a different, and perhaps more oppressive, intimation of the meaning of 'culture' from hers. Though Longley uses the term 'Palestinian' in a rather snide way, comparing Derry's 'literary kings over the water' to Said's bourgeois exile in New York, his personal history makes Deane's project not wholly unlike Said's, and his exilic sense of outsiderhood similar too, even in the midst of academic adulation (Longley, 1994, p. 40). Deane's movement to the Republic has not been one of simple accommodation to state nationalism (not, in fairness, that Longley has been uncritical of Ulster Unionism). It is precisely his relationship to nationalism that has made his presence in the South a troubling one. If Longley's project often seems the literary arm of Conor Cruise O'Brien's self-appointed task of reminding Southern nationalism of the blockage to its dreams constituted by Northern Unionism, then Deane's project has been to remind the Southern state of what it has forgotten or betrayed in Northern nationalism. That he does so by writing literary history that is more concerned with Anglo-Irish relations (hence his focus on Arnold and Burke, and the Revival) than relations between North and South should not blind us to the fact that this (his Anglo-Irish focus) has its force precisely because of the political situation in Northern Ireland from 1922 to the present day.

The comparison to Said can be worked in ways more sympathetic to Deane than that suggested by Longley. When Denis Donoghue, writing an Afterword to the British edition of the volume collecting the first six Field Day pamphlets, *Ireland's Field Day*, observes that the evidence of Deane's contributions, *Civilians and Barbarians* and *Heroic Styles: The Tradition of an Idea*, is that he had been reading Michel Foucault, he fails to remark the Saidian inflection of Deane's Foucault (Donoghue, 1986, p. 111). In the first pamphlet, Deane suggests that the apparatus set up by the British state in the nineteenth century of poor houses, national primary schools, a national police force, the Ordnance Survey amounts to the creation of a grid of Foucauldian 'power-knowledge', that permitted both a modernisation of Irish society and the creation of a necessary but refractory 'other', over against which British identity could be constructed. What Donoghue has failed to notice, in other words, is Deane's Saidian application of Foucault in the colonial setting. This is not a minor matter, as it links Deane's project to Said's. It was in his re-evaluative essay, 'Orientalism reconsidered' that Said suggested most explicitly that his interest had been in the production of a non-Hegelian world-history, of a kind that avoided the pitfalls he associated with even modern practitioners, such as Paul Kennedy, or radicals such as Perry Anderson or Immanuel Wallerstein (Said, 1986). The pitfalls are those, principally, linked with writing a Eurocentric history, that implicitly views Europe as the agent and source of History, as a kind of metasubject which 'gives' or 'takes' history to or from the regions on which it focuses its attentions. Said's *Orientalism*, therefore, had been a contribution to a such a 'non-coercive knowledge', but also, by implication, a critique of the assumed linkage of Europeanness and modernity (Said, 1986, p. 212). For Said, the problem with Orientalism, as a discipline, lies both in its self-referentiality, and in its institutional ability to project itself over the object of its attentions, in the form of actual policies and material practices. There has always been a disparity between Orientalism's capacity to represent the 'reality' of the 'Orient' (compromised at best), and its ability to create new 'facts on the ground' anyway (very considerable). Without explicitly invoking an analagous disciplinary structure of 'Celticism', Deane has been interested to pursue a similar project of enquiry into the contradictions of a modernising project in Ireland that was compromised by its colonial location. Critics following in Deane's footsteps, such as Declan Kiberd (1986) and David Cairns and Shaun Richards (1988), have more openly pointed to the production of a discourse of the Celt, with roots in the scholarship of the Romantic period, later given a specifically national slant by Ernest Renan and a specifically Anglo-Irish slant by Matthew Arnold, in their *Poesie des Races Celtiques* and *The Study of Celtic Literature*, respectively.

The interest in cross-cultural reception of ideas has been an abiding concern of Seamus Deane's. In 1988, he published *The French Revolution and Enlightenment in England 1789–1832* (Deane, 1988), a book based on his Cambridge doctoral dissertation. This is a study of the perception of the Enlightenment and Revolution, and the reception of the ideas that flowed from that cataclysmic event, in England in the Romantic period. Here, Deane focuses on the engagement of a variety of English or England-based writers, from Edmund Burke to Samuel Taylor Coleridge, via William Godwin, Percy Shelley and William Hazlitt, with radical French ideas. Of course, what is significant, in terms of Deane's trajectory as a critic of Irish culture, is the idea that what Said has called 'travelling theory' does not transfer from context to context unmarked by its passage (Said, 1984, pp. 226–47). But the point goes further, since the Enlightenment in Ireland was characterised by a series of contradictions or failures. The period of Deane's book, bringing British history up to the year of the great Reform Bill and the resultant extension of the electoral franchise, covers a much more ambiguous and turbulent period of Irish history, including the brief life of 'Grattan's Parliament'; the United Irishmen, their rebellion and destruction; the Act of Union and its consequent diminution of Irish political independence, of the strength of the Ascendancy class and of the imperial grandeur of Dublin; O'Connell's agitation for Catholic Emancipation, won in 1824, and the subsequent campaign for the Repeal of the Union. The period also saw the foundation of the Orange Order, and of the Roman Catholic seminary at Maynooth, both in 1795, ominous signs of sectarian division in the century to come.

It is in this light that Deane has pursued a critical project of questioning the idea of modernisation in Ireland and in Irish literary culture. His first Field Day pamphlet does this by, firstly, pointing out the degree to which Ireland experienced a project of modernisation as mediated by a state not of its own choosing. Secondly, it shows the imbrication of that modernising process with structures of power, and with a discourse that had the effect of relegating activities or practices of the Irish to the realm of the 'other', or 'tradition' *vis-à-vis* the modernising metropolis. In Said's manner, Deane brings his analysis right up to the present day, and to the Northern crisis. He follows the same trajectory in *Heroic Styles*, since it is part of Deane's argument, and part of the argument of the Field Day pamphlet series to which these pieces are contributions, that the Northern crisis is, '[i]n a basic sense', 'stylistic ... a crisis of language' (Deane, 1986b, p. 46). In the Introduction to *Ireland's Field Day*, it is suggested that the Company's desire is to contribute to the exposure of the stereotypes that are both symptomatic and causative of the crisis. The tendency of the pamphlets by Deane, Kiberd, Richard Kearney and Tom Paulin is to establish a certain continuity between the Northern crisis and a deep past of cultural-political contest between Britain and Ireland. This activity is a critique of modernity, insofar as it recognises modernity in Ireland as having always compromised by its colonial source, which has meant that it has not been a modernity of which the Irish have been the agents, or a narrative of which the Irish have been the subjects, except in the form of the finally conservative modernisation represented by nineteenth-century nationalism. What makes this writing powerful, both as a form of cultural history but also as an intervention into the contemporary public sphere, is the Saidian manner of bringing it to bear on the present, and specifically the Northern present. The Field Day pamphleteers, of which Deane is clearly the chief, have the audacity to bring the Northern crisis into a kind of discursive collision with the cosy assumptions of a Republic more interested in its own *embourgeoisement*. The problem is also that this enunciative location of the Field Day discourse allows Southern liberals to dismiss it, as Edna Longley has done the *Anthology*, as a 'Derry metanarrative' (Longley, 1994, p. 39).

In his *Celtic Revivals*, Deane lays down a demarcation in his work between the Literary Revival of the turn of the century, with essays on Yeats, Pearse, Synge, Joyce, Beckett and O'Casey on the one hand, and pieces on the Northern 'Revival' of Heaney, Mahon, Montague and Friel, on the other. The essays on the earlier writers share a concern with establishing ways or areas in which these writers fall outside the critical models that they have frequently been placed in. This is clear in the essays on 'Arnold, Burke and the Celts', 'The Literary Myths of the Revival', 'Yeats and the Idea of Revolution' and 'Joyce and Nationalism'. It is this apparent eccentricity of Irish texts, *vis-à-vis* an established tradition (that is, an English tradition) or critical attitude, that allows us to assign essays like these to a critique of modernity, though the critical project may not always call itself by that name. This also links these essays to Deane's second Field Day pamphlet, *Heroic Styles: The Tradition of an Idea*. It is here that Deane sets out most clearly his version of what Terence Brown has called 'Yeats, Joyce and the Irish Critical Debate' (Brown, 1988, pp. 77–90). This is the playing off of Joyce and Yeats, that has been performed since O'Faolain and O'Connor in the nineteen-forties. In this opposition, Joyce is held to represent a polyvalent democratic answer, with his parodying of an array of styles, his celebration of the everyday and his semantic indeterminacy, to Yeats' authoritarian mythic élitist univocal literary historiography. Brown traces this debate from its origins in the attacks on Yeats and the Revivalists by Irish-Ireland propagandists such as D.P. Moran, Eoin MacNeill and Daniel Corkery, through O'Connor's and O'Faolain's advocacy of Joyce, then that of Thomas Kinsella, to the Field Day pamphlets of Declan Kiberd, Richard Kearney and Seamus Deane. Unfortunately, Brown sees in Deane's assault on Yeats' 'pathology of literary unionism' a sectarian hostility to Anglo-Ireland comparable to that of Corkery, rather than realising that, since Deane here expresses doubt about Joyce also, it is the critique of modernity that is at issue. Deane resents the comparison, since he rightly sees in Corkery a valorisation of identity that he (Deane) has made it his concern to revise. In the latter's famous trio of criteria which would go to define a properly Irish literature – land, nationalism and Roman Catholicism – Deane sees the 'hungry Hegelian ghost' of 'the idea of essence' as that which defines a culture (Deane, 1986b, p. 58). Brown fails to recognise that Deane has been trying to lay that ghost. But Deane also (and in this also is he comparable to Said) sees that a simple putting aside of the issue of national identity is not necessarily easy or always politically apposite. This is what causes him to write of his sense of disturbance that 'We may be defending a new status quo in the delusion that we are radically revising an old tradition' when he contemplates the efforts of modernisation in Ireland (Deane, 1979, p. 94). In other words, Deane can see the oppressive and narrow nature of the cultural nationalism represented in an earlier generation of critics by a figure like Corkery, but he rightly questions the new 'modernity' that is being ushered in in the process of dismantling the cultural and intellectual legacy of such figures. In *Heroic Styles*, Deane refuses to indulge in the full endorsement of Joyce that others have, since he is worried that the harmony produced by Joyce's pluralism of languages and styles and his omnivorous narrative systems is the 'harmony of indifference', where 'everything is a version of something else, where sameness rules over diversity, where contradiction is finally and disquietingly written out' (Deane, 1986b, p. 56). Perhaps it is not too reductive to say that Deane is worried that the linguistic and semantic indeterminacy of Joyce's texts is the literary analogue of the reified world of consumer capitalism. This is why, in essays like 'Joyce and Nationalism' and '"Masked with Matthew Arnold's Face": Joyce and Liberalism', Deane has been concerned to portray a Joyce that is not simply the darling of liberal criticism that sees the novelist's progressivism in his cosmopolitanism, his distance from nationalism and Catholicism, his championing of the individual and of the quotidian (Deane, 1985, pp. 92–107; Deane, 1986c). In the latter, Deane demonstrates Joyce's difference from Arnoldian cultural liberalism, which embraced the Hellenisation of England and the Celticisation of Ireland. To reject the latter is also to reject the former, and this is what Joyce achieved. He famously had no time for the Celticism of Yeats and the Revivalists, but he also saw that it was derived from Arnold's opposition of Hellenistic and Hebraic culture. In Joyce's repudiation of Celtic heroism, essentialism, even racism, he was at the same time effecting a critique of the Arnoldian idea of culture as a discourse that could help bind the English middle classes to their poorer countrymen. To this extent, Joyce becomes an anti-hegemonic writer, since Arnold was never less than sure that culture was a force *for* the state, the state being the material manifestation of man's best self. Yet even Marxist critics, most notably Franco Moretti, have suggested that Joyce's Modernism emerged in direct proportion to his distance from Ireland (Moretti, 1988, pp. 182–208). Deane has been arguing that not only is this unpleasantly patronising, but it also discloses a conception of history and historical change that is incapable of seeing how its own metropolitan source skews its ability to describe a society such as Ireland's where modernisation has been a project driven, until 1922, by a state whose legitimacy was in question, and where the condition of modernity has been accompanied and produced by traumas of war and famine. It is this side of his project that makes it possible to see it as an Irish version of the more global critique of historicism that Said suggested in 'Orientalism reconsidered' (Said, 1986, pp. 223–4).

It is also this element that allows Deane to return to Yeats, having referred scathingly to his 'pathology of literary unionism', and to find in him an exemplar of what Said, quoting Ernst Bloch, calls 'non-synchronous experience' (Said, 1986, p. 223). In the essays 'Yeats and the Idea of Revolution' and 'O'Casey and Yeats: Exemplary Dramatists', Deane finds a Yeats whose politics may have been reactionary but whose aesthetic practice contained a radicalism, that a writer like O'Casey, the 'provincial writer whose moment has come again in the present wave of revisionist Irish history', can never match (Deane, 1985, p. 122). For Deane, Yeats' power lies in his desire to offer Ireland as a repository of pre-modern or anti-modern ideas, experiences and cultural practices. Yeats may not, in his plays or his poetry, confront 'politics' in the direct manner of O'Casey. The latter's sentimental humanism is most explicitly and famously set forth in the 'Dublin trilogy', where his empiricist morality is the framework through which ideology, indeed abstraction of any kind at all, is inspected and found inevitably wanting. As Deane says, *Juno and the Paycock*, *The Shadow of a Gunman* and *The Plough and the Stars* are, at best, portrayals, not analyses, of the 'state o'chassis' of the tenement-dwelling poor. No solution or alternative vision is offered, or can be offered, since the plays presuppose the humanistic worldview of which they purport to show the discontents. Yeats, however, tried to show that in the Ireland where he found still a mythic heroic potential for regeneration, in the life of 'The Fisherman', or in the extraordinary outburst of the 1916 Rising, a critique of modernity could be elaborated. For Yeats, as Deane shows, modernity was indivisible from England, and from an empirical tradition, as demonstrated in a poem like 'Fragments' (Deane, 1985, p. 39). It was precisely in the colonial backwater that a critique of the values of the metropolis, and an alternative view of history, could be set forth. What Deane demonstrates, and Said later in his Field Day pamphlet returns to, is a reading of Yeats' élitism and sympathy for Fascism that reveals it as an example of colonial *ressentiment*, a kind of nativism. Yeats wishes to suggest that Ireland could fulfil a destiny both national and universal by keeping alive in the debased modern world of 'the greasy till' an awareness of metaphysical considerations. What spoils Yeats' historiography, for Deane, is its sectarian and élitist element, its need for a putative aristocracy of Ascendancy figures – Berkeley, Swift, Burke, ultimately himself – to lead and dominate the Irish peasantry. This is the contradiction in Yeats – the revolutionary potential in the anti-modernism, and the arrogance of the desire for heroes, for a mythic apprehension of history, for an organic community as against a democratic citizenry.

It is in this sense, of Deane's articulation of Irish cultural history with the wider Saidian critique of the essentialist universalism of world-history, that

Deane appears as a critic of revisionism. What Deane is positing, over against the excision of national identity or its dismissal, is the necessity for the critic or cultural historian to seek new and alternative ways of remembering the past, and most especially that which is still valuable in the past. Deane, one might say, is interested in a kind of Benjaminian cultural history, that would accord with the Sixth Thesis on the Philosophy of History:

> To articulate the past historically does not mean to recognise it 'the way it really was' (Ranke). It means to seize hold of a memory as it flashes up at a moment of danger ... In every era the attempt must be made anew to wrest tradition away from a conformism that is about to overpower it ... Only that historian will have the gift of fanning the spark of hope in the past who is firmly convinced that *even the dead* will not be safe from the enemy if he wins. And this enemy has not ceased to be victorious.
>
> (Benjamin, 1992, p. 247)

Deane, that is, has a sense of cultural tradition as a terrain that is vulnerable to the embalming gestures of institutional and specifically metropolitan history. He is interested in what is lost in the production of the 'past-centered' history favoured by the professionals in the field of Irish historiography. Deane has meditated at length, in these essays, on the relationship between history-as-text, and history-as-experience, and in an Ireland where 'history' is associated with either Northern violence or the allegedly repressive and backward period that came between Independence and the Lemass/Whitaker iniative, this is a position that has won him many enemies.

One such has been the novelist, journalist and critic Colm Tóibín, who has suggested that 'the social and cultural revolution of the 1960s has left the artists in the Field Day group singularly unmoved ... They write as though nothing had ever changed: their Ireland is distinctly pre-decimal. Thus England is the problem and the enemy (and the dramatic *other*)' (Tóibín, 1989). Reviewing the *Anthology*, Tóibín wrote that

> Unreconstructed Irish Nationalists have always had real difficulties with the 26 Counties. The 26 Counties are limbo, they believe, waiting for the day when our island will be united and the British will leave. This leaves out any idea that Southern Ireland has been forming its own habits and going its own way.
>
> (Tóibín, 1991, p. 8)

We see here, in Tóibín, an example of the revisionist intellectual hegemony that Deane's work is opposed to. Tóibín was at this time a columnist for the

Sunday Independent, a paper that, in the name of 'iconoclasm' and 'rationality', has in recent years engaged in an ideological project of near McCarthyite proportions, employing a combination of serious intellectuals (Conor Cruise O'Brien, Ronan Fanning) and lesser hacks (Eamon Dunphy) in attacks on John Hume, Gerry Adams, the Roman Catholic Church, nationalism in general, terrorism (chiefly that of the Provisional IRA). In this discourse, even the expression of a desire to understand Northern nationalist militancy is evidence of 'fellow travelling'. It is in such a context that Deane writes critically of 'pluralism', 'modernity', 'revisionism'. It is his recognition of the failures of the political and economic dispensations of the 1960s, North and South, that leads him to write scathingly of modernity. When Tóibín informs us that the Field Day group are 'unreconstructed nationalists' with 'a deep contempt for the Irish state', it becomes clear that he has missed the point entirely. Firstly, Deane, Friel, Heaney and Paulin may be nationalists, but the persistence of their nationalism is intimately related to the persistence of the Union, and to Southern Partitionism. By this I mean that nationalism has remained for them (and they are not alone in Northern Ireland, though they may be a minority) the central ideology and narrative of liberation, though Deane at least recognises the symbiosis between bourgeois state-building nationalism and the imperialism that calls it forth. However, Field Day would be entirely uninteresting if it were not at least projecting a *highly* reconstructed nationalism. Secondly, Tóibín seems to have a peculiar and rather provincial desire to protect the Southern state from Field Day's contempt. Only this can explain his suggestion that if the characters in Thomas Kilroy's play for Field Day, *Double Cross* were trying to be American rather than English, the play would be a farce (Tóibín, 1992, p. 121). So, Tóibín seems to see the development of the Free State/Republic, and particularly its *embourgeoisement* since the early 1960s, as benign. Thirdly, Tóibín displays the intellectual ignorance and partitionism of much of his generation (he was born in 1955, and thus has lived most of his adult life against the background of the 'Troubles') when he fails to recognise that it was *precisely* the 'social and cultural revolution of the 1960s' that *produced* the Field Day group. What is revealed here is in fact the introverted and bourgeois idea of Lemass-sponsored 1960s social change, which hit the Republic late, in the 1970s, that Tóibín is working with. Tóibín's 'social and cultural revolution' seems to lack any trace of international consciousness, any awareness of the American Civil Rights movement, of the anti-Vietnam war movement, of the Paris *soixante-huitards*. Tóibín seems to forget also that it was the singularly conservative revolution of the 1960s in the Republic that brought to power the corrupt or ineffectual political generation of the 1980s, in the form of Haughey (in Fianna Fáil) and Fitzgerald (in Fine Gael). Tóibín's implicit defence of the mediocrities of the Southern state is congruent with the narrow sense of modernity I outlined earlier and suggests a disappointment that 1960s change might have involved more than the bourgeois liberation of the humanist individual from 'ideologies' of church, land, nation, language and class into a kind of consumerist democracy. The problem is that while this may have been the case in the South, it did not obtain in the North. If Deane's, and Field Day's, failing has been to articulate what Longley has called 'old whines in new bottles', then neither Tóibín nor Longley pay sufficient attention to *why* these 'whines' might have relevance (Longley, 1984, p. 18).

Deane is sympathetic to anti-humanist strains in critical thought (Critical Theory, poststructuralism, colonial discourse theory) because he came to maturity in the era of the high institutional tide of Western humanism. His background put him outside of the comfortable stabilities of 1960s modernisation in Ireland, North and South, and predisposes him to look at its legacy askance. His alienation in the Northern Ireland of the 1950s and 1960s has been matched by his sense of intellectual dislocation in the Republic in the 1970s and 1980s. Hence his sympathy to strains of thought critical of modernity, be they Marxist or poststructuralist. It is precisely Deane's relationship to the intellectual revolutions of the 1960s that seems to have passed unreconstructed liberals such as Tóibín by. This is what Longley has, critically but correctly, referred to as the relationship between 'Derry and Derrida' in the work of Deane and his Field Day allies, and also in Richard Kearney (1986) and Declan Kiberd (1986). Deane's writing is, roughly, the intellectual analogue of John Banville's historiographic metafiction. That is, he tries to write criticism at a time and from a place where critical authority itself seems to be at stake, and when a conventional literary history or bourgeois criticism, of the kind practised by Longley, seems no longer possible: Northern Ireland at war, and the Republic seeking to modernise in the postmodern age of late capitalism.

What writers such as Longley and Tóibín fail to do is to historicise and contextualise the Field Day enterprise. So they fail to place the pamphlets in the context of the post-Maze hunger strike surge of support for Provisional Sinn Féin and communal polarisation, or in the context of an extraordinary efflorescence of *English* Tory nationalism, in the aftermath of the Falklands War, the general election victory of 1983, and the rejection by Margaret Thatcher of the conclusions of the New Ireland Forum in 1984. When critics of the Field Day enterprise cite pamphlets by Deane, or Declan Kiberd, as evidence of anti-revisionism, they nearly always fail to note the wholesale (re-)invention of tradition that was taking place in the 1980s across the Irish Sea, with direct repercussions in Northern Ireland. They also tend to overlook the paucity of 'revisionism' in the discourse of Unionism (though Field

Day have themselves published a pamphlet by R.L. McCartney (McCartney, 1985), an example of pluralism for which little credit is given). Little effort has been expended in exploring the ironies behind the simultaneous development of, say, English Heritage, and the New Ireland Forum.

But it is precisely this contradictory relationship to nationalism that makes Deane's writing unsettling and powerful. It is also this that makes his under-theorisation of his own institutional location, and its relationship to his hermeneutic and intellectual practice all the more disappointing. In a critic much of whose career has been devoted to powerful critiques of the cultural authority of the Anglo-Irish literary tradition, it is disappointing to see little evidence of attention to his own role in displacing that tradition. Deane's appeal to reader response and the present moment for the legitimacy of the *Anthology* is a gesture in that direction, but the individual sections of that collection show little tendency to ironise themselves (Deane, 1991, p. xxi). At this point, we can begin to see similarities in the *oeuvres* of Deane and Longley. Deane was an important contributor to the *Crane Bag*, a cultural/political journal (edited by Richard Kearney, a Field Day pamphleteer, and Mark Patrick Hederman) whose lifetime (1977–85) overlapped with the foundation of Field Day in 1980. It was in this journal that the concept of the 'Fifth Province' was initially floated. According to Hederman, this is the meeting-point of the four historical provinces – either the county of Meath, or a punctual space in the Euclidean sense. For Hederman, 'the purpose of the *Crane Bag* is to promote the excavation of such unactualised spaces within the mind of the reader, which is the work of constituting the Fifth Province' (Hederman, 1985, p. 110). This idea or ideal was later taken up by Field Day, and, more recently still, by President Mary Robinson in her inaugural speech in 1990. It is a space in which opposites are brought together and where contradictions are resolved. It is a space out of which Brian Friel has hinted a future political settlement for the island of Ireland might arise. Friel's position was that Field Day, in contributing to the constitution of the Fifth Province, were adumbrating 'a cultural state, not a political state. And I think that out of that cultural state, a possibility of a political state follows' (O'Toole, 1982, p. 23).

One of the problems besetting Edna Longley's critique of Field Day has been her tendency to read individuals (especially Deane, but also Tom Paulin) as speaking for the group. Equally, one can argue that it is the responsibility of such figures to distinguish their corporate and individual pronouncements. Still, it seems fair to suppose that this cultural-then-political state of Friel's would be one with a culture, in Deane's words, 'unblemished by Irishness, but securely Irish'. This leads to the conclusion that this culture was supposed to have been enabled by the *Anthology* project, which is the means, presumably, by which 'Everything, including our politics and our literature' is to be 're-written – that is, re-read' (Deane, 1986b, p. 58). What is disappointing about the Field Day project is, in fact, what it shares with its main antagonists – that is, the emphasis on 'reading', 'writing', 'culture', a unitary political entity, an ideal space where opposites can meet and be resolved. To this extent, Deane and his colleagues display their inability to shake off their origins, be those origins political (nationalism) or institutional (the realm of academia, the discourses of literature, or high culture). Only a group of writers and academics could ascribe so much liberatory power to the act of reading. The irony is that one now realises that one is back at much the same point as Longley's New Critical project of 'close reading' and an Arnoldian position of the priority of culture over politics. When one reads Hederman's comments in the *Crane Bag* about 'the possibility that art is the most potent guide to the riddle of what it means to be fully human in the last quarter of the twentieth century', and his interest in an 'inner journey through the poet's own history and situation to a point of release onto the open space of otherness' (Hederman, 1985, p. 112), one is reminded quickly of Longley's conception of the relationship between poetry, 'full humanity' and the attempt to foster cross-community understanding through literature. It is salutary, then, to be reminded by McCormack that 'literature *is* the Irish ideology' (McCormack, 1986, p. 72).

The problem, then, with Deane's work and the Field Day project (and Longley's alternative) is its idealism or culturalism. In spite of the strenuousness of the rhetoric that is deployed in their debate (more especially by Longley), they are agreed as to the centrality of literature, and of canonical literature at that (in spite of Deane's anthological commitment to 'writing', and Longley's putatively anti-canonical approach). In a very real sense, their quarrel has generated, in Said's words, 'oppositional debate without real opposition' (Said, 1984, p. 160). In their enthusiasm to quarrel over ideologically-driven criticism, or over aesthetic ideologies, they never seem to pause to consider the 'culture industry' or literary culture as an ideological apparatus, though such approaches are sometimes implicit in Deane. Neither of them have much to say to newer critical paradigms such as feminism, or cultural materialism, or the study of other cultural discourses such as film. It must be admitted, of course, that Longley has recently deployed a feminist rhetoric (Longley, 1994, pp. 173–95) but she remains hostile to feminism as a set of theories, and it is difficult not to regard the essay just named as in large part a tactical exercise to create an opportunity to criticise Northern political discourses, chiefly nationalism. This rhetoric is useful to her when it points to omissions and exclusions from the *Field Day Anthology*, but it remains the case that Longley's critical commitment is to mostly male poets, and a 'non-gendered' critique. Deane, of course, has been heavily criticised, by Longley and Tóibín among others, for the representation of female writers in the *Anthology*. He has had the modesty and flexibility, however, to commission a fourth volume, edited by an all-female team of academics (including Siobhan Kilfeather, Clair Wills, Margaret MacCurtain, Angela Bourke, Gerardine Meaney and Mairín Ní Dhonnchadha). Longley has already mocked this as representing a ghettoisation of the 'Mad Women in the Annex' (Longley, 1994, p. 35). Of course, it is easy to see such a fourth volume as a patronising, embarrassing appendage to the 'main' work. However, it seems to me that it remains to Deane's and Field Day's credit that they were prepared to admit weakness and error – a rare quality among anthologisers. Further, it seems very likely that Longley, and other feminist critics, would have objected to women's writing being subsumed in an allegedly nationalist, patriarchal metanarrative if women's representation had been more complete. Longley also fails to register the degree to which, while the fourth volume may compromise and patronise those writings contained within it, it also will compromise and embarrass, and implicitly criticise the *Anthology* as a whole.

So, while Deane sees culture as a realm of exclusion and force, and Longley sees it as a realm of transcendence and reconciliation, they both see it as primarily textual, making little allowance for a broader, anthropological sense of 'culture', or for culture as an element of a mass consumer society. To this extent, they conform to O'Dowd's thesis, that the Northern crisis, and the rise of intellectual technocracy and professionalism in the Republic, has resulted in a separation of debates about identity from economic issues:

> A rather abstract debate has proceeded within the intellectual traditional of the 'old' traditional intellectuals. It has construed their preoccupations with Irish cultural and national identity as a tradition of ideas and texts, rather than as the products of a changing environment of economic, class and power relations. It ignores the changing size, composition and role of the whole intellectual stratum and the extent to which it now depends on state institutions. Furthermore, it has failed to interpret the further loss of control by both states in Ireland over their own economic destinies.
>
> (O'Dowd, 1988, p. 16)

In addition, it must be remembered that the versions of identity set out by intellectuals reflect their own place in the social structure, while also representing (and obscuring) other interests. Deane also is affiliated, necessarily, to the more public Field Day positions, as defined in relation to both pamphlets and theatre as follows:

> Field Day could and should contribute to the solution of the present
> crisis by producing analyses of the established opinions and stereotypes
> which had become both a symptom and a cause of the current situa-
> tion.
>
> (Field Day Theatre Company, 1986, p. vii)

Thus, the company saw itself as revisionist at its inception. Insofar as the
Anthology was projected in 1985, it was imagined as revealing 'the complex
nature of the Irish tradition in writing'. However, the stress was to be on a
'continuous tradition, contributed to by all groups, sects and parties, in which
the possibility of a more generous and hospitable notion of Ireland's cultural
achievements will emerge' (Field Day Theatre Company, 1986, p. viii). The
problem here, as Longley has pointed out, is a unitary critical geography,
combined with an emphasis on continuity (Deane writes in the 'General
Introduction', in a rather wilful manner, that 'there *is* a story here, a metanarrative' (Deane, 1991, p. xix)). which suggests a focus more on external distortions than on internal divisions, on stereotypes produced *outside* the island
of the island. Longley sees this as a tendency to occlude distinctively
Northern identity (Longley, 1994, pp. 22–44), but at least as important are
the other divisions that such an optic is blind to: those of class, region, the
urban versus the rural, diaspora and exile, uneven development, ethnicity,
gender and sexual orientation. The contradiction inherent in a *critique* that
can also conclude in *continuity* results in two difficulties. Firstly, the island-
based imaginative geography is not questioned, though Deane would be
quick to admit the political and cultural coherency thereby assumed has been
the product of a colonial history. Secondly, if the stereotypes examined are
those *of* the nation, the nation is taken as given. But if Field Day is trying to
step into a role of public centrality inadequately held by cultural institutions
such as the Abbey Theatre, it must attend to fissures in the national edifice.
The pamphlets, plays and the *Anthology* together constitute a powerful intervention in and shaping of the national public sphere and, as such, must be
capable of projecting themselves into *all* mentalities on 'the island', not
merely the given national one. Yet the space given to Northern literary identities in the *Anthology* seems to belie this, as does Kiberd's description of the
'barbarous vulgarity and boot-faced sobriety' of Ulster Protestantism (Kiberd,
1986, p. 100). Notably, Kiberd's essay concludes with a call for the British
political establishment to scrutinise the Unionist regime and culture that they
upheld for fifty years. Unfortunately, his language, glossed as it may be from
the terms of F.S.L. Lyons, betrays a lack of such examination on his own part
(Lyons, 1979, pp. 136–7). If Field Day's project is to project a new Gramscian
'people-nation', then a new hegemony is something to be *won* (Gramsci,

1971, p. 418). It must immediately be admitted, then, that the third pamphlet series, concerned with Ulster Protestant conceptions of community and liberty, goes some way to right the imbalance (Brown, 1985b; Elliott, 1985; McCartney, 1985). Further, the fourth series, on *Emergency Legislation*, provides a devastating critique of the repressive legal apparatus of the Free State/Republic (Mulloy, 1986; Farrell, 1986; McGrory, 1986).

The chief strength of the Field Day project, and of Deane's work as a major component of that, is its *oppositional* potential (Said, 1984, pp. 1–30; 1985b). The sociologist Desmond Bell has also argued for a similar position (Bell, 1985, 1993). For Said, oppositional criticism and cultural work are defined by '*interference*, crossing of borders and obstacles, a determined attempt to generalize at exactly those points where generalizations seem impossible to make'. He continues:

> One of the first interferences to be ventured, then, is a crossing from literature, which is supposed to be subjective and powerless, into those exactly parallel realms, now covered by journalism and the production of information, that employ representation but are supposed to be objective and powerful.
>
> (Said, 1985b, p. 157)

Deane's, and Field Day's, crucial contribution has been to 'interfere' with history and historiography, which perhaps constitute the institution in Ireland most obviously employing representation 'but ... supposed to be objective and powerful'. Significantly, this derives from their origins in the unabsorbed energies and community of Northern Irish nationalism. Indeed, it is the dialectic in their work between history-as-event and history-as-text that leads to their complication of liberal complacencies in the South, where history has mostly disappeared into text and 'heritage', and, while it may be contested (by feminist historians, for example) is not directly linked to communitarian power-politics. As Bell puts it, the intrusion into history-as-text and text as historical signifier forces us to consider a major question:

> – what historiographical methods are appropriate to plot a pattern of Irish historical development and contemporary set of mentalities determined by a series of absences: the squandered enlightenment in hock to colonial economic appropriation; the failed political revolution of 1798; the Industrial Revolution we never had, and the Famine we did with its resulting emigration and diaspora; the incomplete resolution of the national question and the sclerosis of post-partition economic, cultural and political life; the marginalisation of the left and the

absence of an adversarial modernist culture. An empiricist historiography can get little purchase on such a significant procession of non-events, of failures and ellipses that make our historical experience so minimal in European terms.

(Bell, 1993, pp. 145–6)

(Bell's comments here on a 'series of absences' remind us of the lack of a properly sociological vocabulary and conceptual apparatus for the study of culture noted by McCormack: McCormack, 1986). His enthusiasm for this element in Field Day does not blind him to its culturalism, to its failure to move beyond a very conventional definition of the literary, and its failure to forge a new, truly popular theatre. This must be at least partly due to their relation to the Yeatsian model of theatre (in spite of Deane's fierce critique of Yeats' historiography, he can still reclaim Yeats as an 'exemplary dramatist' (Deane, 1985, pp. 108–22; 1986b)), and this latter must also partly explain what Bell sees as their slippage from a politicised aesthetic towards an aestheticised politics. This bespeaks a willingness to 'interfere' in historiography, but in little else of much import. Field Day's work to date stands as a titanic contribution to Irish culture and debate over the last twenty-five years – even their most serious critics will concede them that – but there are many fields, disciplines, cultural forms, debates and issues that they have left unexplored. The revived theatrical tour of 1995, and the new publications (the fourth volume of the *Anthology*, and the new series of books led off by volumes of essays from Luke Gibbons and Kevin Whelan) hinted at little 'interference' in film, television, the visual arts, journalism, in terms of practice, though not analysis. As early as 1986, McCormack was identifying areas he hoped would be addressed by future Field Day writings:

(a) the Irish language as cultural totem in the nationalist view of things, and as irritant in the Unionist view; (b) the role of the Catholic Church in political and social life north and south of the Border; (c) the whole question of social class as an alternative to denomination in describing society; (d) the population explosion in the South, especially of the urban young; (e) nuclear energy, neutrality and US/British defence interests in Ireland. The core of these (as yet) unattended issues is the nature, existence and future viability of the nation-state.

(McCormack, 1986, p. 55)

These remarks anticipate those of O'Dowd on the neglect of the 'material dimension'. In the late 1990s, we can see that Field Day have faced none of these issues, and other unaddressed matters including political, social, cultural and economic relations with 'Europe', and sexual minorities. One does not need to disagree with Field Day as to the crucial importance of the 'national question' to recognise that these are grievous omissions, oversights or down-right failures. One also does not need to disagree that the 'cultural is the zone of the political' to recognise with Said that the primary function of the humanities in Ireland as much as in the United States today is to represent 'humane marginality' (Said, 1985b, p. 155), and that projects like the *Anthology*, standing as it does as a powerful mixing of academic disciplines, remains just that – academic – until the intellectuals involved start to address a truly wide public, and to examine the institutional and material grounds of possibility of their own work. Field Day, or some such group, urgently need to produce a sociology of Irish intellectuals, that tries to explain their recent trajectory, in the academy and outside of it, their relationship to the author-ity of the State and to corporate capital, and the ways that these trajectories and relationships are in turn related to their interpretative, scholarly and ped-agogical practices. This brings us back to Richard Ohmann's point quoted earlier, that for universities to be truly 'neutral' in relation to the state and to capital, they would have to be much less pure and more political than they are. For Ohmann, distance is proportional to oppositionality (Ohmann, 1976, p. 332). The point, then, is that the critics, Deane no less than Longley, need to demonstrate how their freedoms (and neutrality, if that is their claim) have been won, in a system where the great bulk of funding for third-level educa-tion comes from the State. If Deane is correct to suggest that Irish historians could learn from the state of anxiety that has beset literary criticism for the last twenty-five years, then so also could the critics, whose salutary assaults on canonical and cultural authority seem so rarely turned in upon themselves, and their institutional, disciplinary, economic and ideological determination. Seamus Deane and Edna Longley have, in spite of the aggression and rhetor-ical flights of their disputes, a great deal in common, especially on the insti-tutional level, and they must be wary of the trap of false oppositionality, as well as Deane's own reminder that 'We do not only read and write history; history also reads and writes us' (Deane, 1994, p. 245).

Bibliography

PRIMARY MATERIALS

John Banville (1977) 'Act of Faith', *Hibernia*, September 2, p. 28
— (1981) 'A Talk', *Irish University Review*, Vol. 11, No. 1, pp. 13–17
— (1983) *Kepler*, London: Granada; first published by Secker and Warburg, 1981
— (1990) *Dr Copernicus*, London: Minerva; first published by Secker and Warburg, 1976
— (1992a) *Birchwood*, London: Minerva; first published by Secker and Warburg, 1976
— (1992b) *The Newton Letter*, London: Minerva; first published by Secker and Warburg, 1982
Dermot Bolger (1987) *The Woman's Daughter*, Dublin: Raven Arts Press
— (ed.) (1988) *Invisible Cities: The New Dubliners*, Dublin: Raven Arts Press
— (1991a) *The Journey Home*, London: Penguin; first published by Viking, 1990
— (ed.) (1991b) *Letters from the New Island*, Dublin: Raven Arts Press
— (1992) *A Dublin Quartet*, London: Penguin
— (1993a) *Nightshift*, London: Penguin; first published by Brandon Books, 1985
— (ed.) (1993b) *The Picador Book of Irish Contemporary Fiction*, London: Pan
Seamus Deane (1976) '"Be Assured I Am Inventing": The Fiction of John Banville', in Rafroidi and Harmon, pp. 329–38
— (1979) 'Postscript', *Crane Bag*, Vol. 3, No. 2
— (1984) 'Introduction' in Friel, pp. 11–22
— (1985) *Celtic Revivals: Essays in Modern Irish Literature 1880–1980*, London: Faber and Faber
— (1986a) 'Civilians and Barbarians', in Field Day Theatre Company, pp. 33–42
— (1986b) 'Heroic Styles: The Tradition of an Idea', in Field Day Theatre Company, pp. 45–58
— (1986c) '"Masked with Matthew Arnold's Face": Joyce and Liberalism' in Morris Beja *et al.*, pp. 9–20
— (1988) *The French Revolution and Enlightenment in England 1789–1832*, Boston: Harvard University Press
— (ed.) (1991) *The Field Day Anthology of Irish Writing*, Derry: Field Day Theatre Company
— (1992) 'Canon Fodder: Literary Mythologies in Ireland', in Lundy and MacPoilin, pp. 22–32
— (1994) 'Wherever Green Is Read', in Brady, 1994a, pp. 234–45
Roddy Doyle (1993) *The Barrytown Trilogy*, London: Minerva
Brian Friel (1969) *The Mundy Scheme*, London: Samuel French
— (1984) *Selected Plays*, London: Faber and Faber
— (1989) *Making History*, London: Faber and Faber
— (1990) *Dancing at Lughnasa*, London: Faber and Faber
Edna Longley (1982) 'Introduction', in Durcan, pp. xi-xv
— (1984) 'More Martyrs to Abstraction', *Fortnight*, July/August, pp. 18, 20
— (1986) *Poetry in the Wars*, Newcastle—upon—Tyne: Bloodaxe Books
— (1992a) 'The Aesthetic and the Territorial' in Andrews, pp. 63–85
— (1992b) 'Belfast Diary', *London Review of Books*, 9 January, 1992, p. 21
— (1992c) Position Paper for the Panel Discussion at the Joint Conference of the Canadian Association of Irish Studies and the American Conference of Irish Studies, Galway, published in *The Canadian Journal of Irish Studies*, Vol. 18, No. 2, December, pp. 119–21
— (1992d) 'Writing, Revisionism and Grass—seed: Literary Mythologies in Ireland', in Lundy and MacPoilin, pp. 11–21
— (1994) *The Living Stream: Literature and Revisionism in Ireland*, Newcastle-upon-Tyne: Bloodaxe Books

229

FILMS DISCUSSED

Caoineadh Airt Uí Laoire (dir. Bob Quinn, 1975)
Maeve (dir. Pat Murphy and John Davies, 1981)
Angel (dir. Neil Jordan, 1982)
The Crying Game (dir. Neil Jordan, 1992)
My Left Foot (dir. Jim Sheridan, 1989)
The Field (dir. Jim Sheridan, 1990)

SECONDARY MATERIALS

Louis Althusser (1984) *Essays on Ideology*, London: Verso
Benedict Anderson (1991) *Imagined Communities: Reflections on the Origins and Spread of Nationalism* (2nd edition), London: Verso
Perry Anderson (1992) *English Questions*, London: Verso
Elmer Andrews (1992) *Contemporary Irish Poetry*, London: Macmillan
Matthew Arnold (1912) *The Study of Celtic Literature*, London: Smith, Elder
— (1932) *Culture and Anarchy*, ed. J Dover Wilson, Cambridge: Cambridge University Press
Stanley Aronowitz (1994) *Dead Artists, Live Theories, and Other Cultural Problems*, London: Routledge
Francis Barker, Peter Hulme, Margaret Iversen and Diana Loxley (eds) (1986), *Literature, Politics and Theory*, London: Methuen
John Barrell (1988) *Poetry, Language and Politics*, Manchester: Manchester University Press
Roland Barthes (1973) *Mythologies*, trans. Annette Lavers, London: Paladin
Morris Beja, Phillip Herring, Maurice Harmon and David Norris (eds) (1986) *James Joyce: The Centennial Symposium*, Urbana and Chicago: University of Illinois Press
Daniel Bell (1988) *The End of Ideology*, Cambridge, Massachussetts: Harvard University Press
Desmond Bell (1985) 'Contemporary Cultural Studies in Ireland and the "Problem" of Protestant Ideology', *Crane Bag*, Vol. 9, No. 2, pp. 91–5
— (1988) 'Ireland without Frontiers? The Challenge of the Communications Revolution', in Kearney, 1988b, pp. 219–30
— (1993) 'Culture and Politics in Ireland: Postmodern Revisions', *History of European Ideas*, Vol. 16, No. 1–3, pp. 141–6
Julien Benda (1955) *The Betrayal of the Intellectuals*, trans. Richard Aldington, Boston: Beacon Press
Walter Benjamin (1992) *Illuminations*, trans. Harry Zohn, London: Fontana
Marshall Berman (1982) *All That Is Solid Melts into Air: The Experience of Modernity*, London: Verso
Paul Bew, Ellen Hazelkorn and Henry Patterson (1989) *The Dynamics of Irish Politics*, London: Lawrence and Wishart
Homi K. Bhabha (ed.) (1990) *Nation and Narration*, London: Routledge
— (1994) *The Location of Culture*, London: Routledge
Augusto Boal (1979) *Theatre of the Oppressed*, trans. Charles and Maria-Odilia McBride, London: Pluto Press
Jorge Luis Borges (1970) *Labyrinths*, edited by D.A. Yates and J.E. Irby, London: Penguin
Tom Bottomore, Laurence Harris, V.G. Kiernan and Ralph Milliband (eds) (1991) *A Dictionary of Marxist Thought* (2nd edition), Oxford: Blackwell
Pierre Bourdieu (1993) *The Field of Cultural Production: Essays on Art and Literature*, edited and introduced by Randal Johnson, London: Polity Press
Paul A. Bové (1986) *Intellectuals in Power: A Genealogy of Critical Humanism*, New York: Columbia University Press
Brendan Bradshaw (1994a) 'Nationalism and Historical Scholarship in Ireland', in Brady, 1994a, pp. 191–216

— (1994b) 'Revising Irish History', in Ó Ceallaigh, pp. 27–41
Ciaran Brady (ed.) (1994a) *Interpreting Irish History: The Debate on Historical Revisionism*, Dublin: Irish Academic Press
— (1994b) '"Constructive and Instrumental": The Dilemma of Ireland's First "New Historians"', in Brady, 1994a, pp. 3–31
John Breuilly (1994) *Nationalism and the State* (2nd edition), Chicago: University of Chicago Press
Terence Brown (1985a) *Ireland: A Social and Cultural History 1922–85*, 2nd ed., London: Fontana
— (1985b) *The Whole Protestant Community: The Making of a Historical Myth* (Field Day Pamphlet 7), Derry: Field Day
— (1988) *Ireland's Literature* (Gigginstown, Mullingar, Co. Westmeath: Lilliput Press)
Herbert Butterfield (1931) *The Whig Interpretation of History*, London: Bell
James M. Cahalan (1983) *Great Hatred, Little Room: The Irish Historical Novel*, Syracuse, New York: Syracuse University Press
David Cairns and Shaun Richards (1988) *Writing Ireland: Colonialism, Nationalism and Culture*, Manchester: Manchester University Press
Dympna Callaghan (1994) 'An Interview with Seamus Deane', *Social Text* 38, Spring, pp. 39–50
Noam Chomsky (1982) *Towards a New Cold War: Essays on the Current Crisis and How We Got There*, London: Sinclair Brown
Patrick Clancy, Sheelagh Drudy, Kathleen Lynch and Liam O'Dowd (eds) (1986) *Ireland: A Sociological Profile*, Dublin: Institute of Public Administration
— (1995) *Irish Society: Sociological Perspectives*, Dublin: Institute of Public Administration
Linda Colley (1989) *Namier*, London: Weidenfeld and Nicolson
James Connolly (1910; 1987 ed.) *Labour in Irish History*, London: Bookmarks
Neil Corcoran (ed.) (1992) *The Chosen Ground: Essays on the Contemporary Poetry of Northern Ireland*, Bridgend: Seren Books
Daniel Corkery (1931) *Synge and Anglo-Irish Literature*, Cork: Cork University Press
Raymond Crotty (1986) *Ireland in Crisis: A Study in Capitalist Colonial Undevelopment*, Dingle: Brandon Books
Liz Curtis (1984) Ireland: *The Propaganda War. The British Media and the Battle for Hearts and Minds*, London: Pluto Press
Ulf Dantanus (1988) *Brian Friel: A Study*, London: Faber and Faber
Lennard J. Davis (1996) *Factual Fictions: The Origins of the English Novel*, Philadelphia: University of Pennsylvania Press
Gerald Dawe and Edna Longley (eds) (1985) *Across a Roaring Hill: The Protestant Imagination in Modern Ireland*, Belfast: Blackstaff Press
Denis Donoghue (1986) 'Afterword', in Field Day Theatre Company, 1986, pp. 107–20
Tom Dunne (1992) 'New Histories: "Beyond Revisionism"', *Irish Review* 12, Spring/Summer, pp. 1–12
Paul Durcan (1982) *The Selected Paul Durcan*, Belfast: Blackstaff Press
Simon During (1992) *Foucault and Literature: Towards a Genealogy of Writing*, London: Routledge
Terry Eagleton (1984) *The Function of Criticism: From the Spectator to Post-Structuralism*, London: Verso
— (1988) *Nationalism: Irony and Commitment* (Field Day Pamphlet 13) Derry: Field Day
— (1994) 'Form and Ideology in the Anglo-Irish Novel', *Bullán*, Vol. 1, No. 1, Spring, pp. 17–26
Sarah Edge (1995) '"Women are Trouble, Did You Know that Fergus?": Neil Jordan's *The Crying Game*', *Feminist Review* 50, Summer, pp. 173–86
R.D. Edwards (1994) 'An Agenda for Irish History, 1978–2018', in Brady, 1994a, pp. 54–67
Marianne Elliott (1985) *Watchmen in Sion: The Protestant Idea of Liberty* (Field Day Pamphlet 8) Derry: Field Day
Ronan Fanning (1988) 'The Meaning of Revisionism', *Irish Review* 4, Spring, pp. 15–19
— (1994) '"The Great Enchantment": Uses and Abuse of Modern Irish History', in Brady, 1994a, pp. 146–60

Brian Farrell (ed.) (1973) *The Irish Parliamentary Tradition*, Dublin: Gill and Macmillan
Michael Farrell (1980) *Northern Ireland: The Orange State* (2nd edition) London: Pluto Press
— (1986) *The Apparatus of Repression* (Field Day Pamphlet 11) Derry: Field Day
John Fekete (1977) *The Critical Twilight: Explorations in the Ideology of Anglo-American Literary Theory from Eliot to McLuhan*, London: Routledge and Kegan Paul
Desmond Fennell (1994) 'Against Revisionism' in Brady, 1994a, pp. 183–90.
Field Day Theatre Company (1985, 1986) *Ireland's Field Day*, London: Hutchinson; Notre Dame, Indiana: Notre Dame University Press
John Fiske and John Hartley (1978) *Reading Television*, London: Methuen
Hal Foster (ed.) (1985) *Postmodern Culture*, London: Pluto Press
John Wilson Foster (1991) *Colonial Consequences: Essays in Irish Literature and Culture*, Dublin: Lilliput Press
R.F. Foster (1989) *Modern Ireland 1600–1972*, London: Penguin
— (1994) 'History and the Irish Question', in Brady, 1994a, pp. 122–45
Michel Foucault (1972) *The Archaeology of Knowledge*, trans. A.M. Sheridan-Smith, London: Tavistock Press
— (1974) *The Order of Things*, London: Tavistock Press
— (1980) *Power/Knowledge: Selected Interviews and Other Writings 1972–1977*, New York: Pantheon
— (1981) 'The Order of Discourse', in Young, pp. 48–78
— (1984) 'What Is An Author?', in Rabinow, pp. 101–20
Robert Garratt (1986) *Modern Irish Poetry: Tradition and Continuity from Yeats to Heaney*, Berkeley: University of California Press
Ernest Gellner (1983) *Nations and Nationalism*, Oxford: Basil Blackwell
Luke Gibbons (1983) '"Lies That Tell the Truth": *Maeve*, History and Irish Cinema', Crane Bag, Vol. 7, No. 2, pp. 149–54
— (1988) 'Coming Out of Hibernation? The Myth of Modernity in Irish Culture', in Kearney, 1988b, pp. 205–18
Sandra M. Gilbert and Susan Gubar (1979) *The Madwoman in the Attic: The Woman Writer and the Nineteenth-Century Literary Imagination*, London: Yale University Press
Colin Graham (1994) 'Liminal Spaces: Post-Colonial Theories and Irish Culture', *Irish Review* 16, Autumn/Winter, pp. 29–43
Antonio Gramsci (1971) *Selections from the Prison Notebooks*, trans. and ed. Quintin Hoare and Geoffrey Nowell Smith, London: Lawrence and Wishart
Jürgen Habermas (1985) 'Modernity – An Incomplete Project', in Foster, pp. 3–15
— (1990) *The Philosophical Discourse of Modernity*, trans. Frederick Lawrence, Cambridge: Polity Press
David Harvey (1990) *The Condition of Postmodernity: An Enquiry into the Origins of Cultural Change*, Oxford: Basil Blackwell
Charles J. Haughey (1986) *The Spirit of the Nation*, ed. Martin Mansergh, Cork and Dublin: Mercier Press
Ellen Hazelkorn and Henry Patterson (1994) 'The New Politics of the Irish Republic', *New Left Review* 207, September/October, pp. 49–71
Mark Patrick Hederman (1985) 'Poetry and the Fifth Province', *Crane Bag*, Vol. 9, No. 1, pp. 110–19
Des Hickey and Gus Smith (1972) *A Paler Shade of Green*, London: Leslie Frewin
John Hill, Martin McLoone and Paul Hainsworth (eds) (1994) *Border Crossings: Film in Ireland, Britain and Europe*, Belfast: Institute of Irish Studies, Queen's University, in association with the University of Ulster and the British Film Institute
E.J. Hobsbawm (1994) *Revolutionaries*, London: Phoenix
Eric Hobsbawm and Terence Ranger (eds) (1983) *The Invention of Tradition*, Cambridge: Cambridge University Press
Linda Hutcheon (1988) *A Poetics of Postmodernism: History, Theory, Fiction*, London: Routledge

Sean Hutton and Paul Stewart (eds) (1991) *Ireland's Histories: Aspects of State, Society and Ideology*, London: Routledge

Rüdiger Imhof (1987) 'Q&A with John Banville', *Irish Literary Supplement*, Spring, p. 13

— (1989) *John Banville: A Critical Introduction*, Dublin: Wolfhound Press

John Kurt Jacobsen (1994) *Chasing Progress in the Irish Republic: Ideology, Democracy and Dependent Development*, Cambridge: Cambridge University Press

Fredric Jameson (1981) *The Political Unconscious: Narrative as a Socially Symbolic Act*, London: Methuen

— (1985) 'Postmodernism and Consumer Society', in Foster, pp. 111–25

— (1988a) *Modernism and Imperialism* (Field Day Pamphlet 14) Derry: Field Day

— (1988b) *The Ideologies of Theory: Essays 1971–1986. Volume 2: The Syntax of History*, London: Routledge

— (1991) *Postmodernism, or, The Cultural Logic of Late Capitalism*, London: Verso

Dillon Johnston (1985) *Irish Poetry after Joyce*, Notre Dame: Notre Dame University Press

Harvey J. Kaye (1991) 'British Marxist Historians', in Bottomore *et al.*, pp. 58–61

Richard Kearney (1986) 'Myth and Motherland', in Field Day Theatre Company, pp. 61–80

— (1988a) *Transitions: Narratives in Modern Irish Culture*, Dublin: Wolfhound Press

— (ed.) (1988b) *Across the Frontiers: Ireland in the 1990s*, Dublin: Wolfhound Press

Michael Keneally (ed.) (1988) *Cultural Contexts and Literary Idioms*, Gerrards Cross: Colin Smythe

Liam Kennedy (1992) 'Modern Ireland: Post-Colonial Society or Post-Colonial Pretensions?', *Irish Review* 13, Winter, pp. 107–21

Declan Kiberd (1986) 'Anglo-Irish Attitudes', in Field Day Theatre Company, pp. 83–105

R.N. Lebow (1976) *White Britain and Black Ireland: The Influence of Stereotypes on Colonial Policy*, Philadelphia: Institute for the Study of Human Issues

J.J. Lee (1973) *The Modernisation of Irish Society 1848–1918*, Dublin: Gill and Macmillan

— (1989) *Ireland 1912–1985: Politics and Society*, Cambridge: Cambridge University Press

David Lloyd (1993) *Anomalous States: Irish Writing and the Post-colonial Moment*, Dublin: Lilliput Press

Georg Lukács (1971) *The Theory of the Novel*, trans. Anna Bostock, London: Merlin Press

— (1981) *The Historical Novel*, London: Pelican Books

Jean Lundy and Aodan MacPoilin (eds) (1992) *Styles of Belonging: The Cultural Identities of Ulster*, Belfast: Lagan Press

F.S.L. Lyons (1973a) 'The Meaning of Independence' in Farrell, pp. 223–33

— (1973b) *Ireland since the Famine*, London: Fontana

— (1979) *Culture and Anarchy in Ireland 1890–1939*, Oxford: Oxford University Press

— (1994) 'The Burden of Our History' in Brady, 1994a, pp. 87–104

Jean-François Lyotard (1984) *The Postmodern Condition: A Report on Knowledge*, trans. Geoff Bennington and Brian Massumi, Manchester: Manchester University Press

Ferdia MacAnna (1991) 'The Dublin Renaissance: An Essay on Modern Dublin and Dublin Writers', *Irish Review* 10, Spring, pp. 14–30

Jim MacLaughlin (1994) *Ireland: The Emigrant Nursery and the World Economy*, Cork: Cork University Press

R.L. McCartney (1985) *Liberty and Authority in Ireland* (Field Day Pamphlet 9) Derry: Field Day

W.J. McCormack (1986) *The Battle of the Books: Two Decades of Irish Cultural Debate*, Mullingar, Co. Westmeath: Lilliput Press

Oliver MacDonagh (1983) *States of Mind: Two Centuries of Anglo-Irish Conflict 1780–1980*, London: Pimlico

Kevin Maher (1995) 'From Angels to Vampires', *Film Ireland* 45, February/March, pp. 16–18

Patrick J. McGrory (1986) *Law and the Constitution: Present Discontents* (Field Day Pamphlet 12) Derry: Field Day

Michael McKeon (1987) *The Origins of the English Novel 1600–1740*, Baltimore: Johns Hopkins University Press

Martin McLoone (1994) 'National Cinema and Cultural Identity: Ireland and Europe', in Hill, McLoone and Hainsworth, pp. 146–73

Joseph McMinn (1991) *John Banville: A Critical Study*, Dublin: Gill and Macmillan

Gabriel García Márquez (1978) *One Hundred Years of Solitude*, trans. Gregory Rabassa, London: Pan Books

Alan Matthews (1985) 'Economics and Ideology', *Crane Bag*, Vol. 9, No. 2, pp. 52–9

Jim Merod, *The Political Responsibility of the Critic* (Ithaca, NY, and London: Cornell University Press, 1987)

T.W. Moody and R.D. Edwards (1994) 'Preface to *Irish Historical Studies*', in Brady, 1994a, pp. 35–7

T.W. Moody (1994) 'Irish History and Irish Mythology', in Brady, 1994a, pp. 71–86

Franco Moretti (1988) *Signs Taken for Wonders: Essays in the Sociology of Literary Forms* (revised edition), London: Verso

Eanna Mulloy (1986) *Dynasties of Coercion* (Field Day Pamphlet 10) Derry: Field Day

Una Murphy (1993) 'Hearts and Minds: The "Cultural Traditions" Industry', *Irish Reporter* 10, Third Quarter, pp. 24–5

Christopher Murray (1993) ' "Friel's Emblems of Adversity" and the Yeatsian Example', in Peacock, pp. 69–90

Lewis Namier (1961) *England in the Age of the American Revolution*, 2nd ed., London: Macmillan

Ashis Nandy (1983) *The Intimate Enemy: Loss and Recovery of Self under Colonialism*, Delhi: Oxford University Press

Daltun Ó Ceallaigh (ed.) (1994) *Reconsiderations of Irish History and Culture: Selected Papers from the Desmond Greaves Summer School 1989–'93*, Dublin: Leirmheas, for the Desmond Greaves Summer School

Barbara O'Connor (1984) 'Aspects of Representation of Women in Irish Film', *Crane Bag*, Vol. 8, No. 2, pp. 79–83

Liam O'Dowd (1986) 'Beyond Industrial Society' in Patrick Clancy *et al.*, 1986, pp. 198–220

— (1988) 'Neglecting the Material Dimension: Irish intellectuals and the problem of identity', *Irish Review* 3, pp. 8–17

— (1995) 'Development or Dependency? State, Economy and Society in Northern Ireland' in Patrick Clancy *et al.*, 1995, pp. 132–77

Richard Ohmann (1976) *English in America: A Radical View of the Profession*, New York: Oxford University Press

Fintan O'Toole (1982) 'The Man from God Knows Where. An interview with Brian Friel', *In Dublin*, 28 October, pp. 20–23

— (1985) 'Going West: The Country versus the City in Irish Writing', *Crane Bag*, Vol. 9, No. 2, pp. 111–16

— (1988) 'Island of Saints and Silicon: Literature and Social Change in Contemporary Ireland' in Michael Keneally, pp. 11–35

— (1990) *A Mass for Jesse James: A Journey through 1980s Ireland*, Dublin: Raven Arts Press

— (1994) *Black Hole, Green Card: The Disappearance of Ireland*, Dublin: New Ireland Books

M.A.G. Ó Tuathaigh (1994) 'Irish Historical "Revisionism": State of the Art or Ideological Project?', in Brady, 1994a, pp. 306–26

Tom Paulin (1986) 'A New Look at the Language Question', in Field Day Theatre Company, pp. 3–18

Alan Peacock (ed.) (1993) *The Achievement of Brian Friel*, Gerrards Cross: Colin Smythe

Lionel Pilkington (1990) 'Language and Politics in Brian Friel's *Translations*', *Irish University Review*, Vol. 20, No. 2, Autumn, pp. 282–98

— (1994) 'Theatre and Insurgency in Ireland', *Essays in Theatre/Études Theatrales*, Vol. 12, No. 2, pp. 129–40

Richard Pine (1990) *Brian Friel and Ireland's Drama*, London: Routledge

A.F. Pollard (1916) 'History and Science: A Rejoinder', *History* (new series), 1, pp. 25–39

— (1920) 'Historical Criticism', *History*, 5, pp. 21–9

— (1922) 'An Apology for Historical Research', *History*, 7, pp. 161–77

Paul Rabinow (ed.) (1984) *The Foucault Reader*, London: Penguin

Patrick Rafroidi and Maurice Harmon (eds) (1976) *The Irish Novel in Our Time*, Lille: PUL

Ernest Renan (1990) 'What is a nation?', trans. Martin Thom, in Bhabha, pp. 8–22

Shaun Richards (1992) '"An End to Rural Idiocy?" Urban Images in Northside Realism', unpublished manuscript, delivered as a paper to The Lipman Seminar, 'Ireland Word and Image', Ruskin College, Oxford, 3–5 April

Kevin Rockett, Luke Gibbons and John Hill (1988) *Cinema and Ireland*, London: Routledge

— (1994) 'Culture, Industry and Irish Cinema', in Hill, McLoone and Hainsworth, pp. 126–39

Edward W. Said (1979) *Orientalism*, New York: Vintage

— (1984) *The World, the Text, and the Critic*, London: Faber and Faber

— (1985a) *Beginnings: Intention and Method*, New York: Columbia University Press

— (1985b) 'Opponents, Audiences, Constituencies and Community', in Foster, pp. 135–59

— (1986) 'Orientalism reconsidered' in Barker *et al.*, pp. 210–29

— (1988) *Yeats and Decolonisation* (Field Day Pamphlet 15) Derry: Field Day

— (1991) *Musical Elaborations*, London: Chatto and Windus

— (1993) *Culture and Imperialism*, London: Chatto and Windus

— (1994a) *The Politics of Dispossession: The Struggle for Palestinian Self-Determination 1969–1994*, London: Chatto and Windus

— (1994b) *Representations of the Intellectual*, New York: Pantheon

Philip Schlesinger (1978) *Putting 'Reality' Together*, London: Constable

Ronan Sheehan (1979) 'Novelists on the Novel. Ronan Sheehan Talks to John Banville and Francis Stuart', *Crane Bag*, Vol. 3, No. 1, pp. 76–84

Alan Sinfield (1989) *Literature, Politics and Culture in Postwar Britain*, Oxford: Basil Blackwell

Paul Stewart (1991) 'The jerrybuilders: Bew, Gibbon and Patterson – the Protestant working class and the Northern Ireland state', in Hutton and Stewart, pp. 177–202

E.P. Thompson (1971) 'The Moral Economy of the English Crowd in the Seventeenth Century', Past and Present No. 50, pp. 76–136

Colm Tóibín (1989) review of fifth series of Field Day pamphlets, *Nationalism, Colonialism and Literature*, *Fortnight* No. 271, March, p. 21

— (1991) 'Confusion of literary traditions', *Sunday Independent*, 24 November, 1991, p. 8

— (1992) paper delivered at the Joint Conference of the Canadian Association of Irish Studies and the American Conference of Irish Studies, Galway, 1992; reprinted in *The Canadian Journal of Irish Studies*, Vol. 18, No. 2, pp. 121–4

— (1993a) 'New Ways of Killing Your Father', *London Review of Books*, 18 November, 1993, pp. 3–6

— (ed.) (1993b) *Soho Square*, London: Bloomsbury

John Waters (1994) 'Last Stand of the Jeremiah Brigade', *Irish Times*, 8 November, p. 12

Ian Watt (1987) *The Rise of the Novel: Studies in Defoe, Richardson and Fielding*, London: The Hogarth Press

Hayden White (1978) *Tropics of Discourse: Essays in Cultural Criticism*, Baltimore and London: Johns Hopkins University Press

— (1987) *The Content of the Form: Narrative Discourse and Historical Representation*, Baltimore and London: Johns Hopkins University Press

James Wickham (1986) 'Industrialisation, Work and Unemployment', in Clancy, Drudy, Lynch and O'Dowd, pp. 70–96

Raymond Williams (1981) *Culture*, London: Fontana

— (1993) *The Country and the City*, London: Hogarth Press

W.B. Yeats (1962) *Poems of W.B. Yeats* (ed. A. Norman Jeffares), London: Macmillan

Robert Young (ed.) (1981) *Untying the Text: A Post-Structuralist Reader*, London: Routledge and Kegan Paul

Index

Quinn, Bob, 165, 168, 190, 196; *Caoineadh Airt Ui Laoire*, 182–9

Renan, Ernest, nation, 113
revisionism, 14, 17–18, 27, 36, 44, 84–109, 110, 114, 134, 144, 146–7, 169, 183, 196, 197–9, 211–12, 218–22, 226–7
Richards, Shaun, 11, 140; Literary Revival, 163; modernisation, 12, 197; Raven Arts Press project, 147, 149
Rockett, Kevin, Ardmore Studio, 166–7; film censorship, 168; state film policy, 165

Said, Edward, authority, 56–7, 65, 66; colonial space, 149–50, 193, 209; colonial stereotype, 71; culture and the state, 41, 42, 79, 104, 105, 213; criticism, 45, 228; 'interference', 112, 134, 182, 187, 208, 226; intellectuals, 38, 44, 194; modernisation, 28; narrative, 39, 55, 131, 154; 'Orientalism reconsidered', 214; performance, 67; terrorism, 177, 180; 'Travelling Theory', 214–15; 'worldliness', 133; on W.B. Yeats, 218
Schlesinger, Philip, terrorism, 176–7
Sheridan, Jim, 169; landscape in films of, 169–72; reproducing stereotypes, 175; *My Left Foot*, 170–1; *The Field*, 171–2; *Into the West*, 172
Sinfield, Alan, narrative, 42

Sinn Féin, 14, 26, 177, 182–3
Synge, J.M., 45; and Catholic bourgeoisie, 160; as Revivalist, 140, 149

Tóibín, Colm, on Field Day, 219–21; organic intellectual, 139; Raven Arts Press/Passion Machine formation, 140, 141, 147; revisionism, 110

Waters, John, economics, 21, 22; organic intellectual, 139; Raven Arts Press/Passion Machine formation, 140, 141
Weber, Max, rationalisation, 20, 21, 35
Whitaker, T.K., 135, 182; *Economic Development*, 13; modernisation, 17, 18, 29, 31, 32, 36, 154
White, Hayden, 97, 98, 99, 116, 211; cultural myths, 39, 198; history and ideology, 106–7; *Metahistory*, 98; narrative and history, 64, 91–2, 94, 95, 134; revolution and history, 87–9, 100, 115, 123, 133
Williams, Raymond, country and city, 159; cultural movements, 140–1, 197
Wickham, James, dependency theory, 21; modernisation theory, 15

Yeats, W.B., 45, 47, 140, 163; 'Easter 1916', 121; 'The Fisherman', 149, 218; 'Fragments', 218; modernity, 158